THE GAS STATION IN AMERICA

Creating the North American Landscape

Gregory Conniff
Bonnie Loyd
Edward K. Muller
David Schuyler
Consulting Editors

*Published in cooperation with the Center for
American Places, Harrisonburg, Virginia*

THE
GAS

STATION

IN AMERICA

John A. Jakle & Keith A. Sculle

The Johns Hopkins University Press
Baltimore and London

© 1994 The Johns Hopkins University Press
All rights reserved
Printed in the United States of America on acid-free paper
04 03 02 01 00 99 98 97 96 95   5 4 3

The Johns Hopkins University Press
2715 North Charles Street
Baltimore, Maryland 21218-4319
The Johns Hopkins Press Ltd., London

Library of Congress Cataloging-in-Publication Data will be found
at the end of this book.

A catalog record for this book is available from the British Library.

Contents

Preface and Acknowledgments

We offer here an exploration of the American gasoline station—its origins, its evolution as a form, its changing geographical distribution, and its changing social meanings. Specifically, we explore the following propositions:

- Gasoline stations, as all the other ephemera of the American roadside, hold cultural meaning. Indeed, in a nation committed to heightened mobility, both social and geographical, they stand profoundly symbolic.

- To the generation of Americans come of age in a post–World War II era of evolving automobility, roadside America, including its gasoline stations, holds strong sentimental value in itself culturally significant.

- The roadside has been modeled by the process we call "place-product-packaging." Total design concepts have been used, especially by the petroleum companies, to create clear corporate images projected onto landscape.

- Place-product-packaging has been used by corporations to engage in territorial competitions. Chains of look-alike gasoline stations defined for the petroleum industry distinctive retail geographies company to company.

- Changing gasoline station form and function reflects both place-product-packaging and corporate territoriality. Much of the cultural symbolism of gasoline stations, as roadside phenomena, is so engendered.

Our book is organized as follows. In chapter 1 we deal with the generational implications of our endeavor, providing context for the consideration of something as ordinary as gasoline stations—something as mundane as the places where automobiles are serviced. Chapter 2 reviews the scholarly literature relevant to the study of the roadside and gasoline stations, and offers definition for the place-product-packaging concept. Chapter 3 reviews the history of gasoline retailing in the United States while chapter 4 outlines corporate territoriality across the country as it has affected gasoline retailing over time. Analysis of evolving gasoline station form is offered in chapter 5 while chapters 6 and 7 detail the gasoline-station design process undertaken by large corporations and small local entrepreneurs, respectively. Chapter 8 contains a case study outlining the changing geography of gasoline retailing in a small middle-western city, placing the gasoline station form squarely into landscape context. Concluding remarks are offered in chapter 9.

Chapters 5 through 8 contain material previously published over the past fifteen years in a number of journals: *Bulletin of the Illinois Geographical Society, Historic Illinois, Journal of American Culture, Journal of Cultural Geography, Pioneer America,* and *Pioneer America Society Transactions.* However, each chapter is completely revised and expanded through the introduction of substantive new material. Chapter 8 is based in part on articles coauthored by John Jakle and Richard Mattson, the latter now a preservation planner in Charlotte, North Carolina. In our previous work we explored isolated aspects of the American gasoline station as a landscape phenomenon. Here we place the gasoline station fully into its cultural context. Additionally, we offer theoretical constructs pointing to more sophisticated future treatment of gasoline stations and other elements of the American roadside—the abstractions of place-product-packaging and corporate territoriality.

Landscape may be the most important cultural product of our age since landscapes structure life both physically and metaphorically.[1] Geographical changes, because they are easily visualized, represent and structure orientations to society. In today's postindustrial age the dominant sources of social meaning have shifted from production to consumption. We live in a consumption-driven capitalistic age and thus we take our social identities substantially from what we consume.[2] It follows that those places nested in landscape, specially contrived to drive consumption, beg the attention of scholars. This kind of thinking has brought us to reexamine our past work focused on the gasoline station, and to redirect its thrust toward understanding the gasoline station as an important icon of our time not only for the student and scholar, but also for the general reader.

Thanks to all those who either spent time and effort to recall their occupational experiences or faithfully pursued requests for library or archival material to make this book possible. Special mention, however, is due several. Most of all is C. A. Petersen for his candid and informative correspondence and interview. E. H. Berners of Berners, Schober, and Kilp gave ready access to the private archives of his firm's predecessor

(Foeller, Schober, and Stephenson) as did James K. Glenn, Sr., of the Quality Oil Company. Corporate collections furnishing information and often photographs, only some of which appear in these pages, include Amoco Corporation, BP America, Clark Oil and Refining Corporation, Chevron Corporation, Jenney Oil Company, Mobil Oil Corporation, *National Petroleum News,* and Texaco.

Public staffs and collections especially fruitful were those of the Illinois State Historical Library; Northwest Missouri State University Archives; Sangamon Valley Collection, Lincoln Library (Springfield, Illinois); University of Illinois at Urbana-Champaign Library; and Urbana Free Library (Urbana). The library and staff of the Illinois Department of Transportation and the private collection of the Dawes Arboretum were very helpful as well.

Several people extensively contributed their expertise. Especially note cartographers Jane Domier and James Bier, University of Illinois at Urbana-Champaign cartography laboratory, and Richard Mattson for his help in developing material contained in chapter 8.

THE GAS STATION IN AMERICA

1

Gas Stations in Generational Perspective

It occurs to us, the authors, that this book might accomplish for our readers several objectives. It might enlighten on the topic of the American gasoline station as architecture. It might treat the gasoline station not merely as an object of landscape, but as a marketing device with clear territorial implications, thus pointing the student of the American roadside toward theory-based explanation. It might suggest how the petroleum industry has impinged, through its roadside architecture, the consciousness of at least one generation of Americans (including its scholars) through what we call place-product-packaging.

Place-product-packaging is a form of advertising. And advertising, of course, drives the American economy as it stimulates our consuming of things. Cereal for breakfast, beer and cigarettes at leisure time, fast food for lunch or dinner, mattresses to sleep on—all products labeled with logos of distinctive color, shape, and slogan cuing the familiar and the trustworthy. Who cannot recall and repeat the slogans of widely advertised brands with but the prompting of a few opening words? Even architecture has been made to speak. Places are created to gain allegiances thus amplifying brand loyalties. Buildings beckon to us by sight initially, but then inextricably by waves of remembered sound, smell, and feeling. In the case of gasoline stations, associations are engendered around our caring for the automobile, that indispensable amplifier of human mobility.

Observe buildings, driveways, and pumps arranged in patterns and located across an array of sites or locations to reinforce each oil company's distinctive image. Integrate colors, shapes, and decorative details special to each firm. Add to the ensemble personnel in distinctive uniforms as well as labeled products specially packaged (see Figs. 1.1–1.5). Thus you have it: place-product-packaging—the networking of look-alike places defining trade territories, all supported through coordinated advertising. Consumers enter environments carefully calculated as cor-

FIGURE 1.1 Early place-product-packaging: the 1920s. Attendants uniformed in jodhpurs of the horse-mounted past, pumps enclosed in futuristic housing, a distinctive station house with canopy, and company signage defined an early Standard Oil of Ohio (Sohio) station. (*Source:* Photo courtesy of BP America, formerly known as Standard Oil of Ohio.)

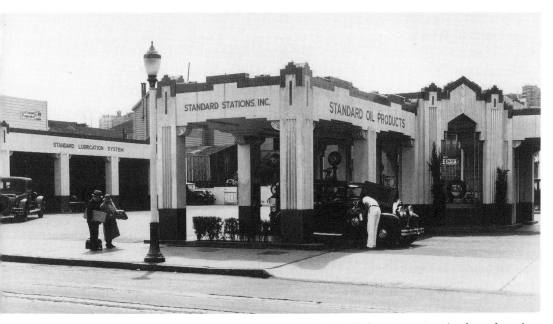

FIGURE 1.2 Place-product-packaging evolved: the 1930s. Service bays housing lubrication and washing floors augmented a canopied Standard Oil of California (Socal) station in San Francisco, the whole decorated in art-deco ornamentation. (*Source:* Photo courtesy of Chevron Corporate Library.)

FIGURE 1.3 Place-product-packaging matured: the 1950s. International modernism played out through the geometries and plain surfaces of this 1953 Springfield, Illinois, Texaco station. (*Source:* Photo courtesy of H. Wayne Price.)

porate sign. Today, place-product-packaging is a major weave in America's cultural fabric.

What follows in this introductory chapter are interwoven biographies descriptive of two paralleling but mutually reinforcing scholarly explorations undertaken by the authors, one a geographer and the other a historian. We seek to outline and place in cultural context our evolving interest in the American gasoline station—a process of discovery we believe to be fully symptomatic of our generation.

The gasoline station has emerged as a cultural icon central to the American psyche. For those of us whose early memories are rooted in the years immediately following World War II, the automobile, and the new landscapes oriented to the automobile, loomed large as youthful preoccupations. In automobility lay identity and a sense of future for our generation. For one's family and oneself the automobile spoke immediately of social status both through the mobility engendered and through the thing possessed. Part of the mystique of automobility was the use and care of the motorcar as machine and central to car maintenance was the gasoline station. For males, especially, the neighborhood gasoline station—with its ringing bell announcing customers, its smell of gasoline and grease signifying technology, and its brisk socializing indicating community—constituted a very important social setting indeed. Here could be found the exhilarating tension of mechanical and other problems faced and solved. In gasoline stations, both close to or far

FIGURE 1.4 The attendant's shirt and hat, monogrammed with the same logo that topped the gasoline pumps and decorated oil cans and other containers, carried place-product-packaging forward as total design. "You can trust your car to the man who wears the star." (*Source:* Photo courtesy of H. Wayne Price.)

FIGURE 1.5 A company's stations were intended to facilitate as well as symbolize fast, complete, and courteous service. (*Source:* Photo courtesy of H. Wayne Price.)

THE GAS STATION IN AMERICA

from home, young boys eagerly entered the exhilarating adult world.

So taken for granted have gasoline stations become in the American era of automobile dependence that they are easily accepted as part of the mundane world of the unimportant. As we begin this book, we ask ourselves how it was that two scholars, who could have taken more conventional topics to study, came to embrace the gasoline station as a research emphasis. Certainly, the roadside offers up generic places so common as to apparently require little or no serious discussion. How was it that we came to reject such an appraisal? Schooling must have contributed. To what extent did academic training help or hinder? Occupation must have weighed heavily. To what extent did work assignments (the former in university teaching and the latter in preservation planning) influence? Also important was personal background. To what extent did personal history—even personality rooted in childhood—help dictate research and writing interests?

Growing Up with Automobiles

One author, the geographer, dates his interest in automobiles and roadside landscapes back to early childhood. He and his family lived in a Detroit suburb and getting to places at a distance, such as southern Illinois where relatives lived, routinely involved automobile travels. West to Coldwater on the old Chicago Pike, then south to Fort Wayne and Indianapolis, and then west on U.S. 40.[1] How to keep a youngster happy while traveling? Easy. Put him in the front seat beside the driver, make him (or pretend to make him) responsible for reading the road maps, and play games around his watching the scenery passing by. His impulse was to count things and as he got older what he counted most were gasoline stations for they stood out by the roadside with their colorful signs and insignia and distinctive design. He was amused by the fact that different brands seemed to dominate in different areas, contributing a sense of personality to regions: Shell here, Sunoco there, and Standard almost everywhere. Everyone must sense how it was—the occasional encounter with the unexpected station selling Hoosier Pete, Wake-Up, or Red Head gasolines making life instantly exciting. And then he began collecting the road maps free for the taking at gas stops. Special trips in the 1950s were made by car to New York (Socony), New England (Esso), and Quebec (Imperial), and west to Wyoming (Sinclair) and Colorado (Conoco).

One could not grow up in Detroit and not be enamored of automobiles. The fathers of many of his friends worked for the automobile companies and one father was chief designer at General Motors, responsible for putting tail fins on Cadillacs. Kids talked constantly of automobiles. One school mate, slightly retarded, thought he was a car and went everywhere making engine noises and shifting gears. Most boys saw themselves eventually as mechanical engineers or corporate lawyers, and most girls as marrying same. As a small child he had expended substantial energies modeling landscapes with toys, especially in a basement recreation room filled with electric trains. But setting up trains was a father's play. His role was to arrange buildings along streets and highways, thus constituting the encompassing landscape of railroading. It was a decidedly automobile world that he constructed and reconstructed through endless rounds of creativity which always included small plastic gasoline stations put together from kits.

At Western Michigan University in Kalamazoo, he discovered what was important intellectually in life. His first major in marketing proved disappointing. Attracted by the bright packaging of the marketplace, including the packaging of the roadside, he nonetheless tired of the bland textbooks. He would have done poorly in business. In one class he predicted that neither the Holiday Inn nor the McDonald's chain would succeed. Who would want to stay in motels that looked all alike? And who in their right mind would get out of their cars to buy food at windows? And so it was that he wandered down to the university's geography department to explore a second major where people drew maps rather than ads. In pursuing a master's degree at Southern Illinois University the budding scholar became a historical geographer.

For the other author, the historian, the family automobile was reserved solely to his father's business use in Chicago as a motor-freight solicitor. Although the father traveled extensively by car and made his living with motor vehicles, none of the lure of faraway places was conveyed at home for work and home were clearly separate spheres. The child's world was pedestrian oriented—walking as he did the mile to grade school or the block to the grocery store, frequently cutting across the backs of lots. Except for a nearby White Castle hamburger stand, roadside architecture had no place in his early childhood. He did not come to enjoy the great American roadside from a basis of warmly remembered youthful experiences in automobile travel.

Perhaps an early inability to fully embrace the modern world of automobility helped generate a sense for the past in the son. He was a collector of things old—either images or objects. If collecting implies at once an interest in diversity, raising questions about the origins of things, then his historical sense can be dated to his first views from a streetcar. Riding the Western Avenue line in Chicago he could see the watertowers of industrial plants, attractive for their individual colors, sizes, and corporate logos. In counting them he claimed to "collect" them. From "collecting" things in landscape as images he turned to collecting things with images—for example, bubblegum cards with pictures of tanks and airplanes. However, pictures of automobiles became his special preoccupation.

Toward the end of high school he set his sights on college and a curriculum that would permit him to teach history. His junior and senior

THE GAS STATION IN AMERICA

years of college were completed at Northern Illinois University in DeKalb and there began the transition to rigorous historical thinking. None of his professors demonstrated any interest in local history and thus he took no special interest in DeKalb's landscape, least of all its evolving commercial strips. A master's degree was added at Northern.

Academia in the Automobile Age

For the geographer it was on to Indiana University and Ph.D. work focused on historical geography. The Indiana geography department was still substantially insulated from the new "scientific geography" that would in the 1960s oversweep the discipline with emphasis on quantification, deductive theory, and other Positivist tendencies.[2] He had been inoculated at Carbondale and persisted at Bloomington in making the study of past geography as scientific as he could. He would believe in spatial analysis, spatial behavior, spatial diffusion, and, indeed, all things "spatial" (rather than geographic) as was faddish and fashionable.[3] Perhaps he never fully believed it. For one thing a love of photography kept taking him outdoors to investigate real places and landscapes not easily reduced and abstracted in mathematical terms. Photography lent itself with difficulty to spatial science since it said much about the specifics of life, making generalization difficult.[4]

And then there was his discovery of the archive: the joys of rooting oneself like a detective in the highly elusive, largely nonquantified and unquantifiable record of the past. People had not thought spatially in the past, and had not bothered to order their recorded observations of the geographical world in spatial terms. Historical evidence, even that arranged statistically in tables, lent itself more to analysis focused on places and landscapes. As with most laymen, "space" came to connote for him a kind of vacancy or nothingness—not the kind of thing one would want to build an academic discipline around.[5] Better to look at place-types, even those defined at the scale of the lowly gasoline station.

His dissertation had nothing to do with roadsides, gasoline stations, or anything else that might have been seen out of a car window during childhood travels. Historical geography was a new subdiscipline that had emerged only in the 1930s after an aborted effort earlier in the century built around a quickly discredited environmental determinism. Earlier the course of human history had been seen as not only influenced by but substantially determined by changes in climate, soil fertility, and other factors of physical environment.[6] The newer historical geography came largely out of political and economic history, although a second brand of historical scholarship, called cultural geography, was also emerging, stimulated by ties that certain geographers, such as Carl Sauer at Berkeley, had forged with anthropologists.[7] Historical geographers focused on the big themes of academic history upon which a geographical or spatial perspective shed light. No theme was bigger than Frederick Jackson Turner's frontier thesis, a kind of environmental determinism in its own right, that saw a distinctive American culture (and society and body politic) as honed on the relative isolation of a constantly moving western frontier.[8] Dissertation research focused on several issues raised by Turner concerning the importance of salt on the early TransAppalachian frontier.[9]

Historical geography today is a discipline charged with comprehending the geographic past.[10] It studies evolving geographies by emphasizing changing spatial distributions. It tries to understand why things were located as they were in the past, and how things did or did not change over time. The historical geographer can study the reality of the past by taking the stance of the scientific observer who tries to describe and analyze object social realities.[11] But most historical geographers are not social scientists. They have taken their cues more from academic history, or from cultural anthropology and what is now emerging as cultural ecology. They function more as humanists.[12] This is our approach taken to the subject of gasoline stations.

Historical geographers can study past reality as it was (seeking some kind of consensual position out of the diverse opinions implicit in data sources uncovered) or they can bravely study the past as it was thought to have been (focusing deliberately on the diversity of opinion that characterized people's past conceptions about themselves and their places lodged in time).[13] The geographer's interest in travel journalists as depictors of landscape produced a book focused on the history of tourism in early twentieth-century North America.[14] What was it that travelers saw in America's landscapes, and why was it important to them? This work concerned the shift from railroad travel to automobile travel and the implications of this shift for Americans conceptualizing and experiencing landscape as place. The roadside, a whole new kind of American travel environment, had evolved. This environment, created initially to ensconce automobile travelers, became a kind of environmental imperative around which the entire of America was ultimately reorganized geographically. The American's love of geographical mobility brought automobiles to the fore. And all that automobile manufacturers and petroleum refiners had to do (along with the makers of portland concrete, rubber tires, and all the other automobile-related things) was to lobby government and promote, largely through advertising, a new geographical reality into being.

But American historical geographers have been tuned primarily to the distant past.[15] Questions concerning European colonial expansion overseas, the early rise of urban-based systems of economic organization, and the early migrations of people and related cultural diffusions came to the fore with little twentieth-century concern. Fortunately, what increasingly is called "cultural historical geography" has emerged to embrace more fully the recent past. The study of contemporary material culture lies at its heart. It deals with the description of landscape features (both individual structures and those aggregated as settlement patterns), discovery of their past origins as distinctive cultural forms, and their diffusion over time and across geographical space up to the present day. It deals as well with the symbolic values of things in landscape, and the evolution of those values. Cultural historical geographers have not been alone in these emphases. They have been joined by folklorists, landscape architects, architectural historians, historians, and others in a vital interdisciplinary mix focused on landscape interpretation.[16]

The material cultural emphases of landscape study in the United States first focused on domestic architecture.[17] Houses were seen to be principal carriers of cultural symbolism as well as numerically predominant in the landscapes of most areas. Emphasis was given initially to folk houses that reflected directly the values of their builder-residents. Folk architecture, including houses, barns, and fences, was rapidly disappearing in the face of modern urbanization, and there was an impelling urgency to record and analyze the peculiarities of regional occurrence. Things such as gasoline stations, in contrast, appeared not only to be universal but enduring. Only slowly did attention shift to the commercially packaged elements of landscape, for example, the builder houses erected on speculation for an anonymous market and the barns built by professionals or bought prefabricated out of catalogues. Ultimately, interest came around to the vernacular buildings of the roadside upon which this book focuses. Slowly attention shifted to studying things in cities although an overall rural bias for this kind of study still persists. The study of commercial architecture, including gasoline stations, is a relatively recent breakthrough.[18]

The formal study of history was also in a tremendous flux during the 1970s.[19] New views and techniques were emerging to create new excitement just as in geography. Prime among the new departures at the University of Illinois, where the historian went for Ph.D. work, was cliometrics, the historian's equivalent of quantitative geography. He found some value in quantitative techniques, which he was encouraged to apply in dissertation work investigating the political uses of anticlericalism in the disestablishment of the Catholic church in France.[20] Perhaps the most exciting ideas encountered at Illinois came through introduction to the French tradition of local historical studies.[21] In the French literature he found well-researched and well-written local histories without equal in American historiography.

He learned to value more the need to exhaustively reference primary sources, to comprehend the historiography of subjects under investigation, and to effectively communicate understandings through clear prose. Underlying this method was a vague belief in objective reality. He was a Rankian in that he believed it possible to write history *wie es eigentlich gewesen,* as it happened. He did not advance toward positivism from this belief in the objective for he also shared the Rankian view that history was the narrative of how individuals interacted with cultural values.[22] His craft lay in understanding and narrating a clear and entertaining sequence of events, then analyzing the subject's significance by relating the subject to larger frameworks. Know your sources! Write well! Bring new meaning!

Other changes were looming in academic history. Most important was the declining number of teaching positions in colleges and universities. Public history, as it has emerged, was not discussed as such at Illinois although an archivist's preparation could be obtained, the assumption being that an academic historian could fulfill that role with no special training. The technique and epistemology of oral history, which later became essential to his research of the roadside, was developed later on his own. Popular culture and its landscape dimensions were not yet of any special interest. He had not yet discovered the automobile and the camera as instruments of travel, landscape-oriented. Predilections still led inward through books and archival materials to imagined worlds of the past rather than outward to real places where history lived as pastness variously relic. But he found historian's work where no self-respecting academic historian would have searched—local history. He obtained a position with the Illinois Historic Sites Survey which did inventory work for the Illinois Department of Conservation.

The commercial roadside with its vernacular buildings was especially problematical for a historical site surveyor trained as a historian. In areas almost devoid of the usual historic landmarks (homes of the rich and famous, for example) roadside buildings seemed to be the only worthwhile stories. They were numerous and many were well preserved. As the historian began to think of gasoline stations as landmarks, he came to think more like a cultural historical geographer, his research questions taken directly from the cultural landscape. From his survey work he developed several case studies focused on the gasoline retail businesses of several dealers. Oral history and historical photographs quickly became main information sources.[23]

Reading the geography literature reinforced interest in all aspects of what he learned to call "landscape." Concurrent reading in the local history of his study area brought realization that the writing of such history should not be left to antiquarians. More important, he saw that a more rigorous kind of local history could be written around landscape themes or landscape change themes. Although the geography literature taught to look primarily at vernacular houses and secondarily at barns and other rural objects of folk origin, it was the charm of dilapidated gasoline stations that continually caught his eye.

It seemed that significant stories about otherwise anonymous people

THE GAS STATION IN AMERICA

would go untold if he did not gather and report them. Those he interviewed told how they had started their gasoline businesses, contracted for buildings, dealt with the large petroleum companies or their jobbers, and managed business affairs over the years, raising families with the incomes generated. This was the stuff of life. Station operators were eager to tell their stories. And no one ever laughed at opening questions or patronized in giving subsequent information. Respondents were flattered to think that some part of their lives held significance in a historical sense.[24]

Following survey work came a position with the Illinois State Historical Library overseeing the museum interpretation program at the Old State Capitol. Then it was on to historic preservation work at the Department of Conservation when the position of chief of registration for the state's *National Register* program was established.[25] Administering the work of the Illinois Historic Sites Advisory Council was one of his chief responsibilities.[26] Actually registering gasoline stations on the *National Register* came as a result of travel in Wisconsin.[27] Travel north had yielded not only oral histories and historical photographs from family albums of "mom and pop" stations, but his first encounter with corporate archives. He strove to uncover something like a psychological profile of the designers and builders of gasoline stations. With a corporate case study he hoped to identify a design process perhaps typical of the large petroleum corporations.[28]

Scholarly Focus on the Roadside

The context in which one operates as a scholar greatly colors what one accomplishes as a student of landscape. Positioning oneself in situations that both orient and reward is of the essence. Surrounding oneself with supportive people helps. Of course, access to research monies is useful. The geographer was lucky to be at one of the nation's large research universities where such encouragement was forthcoming. He put into place a series of historical geography courses that began to attract not only geography students but those from the design disciplines—primarily landscape architecture, urban and regional planning, architectural history, and architecture. Designers were interested in applying lessons learned. How could one explain designs popular in the past? How might the design vocabularies of gasoline stations, for example, be relevant to the present-day planning of the built environment? Historical geography students, on the other hand, were encouraged to give themselves to applied historical geography and many indeed opted ultimately to pursue careers in planning, historic preservation, and museum curation.

The year 1973 was especially important. That year the coauthors—the historian and the geographer—began to collaborate. That year geog-

FIGURE 1.6 This gasoline station at Casey, Illinois, photographed in 1973, represented the widely used 1920s prototype, the house with canopy station. But its classical Revival styling made it special.

raphy faculty and students participated in Illinois Historic Sites Survey field work. On one outing the two found themselves at Casey, Illinois, a bulk storage/pipeline town for Marathon Oil. And there it stood! A marvelous neo-Greek Revival gasoline station sat relic beside the highway, a thing in the landscape for which neither was fully prepared (see Fig. 1.6). Greek Revival houses and Greek Revival churches and Greek Revival banks certainly, but not Greek Revival gasoline stations. There it was with its pillars and entabulature and dentilation. There was no scholarship to fall back on. How rare was this thing? There was no established sense of the normative from which to assess uniqueness. The symbolism of its design made for interesting speculation. Who built it? When? Beyond pumping gas and profit taking, what was the entrepreneur's motivation? Should it be preserved? How did it contribute to the sense of place? What did it mean to the highway as historical display?

Scholars come to research problems for various reasons. Those driven to be successful usually flock with the influential people, securing mentors from among those senior. They focus on the big questions fashionable at the moment of their coming on the academic scene. Many academics of this type drive relentlessly forward focused on a single topic or narrow range of topics, their reputations made on the continued rounds of reinforcement that they give their subject matter. The geographer chose to follow another course. Gasoline stations and other esoterica had excited him. He has allowed himself to be molded by such excitement little understood at the offing. This has been a following of instincts rooted in curiosity about landscapes and places, and how they function and what they mean.[29]

The historian's tendency to question his profession's traditional assumptions and construct his own schema through the development of a specialized subfield of history paralleled the trend of many historians in academic settings.[30] But his intellectual interaction occurred less with historians and more with historical and cultural geographers and historic preservationists. These new cohorts provided a heady mix. Not only were papers given at meetings and articles published in journals, but editorships and board memberships were earned. The latter two especially provided a vantage point from which the personal dynamics and intellectual content of preservation through landscape awareness was heightened and the historian was more fully integrated in several emerging subfields: landscape history, material cultural studies, and vernacular architecture. Occasional classes and courses taught at Eastern Illinois University and Sangamon State University gave opportunities to interact with students in collegiate classrooms over new ideas. Presently, he oversees the state's history programs directed at grades 6 through 12 as head of research and education for the Illinois Historic Preservation Agency.[31] He organizes and directs teacher workshops and edits *Illinois History*.

Discovering relics in a landscape serves to link the observer directly to the past. In experiencing things firsthand in landscape people become part of a continuum that potentially extends also into the future. Reading the landscape can have highly personal rewards since in musing about landscape there can come a restorative therapy, a reintegration of our values as sensory and intellectual beings. Many of life's fragmentations can be overcome as we discover connections. This is a very different reason for studying the past than the more common but equally convincing one that historical knowledge is a necessary component for regulating our social and political future.[32]

Lessons Learned

What lessons might be learned from individuals variously coming to grips with the commonplace? Just what might the authors represent in regards to evolving worlds of childhood, youth, and adulthood? Of what might their evolving interests in gasoline stations have been symptomatic? What might they have shared in common generally with Americans coming of age in their era? What was it that such things as gasoline stations came to mean to their generation matured after World War II?

First, childhood lay important foundations. Although childhood experiences played out very differently with each, both grew up in a time of vast change when traditional ways of being and doing were challenged with increased intensity. From landscapes laid out to suit pedestrians traveling by railroad and streetcar, America was rapidly reoriented to the use of automobiles. The new landscapes created were inherently more egalitarian in spirit and intent. Codes of conduct were relaxed as a new informality came to characterize places increasingly dedicated to casual use. A child could not grow up during this time and not be affected by these changes, irrespective of whether he or she (or his or her own parents or, for that matter, adults generally) fully realized the implications. What earlier had been tentative roadside environments oriented to tourists and other travelers coalesced as a new kind of American habitat: an automobile-convenient world of highway commercial strips and shopping centers to which were oriented sprawling subdivisions with rambling "ranch" houses. Even factory and clerical jobs were diffused along the new super-roadsides as, for example, in the form of industrial and office parks. American geography substantially was remade. The new America pretended a kind of geographical mobility never before known. The sights and sounds of the new automobile-oriented world came to be what Americans, particularly youthful Americans, held most in common as a kind of cultural base.

Different children confronted this new world differently. Variously, some became preoccupied with its symbols, even to the extent of eventually orienting scholarly careers to their understanding. Clearly, pleasant childhood memories built around automobile travel were not requisite. Preoccupation with the roadside could evolve equally well out of feelings of deprivation: the inability to fully access evolving automobility. Apparently what was necessary was some substantial departure from the normative or what appeared to be normal. Experience with automobiles and the landscapes of automobile travel needed to loom large either positively or negatively. Once a strong emotional charge was attached to the roadside, then an important part of the adult personality could later form around it.

Each generation sets itself apart from those preceding according to distinctive experiences widely shared. In highly materialistic societies such as ours, certain categories of things and certain things come to stand symbolic. For the most part the domain for much of this symbolism has become what scholars now recognize as popular culture. It is the ever changeful world of fad, fashion, and taste comprised of the music people listen to, the clothing they wear, the food they eat, the hobbies they pursue. It is as well the automobiles that they drive, and, as important, the packaging of the services and products made readily accessible to them through automobile convenience. In general, succeeding generations in the United States have come to view their place in time largely as a function of the things that they consume and that consumption, since World War II, has had automobiles increasingly close at hand.

The changes taking place were certainly significant in a historical sense. They invited the sorting out of the fads, fashions, and tastes as they evolved and faded in a material world increasingly formed by a corporate-dominated marketplace. For the authors, interest in landscape history evolved from counting and collecting. It was the enumerating of things seen in moving through the landscape, and the accumulating of things related to those experiences, that may have set them apart as future students of landscape change. Eventually the vision was substantially that of the rearview mirror: of looking backward to see how things observed and collected had evolved over time. Eventually, the vision was focused and strengthened through exposure to professional historians and historical geographers variously oriented to the polite and the elite. Nonetheless, with the templates for scholarly careers set, the emphasis ultimately came back to those ordinary places and things emergent in the popular, vernacular world of automobility.

Something called landscape ultimately came to provide the intellectual framework or matrix upon which understandings could be hung. The idea of place also entered in. As children, home neighborhoods stood in contrast with neighborhoods beyond. Places, for their varying landscape configurations, either attracted or repelled. Boys on bicycles set out to explore these differences and the feelings that attached to being in one kind of a place as opposed to another. Most children grow up exploring their environments, accordingly, but for the authors as children such exploration may have been more forcefully internalized, thus setting scholarly trajectories later in life. Both sought in play, whether with packaged building sets or electric trains, to model landscapes physically: something later done with paper and pen. Eventually the preoccupations of landscape and place were strengthened as professional opportunities opened. Somewhere at some time each individually came to appreciate the ordinary, the commonplace, the vernacular as holding intrinsic interest. Here was a chance to integrate the common with the elite to explore the full continuum of human creativity.

Beyond childhood, formal education served to mold interests and modes of orienting to those interests. For one the decision to pursue a career as a historian grew quickly once an aptitude for historical analysis was recognized. The works of certain accomplished scholars loomed large in his early professional orientation. The opportunities presented by specific professors in specific programs of study further molded his thinking. For the other there came realization that academic geography might be an accommodating environment in which to pursue interests that simply did not seem to fit anywhere else in academia.

As with childhood, much of their formal education was molded by their generation's preoccupations. This is the important conclusion. Knowledge does not float free in a sea of random thinking, for significance in scholarship is always grounded in a context of prevailing views and viewpoints. Scholars engage one another in dialogue promoting, reassessing, and rejecting ideas, thereby establishing significance. Each generation of scholars is molded in their thinking by the ideas most widely debated. In overarching philosophical terms the generation educated in the 1960s was preoccupied by a pervasive modernism that worshiped the natural sciences, their discoveries, and their applications. Human geography, as a would-be social science, and history, as one of the humanities, were challenged to embrace scientific method with quantification and deductive theory in the vanguard of logical positivism. Each author accommodated this thinking in his own manner. Although neither became a theoretician wed to numerical analysis, the environments of change in which they individually operated did offer added liberating solace. There was freedom to focus on what previously had loomed merely as esoteric.

The 1960s proved a time of considerable moral and ethical soul-searching as the youth of the 1960s divided over issues raised by the Viet Nam War. It was a period of heightened social confrontation as various minorities sought to redefine and empower themselves politically and economically. Increasingly, scholars in the social sciences and the humanities were challenged to acknowledge social relevance in their work. Ignoring the dispossessed no longer could be abided. Sole concern with the agendas of the upper classes no longer could be justified. Our generation, perhaps as none before, was charged with recognizing commonplace roots: of understanding the whole of society and not just its top.

Beyond childhood and formal education one's quest of career shapes and forms one's interests. The job that one assumes focuses and limits according to the dictates of the institutional setting within which one is embedded and according to the cares and predispositions of the specific individuals who make that setting function. One's work, institutionally confined, both opens and closes opportunities. Success in one's vocation reflects suitability of personality as rooted in one's growing up and adequacy of preparation as reflects one's formal education. But, as much, success is a matter of being in the right place at the right time with the right talents. Life is substantially a lottery, it must be concluded, in which the individual is only, at best, in partial control of his or her own destiny. Nowhere does this truth apply more than to one's work or profession.

The geographer found himself surrounded by stimulating colleagues, all productive scholars and capable teachers who shared many of his values. However, his department served more as a place of convenience where highly competitive individuals justified coexistence abstractly and less as a community of pragmatically reinforcing colleagues. The whole was really not greater than the sum of its parts. It was the kind of heady environment that garnered scholarly achievement, but it was also an environment that garnered alienation. To follow one's instincts in research made one vulnerable, especially if those instincts pointed beyond established disciplinary preoccupations. One's work took longer to impact, especially when it jumped around the margins of generally accepted significance. Once a variety of research and publishing trajectories were set it took time to bring them all to fulfillment with energies focused first here and then there.

State bureaucracy presented different circumstances, but ones typical for many scholars without academic settings in the early 1970s. There the historian found work strictly rationalized within clearly set routines, the players less expected and less required to innovate in matters intellectual. One did not function to perpetuate and expand a discipline of thought through systems of apprenticeship where students follow teachers generation to generation in the pursuit of a subject matter. These aspects do not diminish the significance of the work that governmental bureaus, such as Illinois' Historic Preservation Agency, do—charged, as they are, with administering governmental programs. As work settings they are neither better nor worse than university departments. They are only different. But there is less room for intellectual flights of fancy for organizational objectives are not intellectual, but programmatic as defined through specific legislative edict. Work roles tend to be carefully defined and people shifted among roles with some frequency. In order to pursue the strictly intellectual as a public historian one necessarily augments one's work after hours turning scholarship from a profession into an avocation.

There are, of course, very important payoffs from being a preservation planner in state government. There is satisfaction in performing important services for an appreciative clientele. Professors can pontificate, advocate, and deliberate. Their scholarship can mold values in society and predispose people toward actions both general and specific. The academic concerned with landscape can contribute much to a public's appreciation of the built environment as a resource base inviting conservation or preservation. Nonetheless, it is the preservation planner who implements the programs that constitute environmental management. If scholarship focused on landscape may be said to have value beyond mere intellectual exercise, then that value derives from its ultimate application. And it is the preservation planner who makes that application.

Historic preservation in the United States has matured rapidly since World War II, driven no doubt by the massive changes in the built environment substantially engendered by accelerating automobility. From a concern with the monumental and the polite in architecture associated with society's elites, preservationists have widened their scope to embrace the commonplace in buildings such as gasoline stations associated with the full range of ordinary Americans. Concern with the vernacular in landscape has come to the fore forcefully. Scholarship focused on the American roadside now seems to enjoy a mature societal imperative. The way has been cleared to assault intellectually the gasoline station as fixture by the American roadside.

2

Place-Product-Packaging

The petroleum corporations embraced place-product-packaging in the 1910s when they adopted trademarks and brand names and established chains of look-alike gasoline stations.[1] Chains defined the trade territories necessary to attract large numbers of customers through sustained brand and company loyalties. Similarly, in the late 1930s, the motel industry began to use the place-product-packaging idea through franchising, and in the mid-1950s the fast food industry followed. Substantially, it is the place-product-packaging remembered from landscapes of youth that forms much of the nostalgia of our generation's growing up. So strong are the many recollections along the roadsides of the late 1940s and 1950s that we well might ask in retrospect how our generation could have escaped launching scholarly inquiry into such things as gasoline stations. Wasn't it inevitable? In this chapter we offer further definition for place-product-packaging, a key concept to understanding the roadside, especially its gasoline stations.

Conceptualizing the Roadside

How was it that an emergent corporate economy spawned gasoline stations as standardized places for consumption? As students of landscape we approach this question from the view of the social structurationists.[2] As sociologist Andrew Giddens, the leading advocate of structuration theory, might ask: how does human agency play out through social structures to configure the built environment as meaningful place? Who makes the decisions that configure the landscape? How is this decisionmaking embedded in society's social institutions? Place-product-packaging was a novel process by which gasoline stations, and then motels and restaurants, were increasingly configured as places of clear social meaning. To these settings habitual response was invited from a responsive consuming public. Services were standardized over

18

space and time—the anxieties of roadside consumption thereby reduced in standardized formats offering easily anticipated satisfactions. How was all of this accomplished?

Society, it may be argued, is the sum of its contributing symbolic interactions. Symbolic interactionism, derived largely from the writing of the sociologist George Mead, sees social reality as constituted through communication.[3] Part of that communication is direct and overt, through face-to-face meetings of highly personalized interaction. From there the binding communications of society scale toward the anonymous and the latent as, for example, in the substantially impersonal messages contained in the landscape as built environment. These are messages variously embedded in the infrastructure of place that define social contexts or situations for action. They are messages predicated on an interacting population's past experiences in similar places whereby anticipated satisfactions and dissatisfactions are cued.

Place-product-packaging involves messages embedded in the built environment. It concerns building forms, textures, colors, and spatial arrangements designed to communicate, as well as associated services and products offering easily accessible calculated satisfactions. Place-product-packaging encompasses interlinked coordinated marketing formats, what in franchising has been called "business-format franchising."[4] Engendered place-orientation is intended to suggest clear customer advantage. It is a game played between entrepreneur and client, a contest calculated to business profit but providing the stuff around which life styles materialistically configure for consumers.

Place-product-packaging has been a game played to modernist tendencies. Central are messages communicated through standardization: sameness of promised product and service playing out in the sameness of building form and styling as sign system. Each place in a network must be easily anticipated by the knowing consumer. Surprise enters only through the drift of carefully calculated change intended as difference in sameness. Change, incrementally prompted, tends to the superficial rather than to the fundamental. It serves as monotony's preventative: change calculated more over time than over space with the places of a network changing all at once on cue to protect the integrity of a network's meaning system. Large scale is of the essence. The most successful players are those whose "packages" have been most aggressively spread. Their systems have been carefully researched for consumer satisfaction, have been actively advertised, and, accordingly, have achieved deepest market penetration.

The competition of the modern market economy has worked against the small entrepreneur as would-be experimenter. Those who would sell gasoline, overnight accommodation, or food along the roadside in today's America had best affiliate with an established network of consumer expectation forcefully marketed nationally if not internationally. The small business going alone fights an uphill battle against the large corporations. Through place-product-packaging, merchandising has been thoroughly rationalized using modern management techniques extrapolated from industrial assembly lines. Products and services are provided by production systems made efficient through the social engineering of modern organization. No longer is the roadside a frontier for trial and error where small operators, financed largely by "sweat equity," hope to succeed. "Mom and pop" operations today are largely residual survivors of a previous time, or reflect avocations more than serious business ventures. Thus, unfortunately, much of the diversity, and, indeed, much of the vitality of the American roadside as might be remembered by those over 50 years of age has substantially evaporated in recent years, enhancing nostalgia's claim. With the rise of corporate America has come a pervasive standardization of roadsides, a kind of "commonplaceness," what some commentators have gone so far as to call "placelessness."[5] Roadsides have become so alike across the country that many critics fear that insufficient character exists distinguishing localities from one another.

The student of landscape instinctively quests character in place, seeking to understand what makes a place not only similar to but distinctive from other places. In today's America, distinctiveness derives in two principal ways. First, character accrues in the residual elements of a place surviving from the past. Survivors, even from homogenized pasts, stand in contrast with elements of the homogenized present. Landscapes are given time-depth where elements of several periods accrue in juxtaposition. Second, character is found where some new deviation appears, the novelty of the new element offering contrast with what has come before. Newness, of course, can overwhelm in a landscape, producing ultimately the sameness of a newly imposed homogeneity.

We, as authors, see ourselves as having been born into a physical America substantially fossilized both by the hard economic times of the Depression and by the nation's preoccupation with World War II. Ours was still a world of corner grocery stores, streetcars, policemen walking their beats, and horse-drawn milk wagons. It was the kind of world that Norman Rockwell pictured on the covers of the *Saturday Evening Post,* a world filled with the intimacies of crowded Main Street sidewalks and congested big-city downtowns. It was a time when suburbia still connoted pastoral residences on streets lined by maples and elms. It was a time when the young actually frequented soda fountains and candy stores and, of course (with their parents), the new drive-in restaurants. We can think back now and recognize that we were born at the end of an era. Perhaps it was really the 1920s strung out past its time. For those of us with a historian's inclination it is comforting to know that we lived then, for in hindsight it seems as if it was so different from today. How do you explain it to grandchildren who know only supermarkets and shopping centers and who thrive on the stuff of *TV Guide?*

THE GAS STATION IN AMERICA

FIGURE 2.1 With its modern aerodynamics, this Sohio station offered sharp contrast to its industrial surroundings, which were made suddenly to appear dated. In such contrasts a "modern" generation came to engender for itself identity. (*Source:* Photo courtesy of BP America, formerly known as Standard Oil of Ohio.)

It is also exciting to think about the changes since that instant called childhood. In the teenaged years of the 1950s the promise of a modern world quickly unfolded, driven by the pent-up purchasing power accumulated through World War II. Change was accelerated, no doubt, by frustrations left over from the Depression when the nation's headlong rush toward progress seemed permanently derailed in all but the utopian fantasies of those marshaling science, technology, and the social engineering of Keynesian economics. New landscapes of big business and of big government emerged: office and industrial parks for the suburbs, urban renewal and public housing for the central cities. Modern architecture (not the lush, curvaceous, streamlined versions of glass, tile, and enameled metal proposed at the beginning, but the crisp, angular versions of plastics and other synthetic veneers) produced a standardized world of increasingly specialized and impersonalized services. Produced was an increasingly ephemeral world of short-run amortization in which flimsiness competed with newness. What an exciting time of flux for those enamored of place as well as history (see Fig. 2.1)!

Our generation has now come into its own as society's movers and doers. Shaped by what has come before, we now act to shape in turn. Interestingly, the rationalized impulses of the 1950s no longer seem in fashion: the sterility of slablike office towers, the monotonous cur-

FIGURE 2.2 A 1930s Wadham's station in Madison, Wisconsin, masquerades as a Chinese pagoda.

vilinearity of residential subdivisions of standardized "ranches," the acres of parking lot serving signlike buildings in nondescript shopping centers. Currently, our tastes seem destined, if only temporarily, for the marshaled eccentricities of earlier times. Subdued is the modernist impulse to remake America in the image of a single, fully rationalized modernity. Modernism, with all of its standardization, has taken its place as just another style or fashion of parochial importance. Make way for postmodernism (perhaps, only a phase of modernism) with all of its playful ironies merging the present with notions clearly rooted in the past, even the distant past.

What is it about this generation come of age that prefers eclecticism, if not historicism? Do we read the modernist enthusiasms of the recent past as naive? Might we reject, accordingly, the modernists' quest for universalizing solutions to problems simplistically cast? Have we seen too much standardization in our landscapes and thus in our lives? Have we seen too much ephemerality? In accepting change do we ask more of it now? Certainly we appear to be demanding that innovation, architectural or otherwise, relate to rather than reject the past. From the far past we seem bent on obtaining variety and diversity to counter the sterility of the recent past. We maneuver the pieces of the old into innovative ser-

THE GAS STATION IN AMERICA

vice. Implicit is a violating of traditional architectural codes through the stretching of old meanings to new ends. At work is a kind of double coding, for the consumer of the postmodern must know the old meanings as well as the new in order to fully appreciate the humor of postmodern innovation.[6] Implicit is a deflating of elitist tendencies toward the embracing of the vernacular. The elite is lowered and the popular is raised in the conjoining of various pasts eclectically borrowed. Where might this postmodern vision of ironic plurality have been born? Where might it have been nurtured? Might not it have been born and nurtured along America's roadsides?

Architectural postmodernism may have been born in playful roadside experimentations with lighthouses, coffee pots, and windmills built as attention-getters by entrepreneurs in the 1920s and 1930s—if not the teepee-imitating gasoline stations, then the use of "Colonial," "Spanish mission," and other revivalist themes in roadside architecture, eclectically borrowed and, it is true, often abused (see Fig. 2.2). Even modernism itself tended to play out on the roadside in ever-shifting fad and fashion substantially parodying itself. What we have for so long taken very much for granted—the ever-evolving roadsides of the American experience—now loom not only as omnipresent across the nation but also as generators of taste impacting all other sorts of places. Postmodernist architects who configure high-rise buildings in rebuilt downtowns have taken more than a few of their lessons from Las Vegas and the Strip. *Learning from Las Vegas,* the classic statement of discovery by architects Robert Venturi, Denise Brown, and Steven Izenour, has proven to be a prophetic book.[7] The message taught was quite simple: a new aesthetic has been born based on automobile-oriented sensitivities. The roadside cannot be understood with traditional elitist thinking; a freedom of popular expression now informs architectural sensibilities. Learn therefrom and design! Has the postmodern movement done just that?

Postmodern scholarship rejects the assumptions of the logical positivists. It rejects the centrality of scientific method borrowed from the natural sciences as being less than fully appropriate to understanding human society. It embraces as well the impulses of the humanities by adopting and playing off against one another various philosophies and epistemologies. No thoughtful system of explanation is rejected out of hand, but all are welcomed in the search for understanding the human condition. Postmodern scholarship searches not for universal laws, or for comprehensions universally applicable everywhere at every time. Rather, it recognizes the unpredictable peculiarities of the human world, offering instead comprehensions in outline: explanation sketches more suggestive than definitive. Comprehension is not defined as an absolute condition, but as an ever-changing process of inquiry. Should not the rise of postmodernism in the academy have been expected? Perhaps a generation raised in ephemeral landscapes eclectically engendered might be expected to configure an intellectual environment equally as eclectic if not ephemeral?

The Intellectual Record

Where did understanding of the roadside begin? It probably began with writers and artists scanning the "American scene." There they found inspiration and hope in the people during economically depressed and internationally ominous times. *Fortune* magazine's "The Great American Roadside" in 1934 was the most extensive early sounding. Amid the depths of worldwide depression, *Fortune* contrasted a "young but great industry" that would earn a projected $3 billion. On the article swept in lyrical prose describing America's habitual love of motion entered into an economically vibrant, if aesthetically brash, new expression as car-convenient businesses. John Steinbeck's *The Grapes of Wrath*, although a social plea for the poor, also amounted to a "geographical novel" in that its action was driven primarily by place-encounters in journeying. A fictionalized trek along U.S. 66 from Oklahoma to California, Steinbeck's classic now exemplifies a literary genre of landscape and place-driven character as well as plot development.[8]

In art, photographers of the Historical Section of the Farm Security Administration in the 1930s, meanwhile, documented the American scene. Building on their work, Russell Lee, Sol Libsohn, Gordon Parks, and John Vachon, among the other photographers of that federal agency, went on to record the common places of America, transforming the mundane into art. Edward Hopper's paintings *Gas* (1940) and *Night Hawks* (1942) captured a sense of the roadside as stark reality. Both still haunt. These artists were among the first to react instinctively to the vernacular landscape shunning the orthodoxies of high style. Their works live on as pictorial symbols of an era and we celebrate their pathfinding in retrospective celebrations fully illustrative of the everyday places of our youth.

Road and roadside loomed large in 1950s literature. Vladimir Nabokov's *Lolita* celebrated a specific roadside feature, the motel. *Lolita* was a product of aimless seeking, and the motel the container of her wanderlust. Jack Kerouac took not only theme but manner from the excitement of automobility, *On the Road*. Appreciation became transitory. An experience-seeking generation brushed aside the present for the immediate future, but then just as quickly scrapped it for another adventure. As Kerouac himself asked, "What is that feeling when you're driving away from people and they recede on the plain till you see their specks disappearing?—it's the too-huge world vaulting us, and it's good-by. But we lean forward to the next crazy venture beneath the skies."[9]

Like a "movie through the windshield," as one scholar has comprehended the roadside, such appreciation is expressive of a time but substantially is also a passive consumer reaction.[10] Understanding must transport the reader beyond personal and period experience as well to have lasting value.

We cannot hope to identify the founder of such roadside study. All knowledge is contingent on the knower's background, how the knower came to the discovery. Laymen will have made their own discovery of the roadside in highly individual circumstances sparked more often by a particular place observed or incident occurred, an inductive flash, rather than a priori application of someone else's abstractions. Intellectual antecedents do exist but they are seldom recalled. Academics will likely identify prophets within their discipline. History founders on the complexities of the past, however, at a loss to elucidate single lines of causality easily described. But if we look for someone who first wrote persuasively and at length about the reasons for the roadside, although the study may not at first have influenced widely, it must be found in J. B. Jackson and his kindred authors of *Landscape*.

Jackson first issued the magazine *Landscape* in the spring of 1951. His "Other-Directed Houses" article appeared six volumes later, in the winter of 1956/57, to launch many scholars and simply gain a hearing from others about the roadside.[11] By situating himself literally above the roadside Jackson achieved a reflective stance at odds with the prevailing views of the roadside as eyesore made from along the roadside:

> like the tail of a comet, stretches a long sinuous line of lights of every color and intensity, a stream of concentrated, multicolored brilliance, some of it moving, some of it winking and sparkling, and every infinitesimal point of color distinct in the clear night air. The stream pours itself into the black farmlands, into the prairie, and vanishes. This of course is the roadside development seen from an altitude of several thousand feet; the most beautiful and in a way the most moving spectacle the western flight can offer, because for the first time you see that man's work can be an adornment to the face of the earth.[12]

Jackson invited aerial perspective from the first issue of *Landscape*. How simple yet insightful. Mobilized was the geographer's essential perspective—space. Meaningful order adhered despite the critics' call to bring order to the roadside. But whose order was it? Jackson found it to be that of wage earners seeking pleasure with their discretionary income in roadside leisure activities housed in the architecture of their taste, not wealthier travelers who before the war had set the demand for Revival styles. Here the geographer's spatial perspective coincided with that of the historical geographer's time perspective. As did the artistic and literary forerunners who appreciated the roadside, Jackson reposed great faith in the people. "New," "attractive," "vitality," "ideally suited to its festive purpose" were traits Jackson found in the people's architecture, "folk art in mid-XX Century garb." We are too conformist, he warned in the establishment-oriented fifties. Mindful of roadside excesses, Jackson nonetheless held faith in the people to cooperate with others in tempering but not losing roadside's virtues. Planners and the public could cooperate to channel the roadside into "avenues of gaiety and brilliance, as beautiful as any in the world," Jackson affirmed in conclusion.

Jackson's scholastically buttressed but essentially egalitarian and vaguely antiestablishment thrust continued in *Landscape*'s other roadside studies. "Design for Travel" testifies about the motel. J. Todd Snow's "The New Road in the United States" exemplifies the contributions of Jackson's *Landscape* allies.[13] Incidentally, the gas station was never the subject of one of Jackson's or his colleagues' eloquent eye-openers.

Other readers will find their roadside introduction elsewhere in the 1950s or 1960s although Jackson is now shared by more than geographers. Literate laymen can perhaps point to Tom Wolfe's provocatively entitled *The Kandy-Kolored Tangerine-Flake Streamline Baby* (1963) for first acquaintance with the generational sensibilities of the postwar car culture, including architecture. Professions and academic disciplines each have their own roadside prophets. Douglas Haskell's 1958 article in *Architectural Forum* broke new ground for at least one later architect and scholar. John Kouwenhoven's published lectures of the late fifties and early sixties exploring vernacular design were likely more influential although he did not explicitly discuss the roadside. Historians could cite Warren Susman and Daniel Boorstin a decade later, yet few have taken paths of road and roadside scholarship.[14]

Just what has the author's generation accomplished in documented and tightly reasoned intellectual pursuit or scholarship of the roadside? At first a sense of flux ruled. Modernization brought to the American economy concentration of ownership in corporate hands. On the roadside, as elsewhere, there has been a move toward mechanized, large-scale production as the big players have harnessed management to science. There has come intensified use of advertising both to legitimize and to motivate mass consumption. Work has become de-skilled, fragmented, and rationalized with a clear gap between intellectual and manual labor. The small entrepreneur as craftsman has been overwhelmed by the franchiser as purveyor of industrial system. Initially, scholarship focused on roadsides and roadside elements resistant to this change in celebrating the craft instinct. Focus was placed on roadsides not fully modernized. It was, in part, a nostalgic trip back to youth as much by method as by topic. Early scholarship did not come firmly to grips with the corporation as the principal purveyor of roadside change. Again, each generation finds for itself new things with which to be preoccupied. Those preoccupations reflect a generation's place in the evolution of ideas as well as landscape: ideas and landscape reflecting on one another as mirror image.

Historians of photography have placed their focus on roadsides pictured during the "pioneering" decades of place-product-packaging. Photography fossilizes place in the two dimensions of a print, providing fixes on situations no longer extant. Places appear suspended in time, inviting the viewer to step into the frame of the photo and casually look around. Ulrich Keller's analysis of the roadside photography solicited by Roy Stryker in the employ of the Standard Oil Company of New Jersey stands as example.[15] This photo essay speaks directly and forcefully to a time when residual "folk" and early corporate impulses at standardization mixed to define an evolving vernacular environment oriented to automobiles.

Photography also helps catch the transitory nature of landscape, especially when "before and after" images are placed side by side.[16] Viewers, rather than being invited in, are kept without by the profound sense of disjuncture. Even alienation may be engendered. Feelings of loss or gain (depending upon how the change documented is valued) preclude casual exploration by osmosis. Attention is forcefully drawn to the fact of change, and to questions set in motion toward explaining change. The roadside with its built-in ephemerality is especially problematical in tying frame to frame, date to date, period to period. The evidences of cause are rarely made explicit.

Photography, molded by the instincts of good journalism, has led the way in exploring the historical dimensions of the American roadside. Journalists have had fewer qualms relative to academics about embracing roadside topics. They can write to a lay, popular audience less concerned about the big ideas of academic pretension. As understood here, good journalism employs highly readable narrative leading to a conclusion of social significance, relies heavily on the memories of respondents as to events narrated, and is exacting in the tests for accepting written and oral sources. Good journalism is neither aimlessly anecdotal nor entertainment-oriented in its major intent. It is concerned primarily to be informative. Drake Hokanson's book on the Lincoln Highway stands in our minds as the best of a spate of highway celebrations recently published.[17] Hokanson relies equally on (his own) past and current photography to write the history of a highway promotion important in America's discovery of highway travel. The Lincoln Highway Association, a lobby for the automobile industry in its successful attempt to foster a federal highway system, not only marked a road coast to coast, but experimented with road construction techniques in demonstrating the feasibility of long-distance automobile travel.

The combined stimuli of photography and narrative are far richer in effect than given single use of the one or the other. Words and pictures certainly create a dialectic in Quinta Scott and Susan Kelly's book on

Route 66.[18] Their interview with Ina and Russell Soulsby (a brother and sister who had operated a gasoline station at Mount Olive, Illinois, since 1926) illustrates. Until 1944 the Soulsby station was located on the marked Route 66, but then new pavement was constructed and the establishment found itself isolated off the mainstream. And yet the Soulsbys struggled on, now in the backwater. The written word tells us this. But the impact of what that struggle meant is really communicated in the photographs that provide the detailed texture. In the things portrayed lies the emotional message of what has derived, good and bad, from a dogged rootedness in place. Scholarly history generally regards with caution the subtle innuendoes that photographs imply. Yet oral history does open the door to the recording and analyzing of subjective feeling as it elicits highly personalized responses from people interviewed. True, respondents do tend to emphasize the pleasant, slighting the unpleasant. There is flux in what interviewees tend to emphasize, and even to remember from one interview situation to another. Insight gained is not always as objective as historians would wish. Yet oral sources are vital to reconstructing roadside history.[19] On the ephemeral roadside few records are kept, and much that gets recorded is lost with the turnover of business. The Soulsbys, persevering at Mount Olive, kept little if any written documentation descriptive of their experience.

Feelings teased from personal interviews must be added to factual narrative if the "deepest" or "thickest" history is to emerge. The interview process gives the investigator a direct, highly personalized contact with past roadsides and, accordingly, enables extraction of insights personally important not only to the respondent questioned but to the investigator. In the process, the investigator must extract him- or herself from the subject matter in rendering final interpretation.

Some of the emergent literature on the roadside is clearly interdisciplinary, but most studies remain the province of a single discipline. Each field, of course, has its own historical templates for questioning, and its current core of fashionable questions (if not answers). American Studies seeks to know how the roadside helps define America. What is American about the roadside? Conclusions bordering on moral recommendations are common. Warren Belasco "set out to explore the roots of our automobile love affair" before asking what Americans did with their new-found automobility, and what it did to them. Americans, he concluded, undertake endless rounds of searching for technological convenience amid contrived escapes only to search on, the wonder of innovation having worn off. Karal Ann Marling utilizes the American Studies paradigm of myth and symbol to explore the origins of giantism in roadside statuary. In Minnesota, Paul Bunyan and the Jolly Green Giant spring from a mythic Middle West only to have Marling discard them as the "debris of a trashy, commercial culture, to which they are eminently suitable monuments." Ignoring the debate as to whether the American

FIGURE 2.3 What could be more outrageous to cultivated tastes than a gasoline station built like a giant pump? Witness "The Big Pump," a 1937 creation in Maryville, Missouri. (*Source:* Photo courtesy of Northwest Missouri State University Archives.)

roadside represents good or bad taste, Richard Horwitz, in his examination of a highway strip in Iowa, detects the longstanding American dilemma of the proper limits of individualism and community responsibility.[20]

Architectural historians, long preoccupied with the high style of celebrated designers, now count among themselves enthusiasts for the ordinary. Good or bad in taste, the elements of the roadside are seen as having social implication and cultural value. They reject an earlier generation's negative characterization of the roadside on largely visual-aesthetic grounds.[21] They have begun to follow the guidance of such designers as Venturi, Brown, and Izenour in seeing the strip as a new emergent design form. Most students of vernacular architecture, however, have focused on the individual elements of the roadside and not on its overall configuration. Authors have been attracted for whatever reasons to specific building types, especially those celebrated in early place-product-packaging. Paul Hirschorn and Steven Izenour, in *White Towers*, provided the first published, detailed history of a specific fast food purveyor's roadside buildings. As architectural critics-cum-historians, they argued for the value of early roadside architecture to correct what they saw as modernism's sterility. Daniel Vieyra's highly pictorial *"Fill'er Up!"* dealt with the gasoline station as a vernacular form as has Michael Witzel's very recent *The American Gas Station*.[22] Whereas both books offer excellent description of the evolving gasoline station, neither goes very far in offering explanation for that evolution.

Much of the roadside emphasis in architectural history has been given to the bizarre. Implicit is a dry sense of humor. J.J.C. Andrews's *The Well-built Elephant and Other Roadside Attractions* explores the outrageous, shielding such roadside architecture from quick and categorical dismissal as kitsch (see Fig. 2.3). Architectural historians, and journalists stancing as architectural historians, have also explored the rise of distinctive design vocabularies wrought around selected automobile-oriented building types, especially restaurants. Alan Hess's *Googie: Fifties Coffee Shop Architecture* stands among the best. Writer Philip Langdon's excellent *Orange Roofs, Golden Arches: The Architecture of American Chain Restaurants* is rendered in the same tradition. Overviews that pretend to treat the roadside as a total entity still dissolve into individual essays detailing specific building types and their related functions as in Chester Liebs's *Main Street to Miracle Mile*. What Liebs selects, it is suspected, are the roadside elements (gasoline stations, drive-in theaters, miniature golf courses, and so on) that have long intrigued him even from childhood.[23]

Geographers have published little on the roadside in books since work of that discipline is found more in its professional journals. John Jakle's *The Tourist: Travel in Twentieth-century North America* counts as one exception, the book dealing with travelers' impressions of landscapes, especially roadside landscapes. Ted Relph, on the other hand, functions more as an architecture critic in his assessments, especially of the automobile-derived "placeless" landscapes of the United States and Canada. Geographers have contributed much to other fields, dissipating, perhaps, energies that might have gone into their own distinctive disciplinary thrust. The Vales (Thomas and Geraldine) in pursuing their exploration of vegetation change seen along highways have produced two books: one a transect cross-country east and west on U.S. 40, and the other a transect north and south on U.S. 89.[24] The first effort spoke to regional differentiation, with different regions of the United States compared, while the second spoke to the images of place that pervade but one region, the American West. Potentially, academic geography offers the student of the American roadside concepts such as location, space, place, and region by which landscape can be apprehended not according to separate elements topically treated, but as a totalizing milieu or compage. To this rich assortment of ideas we would add the concepts of place-product-packaging and corporate territoriality.

Historians have focused on the economic, technological, and political powerbrokers, both individuals and organizations, who promoted and benefited from widespread automobility. John Rae launched discussion with *The American Automobile: A Brief History* and *The Road and the Car in American Life*. James Flink, in his encyclopedic *The Automobile Age*, gives little attention to the American roadside although he acknowledges the importance of its study.[25] The look of the roadside, when explained by historians at all, tends to be undertaken by those in public history. Their work, as in geography, is most often published in journals remote to the general public. A recent anthology, however, brings to light several important essays.[26] Learning about the roadside is not something academic history as practiced in the United States would overly encourage. Public historians, practicing outside the academy, have been those able and willing to embrace enthusiasm for studying the vernacular unaffected by elitist tendencies. Academic history's potential for the study of the roadside lies in the broad chronological grasp of changing American values played out in specific places.

Almost all of the work alluded to above has had implicit in it the urge to preserve. By calling attention to America's early roadside landscapes and its elements, authors serve the process of reification whereby commonplace things are raised in value and made worthy of preservation. Their writings are meant to serve an educational purpose whereby concerns, once personal and private, are shared publicly. Things such as gasoline stations, to which personal attachments were first made, are given public meaning. Thus a generation discovers that things thought only privately important are, in fact, important to many, if not to all, as icons of belonging. One step beyond the teaching of roadside awareness stands roadside preservation: the demand that the newly discovered icons of shared history be preserved for the stories they tell. In substantial measure, the publicizing of personal feelings about various kinds of places has provided antidote to the totalizing inclinations of modernism's accelerated reworking of landscape. A dialectic between the standardizing tendencies of the moment and residuals saved from the past puts a generation's world more clearly in perspective. And from such comprehension, in turn, issue attachments to place which further propel the preservation process.

The Scholarly Record Critiqued

The roadside literature accumulated over the past decade or so, as impressive and lively as it may be, suffers serious deficiency. Taken as a whole, it is still quite immature. Too many authors have displayed a propensity to reinvent the wheel. Driven by their own personal instincts as regards the roadside, few bother to carefully embrace (if, indeed, embrace at all) that which others have written before. The accumulated scholarship does not appear to be welling up out of considered thought, but is, rather, a cyclical rewashing of obvious themes. Nothing approaching a theory of roadside evolution has yet appeared. Efforts stand largely in isolation as individual case studies. The outlines of the subject matter have been established, but the framework erected stands with relatively little that could be considered definitive. Perhaps this is the price paid for a generation of scholars stimulated on a topic substantially by the mission of personal discovery.

The superficiality of the existing literature comes despite the reasonably large number of writers who have assigned the roadside in some scholarly fashion. Once having expressed themselves publicly on roadside matters, most authors go off to other interests. Even historical preservationists, after saving some highway relic or another, tend to go on to very different pursuits. Thresholds of commitment do not intensify. It is as if the single adventure or, at best, the small cluster of adventures undertaken releases the emotional energy that drives involvement. The generational implication of accumulated sentiment seems to function but once. Place-product-packaging may prove a concept capable of driving roadside-oriented scholarship to new thresholds.

Current research on roadside America may be categorized as focusing on:

1. Evolving building types;

2. The designers and builders of roadside architecture;

3. Place—the geographical sorting of activities at various scales;

4. Highway transects as linear displays of architecture and related land uses;

5. Evolving highway forms through civil engineering (and sometimes landscape architecture);

6. The history of specific highway alignments;

7. The social implications of evolving highways;

8. The image of the roadside communicated in visual art and literature;

9. The cognitive implications of the roadside as visual display; and

10. The methods of roadside preservation.

The order of treatment should not be taken as implying any sense of priority. Place-product-packaging as a concept potentially informs these emphases either directly or indirectly.

The identification of past, present, and emergent roadside prototypes by industry (and even by corporation) has just begun. At base is an attempt to identify the "normative cases": to spotlight the typical in the landscapes of different decades or eras. Knowing what was typical puts in perspective the deviating cases of the unusual and the unique. Identifying the normative helps not only in appreciating but in understanding difference when found in the built environment. At base is straightforward classification or categorization which enables us to label what it is that we are studying. This is not insignificant work for, as we have said, the labeling of things is a form of reification that establishes importance. Emphasis previously given gasoline stations, motels, and restaurants needs to be extended to other building types, especially to building types that blend different functions traditionally separated. For example, who will write the definitive history of the convenience store?

Architecture is of human creation. We must not lose sight of the people who created and maintained roadside America, in the design and management of gasoline stations for example. Scholars cannot lose sight of the social implications of the buildings that they study. Increased attention to the decisionmaking processes and the institutions in which they operate clearly is called for. Scholars need to look not only at the social infrastructures of big business and big government, but at the ways in which human agency plays out in such settings. Such is the structurationist's imperative. For our study, it is a matter of fully establishing the who, what, where, when, and how of evolving gasoline stations. Design must be placed fully into social context.

Landscape as well as architecture deserves attention. Landscapes are important as holistic entities and not merely according to their parts. Much work remains for those interested in the geographical sorting of different forms and functions. The roadside needs to be understood in terms of places created, symbolized, and used. How are rural highways different from urban streets? How are central business districts different from commercial strips? How do metropolises differ from small cities, and even small towns? Actually, it is a matter of measuring and explaining both similarities and differences. It is a matter of modeling landscapes in terms of normative cases so as to inform deviations observed. Places, of course, can be defined at various scales: places nesting within places to structure landscapes as centers of human intentionality and activity. Places define and are defined by behavioral expectations relevant to place use. Places are used and thus sustained by satisfactions sought, or dissatisfactions avoided. How does the structuring of the roadside as landscape contain and direct place-oriented behavior?

Highways represent a kind of habitat: a long, drawn-out, linear place of highly specialized use. Roads and streets are the superstructures upon which the roadsides of America are configured. Named and promoted, roads such as the Lincoln Highway and U.S. 66 have been seen as taking on personalities. What were these personalities, and how might they have translated into built environment? The study of a specific road, as it makes its way across country, suggests regional contrast. Taken as a transect along which material culture may be inventoried, the highway lends itself to the study of geographical similarity and difference. Why does one roadside form predominate here and another there? Archival records (maps and photographs especially) enable comparison across time as well as space.

Highways, of course, are intrinsically interesting quite apart from the roadside landscapes that they generate. Although it is difficult to separate roads from their contexts, focus on the civil engineering and landscape architectural aspects of the American highway holds substantial promise. Widths of right-of-way, grade and curve specifications, traffic separation (or lack of separation), signage, surfacing materials, and special configurations (such as round-abouts and cloverleafs) are an important part of the American built environment. The history of the highway as a physical entity calls for comparative analysis. How have the major parkways, turnpikes, and freeways of America differed? And why? How did various technologies originate? And why were they applied here, and not there? Now and not then? Despite the regularizing effect of the American Association of State Highway Officials since the 1920s, there are significant differences between the roadways in adjacent states even when the same general topography and similar economic orientations are at work.

Most major highways are actually route corridors, the flow of traffic having been repositioned spatially by the sequential upgrading of facilities. Many routes are like a braided stream in which the current moves by a variety of channels, the latest channel carrying the bulk of the flow. The challenge is to unravel the sequence of channel evolution like a fluvial geomorphologist might analyze a river. Bypassed sections of road stand remnant along nearly every major highway in the United States. What is it that these relics have to say about landscape evolution?

Highways and roadsides are interesting in and of themselves as visual displays and functional containers. But full value is assigned only as we strive to link things of the automobile-oriented built environment to their deepest cultural context. Every preoccupation of the present-day social scientist and humanist pretends some special understanding of the roadside. Roadside-places—their creation, use, and symbolism— inform and are informed by issues of gender, race, ethnicity, class, status, politics, and even religious persuasion. To what extent was the roadside originally a masculine place? To what extent does it remain so today? In whose image was the roadside contrived as a marketplace? Who has been discouraged in its use? Who encouraged?

The reality of roadside America has long been reflected in the nation's arts. As mentioned, the representation of the highway and all that it directly serves has been a subject for writers, artists, and photographers. The bulk of the roadside imagery available for study, however, stems not from formal art and literature, but from advertising oriented to broad popular tastes. There are the trade journals which, despite their lack of sophistication, expose industries, such as the petroleum industry, to view. Imagery, high and low, begs for analysis by way of placing the roadside firmly into social and cultural context.

Concern with the roadside as experienced by different kinds of people playing different social roles begs attention. How do people conceptualize roadside landscapes in their various capacities as tourist, commuter, shopper, or even teenage "cruiser"? What are the visual elements of the American roadside that attract attention and are remembered? How does perception vary between day and night? What is the role of artificial illumination in the creation of distinctive nighttime places? Certainly, the roadside should be studied as a structuring of physical reality, but it also should be studied according to its cognitive dimensions, and, of course, the two aspects related.

What of historic preservation? The preservation of roadside America needs not only to be promoted, but its promotion understood as a process of environmental management. How do people discover value in roadside places and translate those discoveries into action? How do the institutions of preservation operate? What are the implications for preservation vis-à-vis the making of future landscapes? How should preservation be interpreted in the context of evolving postmodernism?

In recent decades place-product-packaging has been a mechanism of standardization generally undertaken as a form of modernism. True, the eccentricities of postmodernism have come to the fore. Nonetheless, place-product-packaging remains essentially a modernist idea, a means of organizing markets for mass consumption tied to assembly lines and other methods of labor specialization. Will the eccentricities of postmodernism be sufficient to contain the emergent demand for distinctiveness in the built environment? Will the pendulum swing back in favor of the local, the unique, the particular? More likely, place-product-packaging will continue to foster standardization. The ability of big business to control local markets is simply too well established. We find in such thinking compelling rationale to fully explore place-product-packaging where it first emerged on the roadside—in the American petroleum industry's gasoline stations. Such exploration will provide some of the theoretical glue capable of raising in sophistication future scholarship focused on the American roadside.

How, then, does place-product-packaging relate to the various scholarly orientations outlined? The creation of distinctive building types carrying strong behavioral predispositions is the central dimension of place-product-packaging. The question of when, where, and how different forms evolved along America's roadsides is essentially a question of commission and design given overarching entrepreneurial strategies. Places for doing business are deliberately packaged to assign specific market niches, and necessarily emphasized are the territorial aspects of market creation. Place-product-packaging as practiced across retail sectors regionally, nationally, and internationally sums to kaleidoscopic roadside arrays—linear displays of architecture and related land use. Indeed, place-product-packaging is the very progenitor of the American roadside as built environment. Highways, as civil engineering, are made functional through infrastructures driven by place-product-packaging, a story played out in the history of literally every American highway alignment. Place-product-packaging, as a kind of social engineering, is central to consuming in the United States today—consumption itself the primary means of defining social relationships. Accordingly, the symbolisms of the roadside, especially those of place-product-packaging, figure increasingly in the work of writers and artists. And the cognitive aspects of roadside display loom increasingly important to humanists and social scientists alike. All of these various concerns have fostered an impulse to preserve aspects of the American roadside, especially forms place-product-packaging produced.

The Place-Product-Packaging Concept

Place-product-packaging evolved as American life radically reordered between 1865 and 1900. Population and wealth grew rapidly. Population nearly doubled and began centering in cities. Whereas one-sixth of America lived in centers of over 8,000 people before the Civil War, one-third did by the turn of the century. Complaints against the uneven distribution of wealth, which captured national political attention, reflected an undeniably burgeoning economy. Marketing's techniques and extent altered accordingly. Whereas consumers had traditionally purchased from nearby retail stores in villages, consumers in rural, small-town, and urban centers were drawn increasingly to urban-based department stores, chain stores, and mail-order houses. Credit was extended in various ways to encourage consumption of goods beyond the average buyer's capacity to purchase. Although installment credit dated from the republic's earliest days, "open book" credit prevailed until the end of the nineteenth century when department and specialty stores began monthly billing. Americans were encouraged to substitute a credit-based national economy dependent on institutional lenders. Mass consumption arose.[27]

Patented trademarks became a function of mass consumption.[28] After the Civil War, corporations in nearly every industry sought to establish

FIGURE 2.4 Place-product-packaging was built around brand names and trademarks. The Pegasus logo soared not only on behalf of Socony-Vacuum, but on behalf of all of that firm's subsidiaries, including the General Petroleum Company of California.

at the retail level clear identities for their products in order to build large regional if not national markets. By establishing customer preference for a product clearly named and readily identifiable in stores, companies sought to establish market penetration, if not dominance. Mass marketing, driven by widespread advertising, enabled economies of scale in production, engendering lower production costs and wider profit margins, the advantages requisite to oligopolistic or even monopolistic control of markets. Patent and copyright law provided the legal environment. By 1900 the brands of the United Cigar Company and the National Biscuit Company, for example, could be found nearly everywhere in the United States, the stores that carried their trademarks assigned degrees of status and prestige in the process. Other companies, such as the Great Atlantic and Pacific Tea Company, actually entered retailing with chains of stores owned and franchised to agents.

A regional or national brand carried implications of quality guarantee. The customer was assured of a known product for which standards were maintained. Unbranded or generic merchandise carried only the guarantee of the retailer and not the declared assurance of the manufacturer. In providing the local merchant with prepackaged, branded merchandise (reinforced by point-of-purchase signage and newspaper and magazine advertising) the large corporation signified to customers a breaking down of parochialism and an embracing of modernism. Newspaper and magazine ads (and later radio and television promotions) fostered the sense of being connected to the fashionable and up-to-date centered in the cosmopolitan places of the country. The logo—its composition or form, the wordings used, the specific colors of its design— raised the ante on purchases made. Things were bought not only for their functional or utilitarian properties but for the sense of social prestige attached. Increasingly, as markets evolved in scale branded goods proved cheaper to manufacture and to sell, price linking with status as sales incentive. Prime among the national brands to emerge in the American marketplace prior to World War I was that of Standard Oil. It is to the

FIGURE 2.5 The runner Pheidippides provided the Ohio Oil Company its logo and a slogan that promised "Best in the long run."

trademarks and brand names of the petroleum industry that we turn in a search for the origins of roadside place-product-packaging.[29]

Trademarks and Brand Names

The Standard Oil Company, founded at Cleveland by John D. Rockefeller and his associates, was not merely a good competitor in the marketplace. Standard Oil competed vigorously, indeed unethically, to control the refining of crude oil into kerosene, lubricating oils, greases, floor dressings, and the other petroleum products in demand in the late nineteenth century. Favorable freight rates were extracted from the railroads and, through collusion with the railroads, the profitable transportation of competing company products even denied. More important, the Rockefeller interests moved forcefully to buy out troublesome competitors on the realization that control of the market meant control of the price for petroleum products and, through pricing, the expenditures made for buyouts could be recouped. Through the first decade of the twentieth century the Standard Oil companies, overseen by the parent holding company, Standard Oil of New Jersey, controlled some 85 percent of the nation's total petroleum market. The Standard Oil name was everywhere represented through wholesale agents and its branded products were accepted as the industry's "standards."

With the breakup of the Standard Oil Trust in 1911, the separated companies, joined by other firms attracted by the prospects of open competition, brought a spectrum of new brand names and trademarks to the marketplace. The rise of automobile ownership pushed gasoline and motor oil sales to the forefront. Motor oil was branded first, with gasoline remaining essentially a generic product until the 1920s. Early automobile engines, lacking precise engineering, consumed inordinant amounts of lubricating oil. Sold at garages and in paint, drug, and a variety of other stores, oil was marketed out of storage drums and pumped into small containers to be poured into engine crankcases. Customers were faced with a variety of oil brands, Pennzoil, Kendall, Quaker State, and Valvolene among those still on today's market, and Polarine, Magnolene, Stanocola, Purol,

FIGURE 2.6 Trademarks changed. The Continental Oil Company used a Revolutionary War "continental" soldier as logo before adopting western themes.

FIGURE 2.7 Advertisement for the Continental Oil Company soliciting dealers. The Conoco brand is made into a branding iron. (*Source: National Petroleum News* 52 [October 1960]: 26. Courtesy *NPN*.)

and Gargoyle among the brands no longer in existence. Gargoyle was the trademark of the Vacuum Oil Company, the Standard Oil subsidiary that originally specialized in producing high-quality lubricants. Although sold worldwide (the Gargoyle brand was originated in France), it would be the firm's Mobiloil that would survive as a trademark.

Petroleum companies next turned to branding gasoline, many garages and stores initially carrying several competing brands. Point-of-purchase advertising proliferated at retail outlets—signs painted on walls, metal signs attached to or hung from buildings, names and logos stenciled on windows, posters displayed. Garages were often festooned with signs, much to the irritation of cultivated eyes already offended by the ordinary architecture of converted livery stables, sales barns, and other utilitarian structures given to garage use. Clashing signs neutralized one another. Far better for an oil or gasoline marketer to achieve exclusive rights to sell only its own products with a given retailer.

Let us pause briefly to note some of the better known brand names and trademarks traditionally associated with gasoline marketing over the years. The flying red horse was first used in South Africa by Socony (the Standard Oil Company of New York), originally Standard Oil's exporting affiliate. In Greek mythology, Pegasus, the steed of the Muses, was seen to carry its riders to poetic inspiration (see Fig. 2.4). But to loyal customers of what is today the Mobil Corporation Pegasus came to connote dependability, with overtones, perhaps, of uplifting power. Royal Dutch Petroleum, derived from the Shell Transport and Trading Company, used the scallop shell as logo worldwide. The firm, originally an importer of shells used in mother-of-pearl items such as buttons and knife handles, shipped petroleum products as well when oil was discovered in the Dutch East Indies (today's Indonesia). The Gulf orange disc, once known nationwide but today seen only in the Northeast, derived from the firm's entering the New Orleans kerosene market; kerosene for business and home lighting was sold from horse-drawn tank wagons with each company's vehicles painted a different color. Orange was the only color not in use when Gulf entered the field.

The Esso name was coined in 1923 by the Standard Oil Company of New Jersey. The company's French subsidiary had adopted "Eco," derived from the word *l'économique*. The name was short and was pronounced like "echo" in most languages. But the similarity of "Esso" to "S.O.," the initials for Standard Oil, won the day. The name was printed in red (with a rounded *E*), and surrounded by an oval band of blue (see Fig. 4.3). The Pure Oil Company's logo was comprised of a blue circular band made to look like a gear with ratcheted edges framing the word "Pure," also in blue. Its design was said to reflect at once "curvature, angularity, and radiation" as derived from the geometrics of the circle, square, and star. When the Pure seal was adopted in 1930, the *Pure Oil News* reported to company employees that "the Pure Seal by consistent use on many types of advertising material, will become indelibly impressed upon the minds of thousands of motorists. It will unify the company's operations and its products."[30]

Numbers were integrated into many brand names. In 1931, the Union Oil Company of California adopted the number 76 as a marketing symbol for its operations on the West Coast. The number represented the Spirit of 1776 and was augmented with an advertising campaign that emphasized "Minute Man Service." The U.S. Patent Office, however, refused until 1950 to register the trademark on the grounds that the name deceptively suggested the octane number of the company's gasolines. The "66" in the Phillips brand seemed "catchy" (like "Heinz 57") and was rationalized after its adoption in terms of U.S. 66, the federal highway that cut across the firm's marketing area in the Middle West and the Southwest. The company even adopted the shield popularized on federal highway markers.

Transcontinental Oil's marathon runner was expropriated by the Ohio Oil Company when it bought Transcontinental in the 1930s (see Fig. 2.5). Here was the Athenian runner Pheidippides, hero at the Plains of Marathon. The firm later adopted a block "M" logo when it was renamed the Marathon Oil Company, but advertisements continued to promote Marathon gasolines as "Best in the Long Run." Continental Oil Company advertising used the Revolutionary War soldier as a logo before adopting regional themes appropriate to its western marketing area (see Fig. 2.6). "Conoco's 'the Hottest Brand Going' is a symbol," the company informed

FIGURE 2.8 Depicted on this late 1940s Tide Water-Associated map are many of the elements of place-product-packaging which characterized the company's gasoline stations. Here was a place of known satisfaction tied to brand identity.

would-be wholesalers and retailers in a 1960 ad in the *National Petroleum News* (see Fig. 2.7). A cowboy, looking somewhat like the Marlboro Man, stands before a gasoline station with a lit cigarette and a hot branding iron displaying the Conoco triangle. "This symbol is the face we present to motorists who are looking for quality products, fine service, and friendly care for their cars," the ad continued.[31]

So successful did brand marketing become that independent wholesalers and their dealers found themselves quickly disadvantaged. Without a readily recognized and appreciated symbol, independents found it difficult to attract the tourists and other motorists unfamiliar with a strange locality's business community. The quality of locally branded or unbranded gasolines could not be readily ascertained. Attempts were made to create trademarks that independents could share just like the dealers of the emergent integrated petroleum corporations. In the 1920s, the Red Hat brand was introduced by the National Petroleum Marketers Association for retailer use. But Standard Oil of Indiana successfully challenged the logo in the courts claiming infringement on its Red Crown gasoline trademark. Also in the 1920s, the Spread Eagle logo was introduced. "By this sign you will know the oil men of America who are truly independent," promotional ads read.[32]

Color Schemes

Trademarks were specifically protected by federal legislation and, early in the 1930s, various state courts held in addition that companies could also claim exclusive rights to decorative color motifs, especially when combined with logos.[33] Most of the companies descended from the Standard Oil Trust adopted red, white, and blue. Consequently, most of the other corporations embraced other color schemes—Shell's orange and red, Sun's blue and yellow, Pure's blue and white, Union's orange and blue. Most companies modified their colors over time. Cities Service adopted green, white, and black, then shifted to green and white, and, finally, to red and white in adopting the present Citgo name. Phillips worked initially with distinctive shades of orange and brown, shifting to red, white, and gray. Next to the red, white, and blue combination that carried patriotic implication, red, white, and green were most frequently combined as, for example, at Texaco and Sinclair.

Building Designs

Distinctive building designs linked with logos and color schemes were also protected by the courts. Although different gasoline station form-types evolved in succeeding phases of popularity (as will be discussed in chapter 5), most companies sought to give their stations at least some minor design motif to set them apart from those of rival firms. In the late 1940s, the stations of the Tide Water-Associated Company featured truncated towers upon which the company's distinctive Flying A was displayed (see Fig. 2.8). The company's stations also sported canopies which, along with the tower, presented a distinctive profile to motorists driving at high speeds along West Coast highways. Stations stood in the landscape as much as signs as structures. They were icons by which the company and its products were readily recognizable, and thus readily accessed. The loyal customer knew what to expect from such a place, eliciting, as it did, the familiar. At night whole buildings, when illuminated, stood out sharply signlike (Fig. 2.9).

Signs and Logos

Logos were first attached only to station buildings. But from approximately 1915 onward gasoline stations were marked additionally at the street by distinctive sign postings—logos lifted high on columns or posts (see Fig. 2.10). These sign standards have become an integral part of the

FIGURE 2.9 At night, light reflecting off the ceramic tile of this 1950s Standard Oil of Indiana station made the entire building a vivid sign. (*Source:* Photo courtesy of Sangamon Valley Collection.)

THE GAS STATION IN AMERICA

WISCONSIN

Tourgide Map

GULF

DEALER

STOP AT THE SIGN OF THE
ORANGE DISC

FIGURE 2.10 Free road maps inclined motorists to carry corporate logos with them. Here the Gulf disc is portrayed soaring above a 1950s vintage "oblong box."

gasoline station as place. Companies carefully measured the visual impact of their signs. Could motorists readily identify them day and night? In the 1960s, the Shell Oil Company switched from a shell silhouetted against the sky to a "controlled background" sign designed by Raymond Loewy Associates (see Fig. 2.11). Sunray Mid-Continent Oil Company hired the industrial design firm of Lippincott and Margulies to rethink the D-X logo, the descendant of the firm's Diamond-X brand. The twenty-five-year-old red, cream, and black color scheme was retired in favor of red, white, and blue and the hyphen removed to form a simpler DX. The new motif was deemed more modern in its simplicity and thus more legible, as well as fashionable.

"Brand identification is taking a professional look," headlined a feature article in the *National Petroleum News,* long the industry's leading trade journal emphasizing marketing. Companies, it was reported, were seeking "sharp, simple lines" in their signs, and logos were changing accordingly. A trademark should have:

1. Legibility (instant recognition and impression);
2. Impact (single impression with immediate appeal);
3. Simplicity (easy understanding);
4. Distinction (recall and remembrance); and
5. Adaptability (facile reproduction in any size or medium).[34]

Companies needed to eliminate conflicting or obscure elements in signs. In the old Socony sign, the flying red horse and the word "Mobilgas" were seen as competing for attention. The new sign reduced the size of the horse and built up the simplified word "Mobil" in bigger, heavier letters (see Fig. 2.12). Thus corporations came to use shorter names written in larger letters set against controlled backgrounds of sharpened outline. Where colors were not appropriate they were changed as, for example, Shell's replacing of orange with lemon yellow.

FIGURE 2.11. "Controlled background" signs, as adopted by Shell in the 1960s, amplified the visibility of the shell logo.

FIGURE 2.12 Down with the old and up with the new. Socony Mobil adopts a new logo. (*Source:* Socony Mobil *Annual Report,* 1956.)

FIGURE 2.13 In addition to architecture, place-product-packaging involved logo, color scheme, product and service mix, and the actual packaging of commodities as depicted on the front of this 1950s American Oil Company road map.

"Total Design"

Place-product-packaging emerged as a "total design" concept. Each company sought to coordinate logos, color schemes, signage, and building architecture toward creation of chains of attractive, look-alike retail outlets. Careful attention was given to gasoline pump design and pump coloring and marking, point-of-purchase advertisements (including office, window, and driveway displays), uniforms worn by attendants and attendant demeanor, and, of course, product line and service mix.

The American Oil Company, like most other oil companies in the 1950s, constructed rectangular, boxy-looking gasoline stations clad in porcelain enamel. But their buildings had distinctive rounded edges, ornamental towers, and façades of red and green striping on white. Pumps were painted in company colors with glass globes atop carrying company brand names. Since the 1930s, America's oil had been sold in quart cans, the labels carrying the Permalube brand. Tires, batteries, fan belts, antifreeze, and, indeed, all products were marked "Amoco." Free road maps showcased the integrated marketing system created (see Fig. 2.13). As "service" stations, American outlets sold light engine repair as well as greasing, lubricating, and washing services. Pictured on map covers was an ideal place—the station building, its surrounds, its contents, and its activities—all subtly orchestrated to present the American Oil Company in a positive light.

Created in the American scene, therefore, were places, defined at the scale of the retail store with clear meaning vis-à-vis gasoline's availability. Strong behavioral proclivities attached to these places. Customers developed expectations as to satisfactions to be gained, or dissatisfactions to be avoided. Behavioral predispositions were reinforced by signage, architecture and site design, and merchandising as integrated marketing system. Important also was the service provided implicit in functions performed. To oversee the whole, companies adopted systems of quality control, encompassing training schools for station managers, elaborate manuals detailing station operation, and, of course, systematic inspection. Employment contracts and lease agreements hinged on station operators maintaining company standards. The Texas Company established its "Certified" service stations in the 1920s, guaranteeing that Texaco stations, even those not owned and operated directly by the company, adhered to standards. In the 1930s Texaco offered the public "Registered Rest Rooms" and maintained a fleet of white cars (the "White Patrol") to oversee their cleanliness. Green and white metal curb signs identified participating dealers.

Place-product-packaging was an integral part of corporate advertising campaigns. It was itself an advertising strategy. With the image of a corporation firmly established in chains of look-alike or similar gasoline stations spread across sizable trade territories, customer loyalty was excited through regional and national advertising campaigns. In 1920, the various Cities Service companies advertised in mass-circulation magazines such as the *Saturday Evening Post,* and in some 142 newspapers in 113 cities across 20 states.[35] The company used billboards and small "snipe" signs nailed to trees and fence posts along highway rights-of-way. Professed objectives were: "To make the Cities Service trade mark nationally known and nationally respected as the symbol of a great and efficient organization; to strengthen the fine morale of the employees by giving them, collectively, a more complete uniform picture of their organization," and, of course, "to sell Cities Service oils and gasolines."[36] Radio, and later television, augmented print. Vincent Lopez and his Pure Oil Orchestra promoted that company on radio starting in 1930. Through to the 1950s, Pure Oil sponsored news commentator H. V. Kaltenborn over NBC radio. In 1950, the company launched "Who Said That?" a quiz show aired over a sixteen-station NBC network. Constantly repeated was the company's admonition: "Be Sure with Pure." The way to impress a slogan on the public mind, and to make it a part of everyday language, the *Pure Oil News* reported, was constant repetition.[37] Of course, Texaco scored early television's biggest success with Milton Berle. "We are the men of Texaco," the uniformed attendants sang, gasoline hoses and nozzles well in hand.

Place-product-packaging evolved on the roadside first in the petroleum trade.[38] At gasoline stations, logos, colors, building design, point-of-purchase signage, uniformed attendants and their activities, branded merchandise, and managerial system all served to communicate place meaning. Place-product-packaging, of course, was a constantly evolving process within the system of a given company's self-promotion. Architecturally, it drove ephemerality along the nation's roadsides with change tending to the "clip-on" or "plug-in" variety. Except at those infrequent intervals when substantive change was driven by profound technological or economic shocks in the petroleum industry, place-product-packaging entailed appearance or image more than substance. Companies sought to appear continually refreshed, reactivated, and progressive. To do otherwise was to risk falling out of fashion with loss of market to competitors accruing. Gradually have Americans come to expect change in the built environment. Advertising, as it drives demand in a capitalistic economy, lays the basis for this change.

Place-product-packaging is a form of symbolic interaction. Gasoline stations stand as "to whom it may concern" messages in the American scene. The marketers of gasoline and other petroleum products for motorcars are sending these messages to a conditioned motoring public. Thus have the purveyors of gasoline structured or institutionalized distributive systems for their products. Distribution has been placed on a thoroughly rational basis such that basic schemes employed at any one time are very much alike corporation to corporation. (Even small entrepreneurs find that they must simulate the corporate tools of marketing if they are to survive.) Corporations act very much alike in defining and meeting market contingencies with place-product-packaging central to the drama. The fads and fashions of place-product-packaging are communicated through the industry media, especially the trade journals.

Place-product-packaging, vital as it is to understanding gasoline stations and, indeed, the whole of the vernacular American roadside, rings hollow without careful consideration of its territorial dimensions. How was it that gasoline station chains formed geographically to do battle for gasoline dollars? How did the creation and defense of trade territories enter in? Did territorial strategies differ significantly from corporation to corporation? How did territorial strategies change over time? Are there lessons for understanding modernism, and the version of modernism that we call postmodernism? What can we learn about evolving building types? The designers who rendered them? The geographical sorting of highway-oriented activities? The highway as form? The social implications of highway technologies? And all the other questions that have stimulated recent scholarship focused on roadside America? It is to questions of marketing strategy and corporate territoriality that we now turn.

3

Marketing Strategies in the Petroleum Industry

Traditionally, the petroleum industry has been segmented by production, transportation, refining, and marketing activities. Initially, most companies organized to pursue only one or possibly two areas. Producers sank wells and pumped crude oil, pipeline companies moved the crude to refineries, and refining companies manufactured kerosene and other products with wholesalers and retailers handling distribution. John D. Rockefeller's Standard Oil Company came to dominate the industry by controlling transportation and refining. After 1900, however, Standard Oil began to vigorously integrate back into producing, with distribution left primarily in the hands of small businessmen acting as Standard Oil agents. With the breakup of the trust and the rise of the new major independent oil companies, competition intensified with most large companies integrating forward into marketing as well. The integrated oil corporation of the 1920s operated wells in a variety of fields (foreign as well as domestic in many instances), owned or shared ownership in pipeline facilities, operated refineries, and distributed both through company-owned and -operated (or owned and leased) retail outlets, and the retail outlets of independent dealers. What follows is a brief overview of the changing marketing practices driven by downstream integration, especially as it reflected the rise of gasoline as the petroleum industry's principal product encouraged by new automobile and highway technologies.

Pre-1920s

Automobiles, highways, and petroleum induce a way of life whose overall significance as mobility Americans have long valued. Its components, however, converged from separate paths at the start of the twentieth century to reformulate the national passion as automobility.[1]

Automobiles by whatever power—gasoline, electric, or steam—were first invented by Europeans. Brothers Charles and Frank Duryea are generally credited with the first American-built gasoline automobile although other lesser-known claimants contend.[2] The Duryea was built in Springfield, Massachusetts, in 1893. By 1900, six companies produced a total 4,192 automobiles. But in 1902 the Olds Motor Works alone produced 2,500 two-cylinder automobiles and thereby foreshadowed dominant trends: the ascendance of the gasoline-driven engine and mass production. Olds' three-horsepower "curved dash" model captured 28 percent of the total market with its low $650 price. Today's basic engine and the mechanical means for transmitting it to the drive wheels were quickly developed.

The year 1908 marked the founding of General Motors and the appearance of the Model T Ford, two key factors in the growth of passenger car production to over 100,000 by 1909. Ford's twenty-horsepower, four-cylinder 1914 Model T averaged twenty-three miles per gallon and positioned the company to hold nearly 50 percent of the American automobile market through 1924. Ford's assembly-line improvements drove the retail price of the Model T progressively downward to $385 in 1927 when its fifteen-millionth and last unit rolled off the line.

Highways changed in response to traffic demands.[3] Slow-moving and relatively light vehicles in the nineteenth century were well served through introduction of "macadam," a hard clay pavement held together by a bituminous binder. But most improved roads were of gravel or graded dirt. Responsibility for roads fell to local governments, which tended to assume little responsibility for intercity trunk highways, focusing instead on farm-to-market and other localized needs. Privately financed railroads provided the long-distance connectivity upon which mass markets and mass consumption were initially based. Then, the League of American Wheelmen lobbied for road improvements to accommodate bicyclers and in 1893 induced congressional funding of the Office of Public Road Inquiry to study ways to improve road building.

Improved highways for long-distance travel came slowly to the fore. Four miles of brick pavement were laid in 1893 near Cleveland, Ohio. The first concrete highway was laid in Michigan in 1909, a one-mile section near Detroit. In 1904, the first census of the nation's roads disclosed that only 7 percent were hard-surfaced, and only some 200 miles were fit for the ever more popular automobile. The landmark Federal Aid Road Act, which was passed in 1916, appropriated $75 million to be spent over five years to improve rural post roads and encouraged the implementation of federal highway standards by granting up to 50 percent of road improvements upon a state's organization of a highway department. In 1919, Oregon led the way to automobile-financed highways with adoption of the first gasoline tax, one cent on each gallon of gasoline sold.

Concurrently, marketing assumed a new form in the petroleum industry. Kerosene (used primarily for lighting) and gasoline were at first marketed through a variety of independent jobbers or bulk dealers. After the

FIGURE 3.1 A 1915 curbside gasoline station affiliated with Standard Oil of Kentucky. (*Source:* Photo courtesy of Chevron Corporate Library.)

end of Standard Oil's monopoly, gasoline consumption soared from 25 percent of the petroleum market in 1909 to 85 percent only ten years later. Existing retail outlets, primarily grocery and hardware stores, added gasoline to their inventories, as did the new automobile repair and storage garages. Communities, consumers, and dealers alike grew dissatisfied with these unspecialized outlets. Gasoline pumps, which originated as unadorned mechanical devices, offered safe dispensing directly into fuel tanks, thereby avoiding use of hand-held containers that were susceptible to spilling and a definite fire threat. Pumps satisfied consumer demand for product quality by avoiding impurities common to open containers. Pumps also reduced evaporation. But slow service and overpricing at the unspecialized stores and garages invited a new way of retailing gasoline. Pumps and a station building accessed either from the curb or off the street at a drive-in promised much (see Figs. 3.1 and 3.2).[4]

The 1920s

Petroleum marketing's basic structure as developed in the early 1920s would survive for nearly a half century. Bounteously supplied cheap gasoline coupled with ever bigger automobiles as well as quietly self-imposed taxation for rapid highway expansion ensured stability. Place-product-packaging evolved from the retailers' emphasis on the gasoline station as the critical link in marketing.

FIGURE 3.2 A 1917 off-street gasoline station operated by the Gulf Refining Company in Louisville. (*Source:* Photo courtesy of Chevron Corporate Library.)

Automobility enjoyed explosive growth. Almost 10.5 million motor vehicles were registered by 1921, including slightly over 8 million automobiles. Ten years later registrations totaled slightly over 26.5 million, 23 million being private motorcars. Car designs standardized. Closed steel bodies brought enhanced passenger comfort and enabled year-round automobile use in cold climates. Higher compression engines of the 1920s made more efficient use of gasoline than before, but the Burton cracking process discovered in 1913 made refining more efficient and gasoline cheaper to refine. American automakers were little pressured to design and produce truly fuel-efficient vehicles. Four-cylinder engines were most common at the decade's start, but sixes eventually dominated with eights too becoming popular. Nearly 4 million gallons of motor fuel were being consumed in private use by 1921, and nearly four times as much by 1930. Consumer credit was extended to automobile and motor fuel purchasers, which encouraged the use of consumer credit generally. The automobile was looming quickly as the backbone of the nation's consumer-oriented culture.[5]

Highways developed apace. The Office of Public Roads and supporting industrial interests (automobile manufacturers, petroleum companies, and the makers of tires, rubber, and concrete, for example) persuaded Congress to capitalize on the popular enthusiasm for highways by enacting the Federal Highway Act of 1921. "Primary" roads thus became those connecting large population centers and for them matching

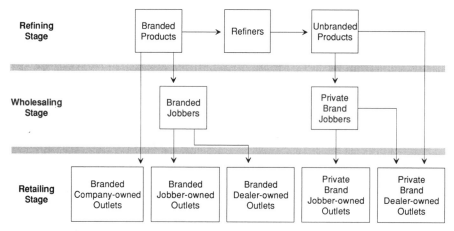

Refining Stage	Branded Products	→ Refiners →	Unbranded Products	

FIGURE 3.3 Outline of petroleum distribution in the United States defined in terms of the basic linkages between refiners, jobbers, and dealers.

grants were provided up to 7 percent of each participating state's mileage. Although total road and street mileage increased by 3 percent in the decade, surfaced road mileage doubled. By 1929 every state had enacted the motor fuel tax by which motorists financed the highway construction boom. Federal engineers sat in the committees of the American Association of State Highway Officials, which responded to federal dollar-matching in 1925 by recommending a nationally uniform system of highway signs. Thus originated ubiquitous federal shield signs with odd numbers for north-south highways and even numbers for east-west highways, as well as color- and shape-coded signs for other information.

The 1920s brought a glut of crude oil onto the American market with the opening of major producing fields, especially in Texas, Oklahoma, and California. The overproduction of crude oil drove prices down and diminished profit margins. Refineries were built at larger and larger scales with technologies designed to cut refining costs and enhance competitiveness. To increase gasoline sales, companies moved aggressively to develop larger and larger sales territories utilizing place-product-packaging as the principal marketing strategy. Major companies made their profits primarily at the refinery level. Their essential problem was to secure increased market expanse and penetration. In Figure 3.3 the linkages between refiners and retail dealers traditional to the petroleum industry are diagrammed.

In using place-product-packaging, companies sold branded gasoline, distributing it, in part, through company-owned outlets. These stations were either managed by company employees or leased to private businessmen carefully supervised through lease agreements by company district managers. Gasoline sold per gallon four or five cents over "tank wagon" price, the price companies normally charged in making deliveries in a locality. At leased stations, contracts generally extracted two or three cents per gallon, the dealer keeping the residual over the tank-

FIGURE 3.4 In the 1930s, Standard Oil of California owned a network of stations throughout the Pacific Coast states typified by this outlet in Los Angeles. (*Source:* Photo courtesy of Chevron Corporate Library.)

FIGURE 3.5 Standard Oil of California road maps portrayed these stations through the late 1940s.

wagon charge. Some corporations, such as Standard Oil of California, preferred to emphasize company-controlled stations (see Figs. 3.4 and 3.5). Other firms, such as Phillips and Pure, preferred to market almost exclusively through branded jobbers, wholesalers who handled only a single branded product (discussed below). Most corporations built chains with both types of distribution networks (see Fig. 3.6). Quality control was easier to achieve in company-owned outlets, but capital outlays were less when jobbers were used. The financing costs of chain expansion could be shared with local businessmen (and their bankers) when jobber networks were employed. Some refiners sold only unbranded gasoline that went directly to independent dealers or to private jobbers who, in turn, supplied their own stations and/or those of independent retailers. Some refineries sold both branded and unbranded product.

The early experience of the Shell Oil Company in California illustrates the vitality of place-product-packaging in the 1920s. Initially an importer of Indonesian oil and then a crude oil producer in various California fields, Shell began marketing in 1914 as the American Gasoline Company, opening twelve outlets in Seattle. By 1920, the company had stations in Washington, Oregon, and California supplied from some twenty company-owned bulk depots. Both through the purchase of several small independent chains and through the vigorous building of new gasoline

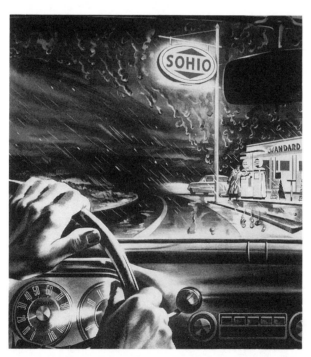

FIGURE 3.6 In the 1950s Standard Oil of Ohio (Sohio) was marketing both through company-owned outlets and dealers. As this advertisement (reproduced in the company's 1952 *Annual Report*) implies, stations were intended to symbolize for motorists complete dependability.

FIGURE 3.7 Shell's "A" station, introduced in California, was used as well by the company's Roxanna subsidiary in Illinois and across the Middle West.

stations, Shell aggressively built a trade territory. Key was the company's first prototype gasoline station—the "A" station, called affectionately by employees the "cracker box" (see Figs. 3.7 and 3.8). It was essentially a roof some 32 feet long and 16 feet wide, half supported by columns and covering a driveway with pumps, and half covering an office space walled with glass-paneled "factory sash." Prefabricated panels, metal frame, window glass, doors, and fixtures of all kinds were packed in crates that could be stored in warehouses and transported to roadside locations as needed. A complete station with pumps, tanks, pumping equipment, a graded drive, and signage cost about $3,500 in 1920. Stations were painted orange with bright red trim.[6]

Shell "invaded" the area between San Jose and Santa Barbara in California by building 8 bulk depots and 100 service stations in six weeks. District managers drove the area's highways picking suitable locations. Real estate men followed to buy or lease sites, and were followed in turn by construction crews in relays to excavate and bury tanks, pour concrete foundations, bolt buildings into place, install pumps, and paint. Stations could be established, start to finish, in as little as ten days.

The ability of companies to marshal internally the capital and expertise to drive trade territory expansion was not infinite. Thus corporations contracted with wholesale jobbers to create and sustain chains of branded stations in local trade areas. Jobbers might be partially financed by a corporation toward establishing a new business in a new territory, or the jobbers of competing companies might be converted. In a sense, oil companies operated in marketing as in production through a "law of capture." In producing fields, oil pumped to the surface on a given tract of land belonged to the owner of that land even if it was siphoned from pools beneath adjacent properties. This rule led to wasteful overdevelopment of fields and, of course, to the gasoline glut as competing interests sought to extract maximum flow. The same mentality led competing companies to overbuild retail chains in their competition to siphon away gasoline sales from other firms.

FIGURE 3.8 A modified version of Shell's "A" station was still operating in James-town, California, in the 1970s. (*Source:* Photo courtesy of David Davenport.)

Pure Oil moved into the Southeast through such jobber organizations as the Mid-South Oil Company of Alabama, the Wofford Oil companies of Georgia and Alabama, the Seaboard Oil Company of Florida, and the Colonial Oil Company of Virginia and North Carolina. The Wofford com-panies purchased their gasoline from Pure, but initially sold the product under the Woco-Pep brand. In Alabama, the firm owned 31 bulk depots and some 600 outlets in 1930. Organized in 1903 at Birmingham, the firm originally had sold kerosene and lubricating oils, turning in 1916 to gasoline. The Seaboard Oil Company in Florida involved the conversion of 23 bulk depots and 160 retail outlets to the Pure brand from that of the Indian Oil Refining brand, Indian Oil's refinery and brand names, includ-ing the Havolene trademark, having been sold to Texaco. By 1931, Sea-board operated 35 bulk depots and 328 stations for Pure, the flagship stations sporting "Spanish mission" styling with stucco walls and tiled roofs. The Colonial Oil Company, headquartered at Norfolk, represented a consolidation of several former Pure Oil distributors. Its stations were spread across some 43 counties in two states. Not all Pure Oil jobbers were by any means as large. The R. R. ("Railroad") Jones Oil Company of Winston-Salem, North Carolina, affiliated with Pure in 1929, bringing a single bulk depot of 15 storage tanks and 21 owned and operated sta-tions.[7]

Stations could be categorized by type of ownership. At some stations in a given chain, land, buildings, and other improvements might be owned by the corporation. At other stations, land might be leased but improvements owned, the corporation leasing the land from a local own-er usually at a stipulated annual rent for a set term of years with renewal options. At still other stations, both land and buildings might be leased from a local investor. Some corporations acquired land, built stations, and then sold them to investors, leasing back the facilities. Many corporations offered finance plans whereby jobbers or dealers assumed mortgages, and thus ownership of stations, the contracts acting very much like lease agreements. Some stations might be jobber- or dealer-owned, with owners operating with supply contracts, corporations guaranteeing gallonage for specified periods.

Stations also could be categorized according to type of management. Salaried employees ran company-controlled stations. Lessee dealers leased their stations and operated them independently. Dealers hired and fired employees, set hours of operation, set prices, extended credit, and otherwise functioned as independent businesspeople. They bought gasoline at wholesale either directly from supplying corporations or, more commonly, through their designated jobbers, reselling it at retail. Consignee dealers also leased stations from a supplying company, but took gasoline on consignment, taking a commission on sales. This arrangement helped dealers with limited capital get established. Great variety existed in the ownership and management of gasoline stations from one corporate chain to another, and even within chains decade to decade.

Shell, in building its West Coast marketing territory in the 1920s, used several kinds of lease contracts.[8] In order to bring dealers who had previously sold several brands of gasoline (as many garages did early on), Shell offered "paint leases." Facilities were leased to Shell which painted them with company colors and leased them back at lower rents, dealers agreeing to sell only Shell products. Out of this lease program grew the company's standard "two-party leases" helpful in converting "open account" dealers into "controlled account" dealers committed solely to the firm's products. "Three-party" leases involved the company, a dealer, and a third-party investor. Shell built the facility, leasing it from an investor and subleasing it, in turn, to a qualified dealer. Shell also leased blocks of stations to jobbers who then subleased them to dealers. It was not uncommon for companies to offer retailers liberal rental terms for their stations, special price concessions on gasoline, and free installation of pumps and storage tanks as incentives to switch from other brands.

During the 1920s the wide margin between tank-car prices (that charged to the bulk depot) and tank-wagon prices attracted numerous jobbers into both gasoline and heating oil distribution. In 1920, there were 675 oil companies large and small operating in the ten-state middle-western trade territory of Standard Oil of Indiana. In 1929, there were 15,421.[9] With 5.4 million automobiles registered and 11,216 gasoline stations operating in its sales territory, the company estimated an average of 490 cars per station.[10] The number of gasoline stations nationwide grew from an estimated 15,000 in 1920 to 124,000 in 1930 (see Table 3.1 for growth from 1920 to 1990).

In 1920, S. F. Bowser and Company, manufacturer of gasoline pumps, conducted a survey of gasoline stations along some 600 miles of highway in New York, Nebraska, Texas, and California. Eight-two percent of the 719 outlets handled only a single brand of gasoline. There was a gasoline station (with off-street driveways) on average every 0.74 miles, and a curbside pump (in front of garages and other businesses) on average every 0.46 mile. Gasolines of the various Standard Oil–descended companies were sold in 42 percent of the locations. Some 37 percent of the total outlets handled food items, 14 percent sold automobile supplies other than greases and lubricants, 8 percent provided repair service, and 6 percent were linked with automobile sales agencies. Thirteen miles of streets were surveyed in New York City, revealing 42 stations or 3.23 per mile of which 64 percent were off-street drive-ins.[11] The Atlantic Refining Company estimated in 1925 that its average station sold some 150,000 gallons of gasoline a year, or 400 gallons per day. The average motorcar, the company claimed, consumed 300 gallons of gasoline a year.[12]

The 1920s saw Standard Oil of New Jersey, in partnership with General Motors, bring tetraethyl lead to the market as an antiknock additive. To maintain a close grip on the market, the jointly owned Ethyl Corporation did not license its patent, but instead manufactured the additive, selling it to refiners for blending as premium gasoline to be sold at several cents above regular price. Some companies, such as Sun Oil, pursued independent courses. Sun marketed a single premium brand called "Blue Sunoco," to which it added blue dye for branding purposes (the blue color showing through the glass of the new pumps that Bowser and other companies had brought to the gasoline station scene). Sun's catalytic cracking process produced a "poison-free" gasoline, so it was advertised, without harmful lead oxides to gum up spark plugs and valves (see Fig. 3.9). Sun Oil was the first firm to introduce octane ratings to the public as

TABLE 3.1 Gasoline Stations in the United States, 1920–1990

Year	Total
1990[a]	111,657
1980[b]	158,540
1970[b]	216,059
1958[c]	193.948
1930[d]	123,979
1920[e]	15,000

[a] "Service Stations with Payrolls," *NPN* 82 (1990): 129.

[b] "Service Station Population Plummets," *NPN Factbook* 73 (1981): 108.

[c] "Service Station Census Report," *NPN* 52 (1960): 208.

[d] "123,979 Filling Stations in U.S.," *NPN* 23 (Sept. 23, 1931): 46.

[e] E. B. Reiser, "Oil Marketing a Typically American Merchandising Enterprise," *NPN* 28 (Feb. 5, 1936): 239.

FIGURE 3.9 Here is Sun Oil's 1930s corporate image. Depicted is an early station prototype and sign linked to the company's "Blue Sunoco" brand.

a sales device. In 1931, Sun claimed 72 octane for its gasoline, the average being 59.2 for regular and 74.0 for premium industry-wide.[13]

To enhance sales, most corporations gave away promotional items with gasoline purchases—premiums such as glassware and chinaware. Corporations launched games and raffles and began to introduce trading stamps. At first, stamps were sold to merchants who then passed them out to their customers when purchases were made at their stores. Customers, in turn, could collect and cash in the stamps for gasoline. Later, things were reversed—stamps given out for gasoline redeemable at special stores for merchandise. Road maps were distributed free to customers, with publishers such as Rand McNally and Company of Chicago (printers of railroad tickets and railroad maps) creating a whole new advertising form. "Put Your Sign Post in His Pocket" headlined a 1924 Rand McNally ad in the *National Petroleum News*.[14] With a road map, customers would carry a company's logo everywhere they traveled and be constantly reminded of where to buy. Credit cards began to appear, replacing the cumbersome coupon books that many companies used in rewarding regular customers. Customers had bought the books at discounted prices, peeling off the requisite number of coupons with each gasoline purchase.

The 1930s

Automobile registration slumped to slightly over 24 million in 1933 from a height in 1929 slightly over 26.5 million, but rose to nearly 32.5 million by 1940. Motor-fuel consumption followed the same peaks and valleys.[15] Production management responded. Innovation in automobile design shifted from the mechanical aspects of engineering to body styling, partly to spur demand for successive annual models. Alfred P. Sloan, Jr., head of General Motors, and Harley J. Earl of the corporation's styling section dramatized the industry's trends. Although in the 1920s Sloan had articulated the importance of style in pushing sales, it was not until 1934 that General Motors' Fisher Body division introduced the turret top amid a nascent interest in streamlined automobile bodies. Sloanism focused on image and played on the striving for upward mobility to lure GM owners to trade up from Chevrolets to Buicks or Oldsmobiles and ultimately to Cadillacs. Independent American passenger car manufacturers had declined to forty-nine by 1925 and, in the depressed market of the 1930s, Sloan's strategy left GM, Ford, and Chrysler a dominant "Big Three."

In 1932 the first federal gasoline tax was levied at one cent per gallon to restore declining highway funds. Between 1934 and 1937, $2.8 billion was allocated and spent on road construction. Most of the effort was focused on secondary roads to articulate the system of two-lane interstate highways. Although the Federal Aid Highway Act of 1938 called for consideration of four-lane "superhighways" between major population centers, development stalled for lack of funds.[16]

Meanwhile, the petroleum industry found itself dominated by some twenty large oil companies, all substantially integrated vertically. Taken together, these companies accounted for some three-quarters of the nation's refinery capacity (see Table 3.2). Eight of the former Standard Oil companies accounted for 40 percent with the top four—Standard Oil of New Jersey, Socony-Vacuum, Standard Oil of Indiana, and Standard Oil of California—topping the industry with an aggregate 35 percent share. The top twenty firms controlled nearly 60 percent of the nation's drilling activity, almost 90 percent of its pipelines, and over 75 percent of its marketing infrastructure.[17]

Generally speaking, the former Standard Oil companies remained preeminent in their original trade territories, areas the Supreme Court had approved for their respective use of the Standard Oil name. Thus in Minnesota, for example, Standard Oil of Indiana was dominant (see Fig. 3.10). Of the 588 Minnesota towns and cities where gasoline was retailed in 1936, Standard Oil was represented in 383, or 65 percent of the total

FIGURE 3.10 Standard Oil of Indiana (Stanolind) was the predominant company from the Great Lakes to the Rocky Mountains. The firm's rectangular blue sign with red surround and white lettering championed "Standard Service."

(see Table 3.3). Socony-Vacuum (through its White Eagle subsidiary) was the second most widely represented, but only in 14 percent of the places (see Fig. 3.11). Cities Service, Skelly, Sinclair, and Continental also topped the list of the brand names more frequently encountered. Among the small independent jobbers were the Gopher State Oil Company at Pine City, the Local Oil Company at Wheaton, and the Perfect Oil Company at Harmony. Farmer cooperatives—such as the Four Square Coop Oil Association at Sleepy Eye—could be found in at least 131 places, or 22 percent of the total. Independents retailing in Minneapolis–St. Paul included the Bulk Oil Company and the Economy Oil Company. Seeking the modern by way of image was the Radio Gas and Oil Company. Geographical distribution and market penetration were only weakly correlated in Minnesota. In 1935 Standard Oil of Indiana sold 19 percent of Minnesota's gas-

TABLE 3.2 Company Refining Capacities in the United States, 1930

| | Capacity | |
| | Percentage of Industry | Cumulative Percentage |
Company		
Standard Oil of New Jersey[a]	13.5%	13.5%
Socony-Vacuum[a]	7.4	20.9
Standard Oil of Indiana[a]	7.2	28.1
Standard Oil of California[a]	6.5	34.6
Shell-Union	5.9	40.5
Texas	5.6	46.1
Gulf	5.5	51.6
Consolidated (Sinclair)	4.3	55.9
Tide Water	3.8	59.7
Cities Service	3.0	62.7
Union of California	2.7	65.4
Pure	1.9	67.3
Atlantic[a]	1.8	69.1
Continental[a]	1.6	70.7
Sun	1.5	72.2
Phillips	1.0	73.2
Mid-Continent	1.0	74.2
Standard Oil of Ohio[a]	0.9	75.1
Skelly	0.6	75.7
Ohio[a]	0.1	75.8

[a] Companies derived from the Standard Oil Trust.

Source: Adapted from Giebelhaus, *Business and Government in the Oil Industry,* 290.

oline while Socony-Vacuum sold 9 percent (see Table 3.4). Cooperatives accounted for 8 percent of the state's gallonage in 1935. Apparent in Minnesota of the 1930s were very different strategies at building corporate territories. Some companies, such as Pure Oil, built large-volume stations in the larger towns and cities. Represented in only 3 percent of the places where gasoline was retailed, the company nonetheless sold over 6 percent of the state's gasoline in 1935. Socony-Vacuum's White Eagle subsidiary, however, marketed more in small towns outside Minneapolis–St. Paul. Represented in 14 percent of the state's local markets, the company sold less than 5 percent of the state's gasoline (see Tables 3.3 and 3.4). Skelly, Sinclair, and Continental's Conoco brand also heavily favored low-volume small-town dealers. These latter chains were built primarily on locally established jobber networks. Cooperatives dominated gasoline retailing only in selected of the state's smallest towns and villages.

The "cooperative" movement arose in response to various factors. Price margins of over six cents a gallon (thirty cents or more on the

TABLE 3.3 Branded Gasolines in Minnesota Cities and
Towns, 1936

Brand	Number of Towns	Cities with Gasoline Retailing
Standard Oil of Indiana	383	65%
Socony-Vacuum	82	14
Cities Service	78	13
Skelly	51	9
Sinclair	50	9
Phillips	46	8
Continental	34	6
Deep Rock	24	4
Shell	21	4
Barnsdall	19	3
Pure	17	3
Texaco	16	3
Cooperatives[a]	131	22

[a]Tabulated here are towns with retail outlets carrying the words *coop*
or *cooperative* in their names.

Note: In 1936, gasoline was retailed in 588 cities and towns in Minnesota.

Source: "State Tax List Proves Competition," *NPN* 28 (Feb. 5, 1936): 217.

TABLE 3.4 Share of Minnesota Gasoline Market, 1935

Company	Gallons	Percentage
Standard Oil of Indiana	81,854[a]	18.7%
Phillips	42,397	9.3
Pure	29,796	6.5
Socony-Vacuum	20,376	4.5
Texaco	19,701	4.3
Skelly	19,205	4.2
Tide Water	18,920	4.1
Cities Service	17,375	3.8
Shell	15,080	3.3
Sinclair	10,219	2.2
Continental	6,682	1.5
Deep Rock	3,626	0.8
Others	167,752	36.8
Total	456,444	100.0
Included in the total above are co-ops	37,384	8.2

[a]In thousands

Source: "Dr. Wilson Tells How Competition Grew to Cut Standard's Share of Oil Market,"
NPN 42 (April 19, 1950): 29.

FIGURE 3.11 The Standard Oil Company of New York (Socony) sought to invade Stanolind territory in the 1920s. Forbidden by the Supreme Court to use the "Standard Oil" name outside its own court-assigned area in the East, Standard developed White Eagle and other brands.

dollar) attracted farmer-owned grain associations into gasoline distribution since considerable savings could be passed on to members. The major corporations had tended to slight rural areas in favor of urban places. Finally, lubricants on the market tended to be inadequate to farm needs, attracting the state cooperative associations into the blending and, later, into the refining business. Most active were the farm bureaus in the eastern Middle West, the farmers' unions west of the Mississippi River, and the granges along the Atlantic seaboard.

In 1939, the Illinois Farm Supply Company served 64 affiliated farmer co-ops in 102 counties from two bulk terminals, one on the Illinois River near Peoria and the other on the Ohio River near Shawneetown. The Aladdin brand of gasoline had been introduced.

With the decrease in registered automobiles and the related decrease in gasoline consumed, the market became hopelessly saturated, exacerbated by the largest oil fields as yet discovered coming on line in East Texas. Many corporations, led by Gulf Oil, introduced a third grade of cheap, low-octane gasoline in an attempt to undercut competition through price. Independent private brands thrived in undercutting the majors through no-frills merchandising, with gasoline selling for one or two cents per gallon less. Nonbranded jobbers had traditionally obtained gasoline from independent refiners, but now the major corporations, unable to sell all of their refinery output, dumped unbranded product on the market as well. Many of the larger corporations established subsidiaries (or "concubine" companies, as they were called) to sell cut-price gasoline in various local and regional markets. Many companies, faced with falling profits (and, for some, substantial losses), abandoned marketing altogether in their less competitive trade areas. Marketing territories that had rapidly expanded in the 1920s rapidly contracted.

With adoption of the National Industrial Recovery (NIR) Act during the Roosevelt administration, the petroleum industry, dominated by the larger corporations, began to set prices through its "code of fair competition," temporarily easing cutthroat competition. On the production end, conservation laws adopted in Texas and other states, passage by Congress of so-called hot oil laws (forbidding the interstate transportation of oil produced in violation of state conservation rules), and creation of the Interstate Oil Compact Commission reduced crude output, bringing real stability to the industry. In 1936, indictments were brought by the Department of Justice against the major oil corporations charging price fixing. Annual meetings, allegedly held each year at the Blackstone Hotel in Chicago, established a pricing system based on refinery costs at Tulsa, Oklahoma. Jobbers and dealers were excluded from these deliberations. Ultimately, the U.S. Supreme Court upheld the price-fixing charge, disapproving as illegal the NIR-inspired "coordination."

At the same time, Congress debated legislation to improve the position of the nation's jobbers and dealers. The large corporations faced dismemberment, their marketing activities to be reserved exclusively to small independent wholesalers and retailers. "Divorcement" proposals would be introduced repeatedly, and unsuccessfully, over the following half-century. As the president of the Sun Oil Company argued in opposing such legislation, mass production reduced costs and made for lower consumer prices, but mass production demanded mass market. Mass markets, in turn, hinged on brand identity, the guarantee to customers of quality in the marketplace. Only the integrated oil corporations, he argued, could guarantee quality. "That brand name is your pledge to the buyer—on it your honor is staked. The integrated business can make sure that all its divisions and branches work in harmony to turn out a product always worthy of its name and fame."[18]

State and federal taxes on gasoline increased continuously in the

1930s, the latter funneling money into the Highway Trust Fund to under-write the nation's rapidly evolving interstate highway system. In 1926, gasoline averaged 23.26 cents per gallon, with 2.34 cents going to taxes. In 1933, the price had fallen to 19.64 cents per gallon, but taxes took 5.64 cents.[19] During 1934 and 1935 prices fell to 13 and 14 cents a gallon. Many independents began to mix nontaxable fuels, such as kerosene, naphtha, and furnace oil, into gasoline in order to cut prices further.

Cut-rate chains thrived as never before. Perhaps the most unusual was started by radio station WNAX at Yankton, South Dakota. The station's entire programming was dedicated to promoting lower gasoline prices through the station's chain of some 500 outlets spread across the Dakotas, Minnesota, Iowa, Nebraska, and eastern Wyoming. WNAX ac-cused the major companies of price gouging and sought to prove the point by lowering prices three or four cents per gallon below prevailing levels. Traditionally, the largest petroleum marketers in each area set wholesale and retail prices. In WNAX's territory, Standard Oil of Indiana played this role with its tank-wagon listings.

Unable to meet cut-rate retailing head on, the large integrated corpo-rations moved to broaden product and service mixes. Service bays were added to gasoline stations to handle increased repair work. Office spaces were enlarged to accommodate the sale of accessories—tires, batteries, and accessories comprising the so-called TBA line. Emphasis was placed on service and the term "gasoline station" gave way to "service station." Some corporations built large complexes, dubbed "super service sta-tions," with large repair, lubricating, and washing floors tied to sales offices.

The 1930s also saw an increase in leasing, the direct result of new state laws taxing chain stores. The number of retail outlets belonging to chains (such as the Great Atlantic and Pacific Tea Company) were in-creasing rapidly. Local grocery and drugstore merchants, hurt by the Depression, sought legislative relief from what they saw as unfair com-petition. Under the Iowa chain-store law, every store belonging to a chain of more than 50 outlets had to pay a tax of $155 a year, and the gross receipts of the chain were taxed up to 10 percent for receipts of $1 million or more. Jobbers in Iowa successfully included gasoline retailing under the law's umbrella. Standard Oil of Indiana responded with its "Iowa Plan," which it subsequently extended to other states as chain-store taxes came on line. The company's 350 owned and operated stations in Iowa were converted to lease operations, former company employees becoming independent retailers in the process and, consequently, legally not part of a chain. The approximately 500 stations leased from owners and operated by agents were returned to their owners. Standard Oil of Indiana operated 11,685 controlled stations across its marketing terri-tory at the end of 1934. At the end of 1935, it had 7,576.[20] But the cor-poration quickly seized the new leasing emphasis to nearly double the number of its branded outlets to some 20,500 across the Middle West.

Chain-store laws apparently worked against and not for the independent jobbers. They had lost some 10 to 15 percent of the market in Standard Oil of Indiana's territory by the end of 1936.

In some states, such as West Virginia, the courts ruled that gasoline stations were not stores and, therefore, chain-store taxes did not apply. The West Virginia operation of Standard Oil of New Jersey was scrutinized carefully. The firm controlled some 1,046 gasoline stations in the state, 98 owned outright and 948 leased or operated under commission contracts. The company had 54 bulk depots. The owned stations averaged gross annual revenue of $26,822, as opposed to $3,892 for agency stations. The state supreme court observed, "The small volume of business done in most of the Standard Oil stations in the state is reflected in the small profits and the heavy burden of the tax when contrasted therewith." In 1931, the average profits of all gasoline stations, including bulk plants, stood at $539.34 per station and the tax, computed according to the intended act, $239.29. In 1932, the profit was $248.37 per station, and the estimated tax $240.51.[21] Further, the court observed, should the tax have been imposed on gasoline retailers, the industry, which did only 4.3 percent of the total retail business of the state, would have paid 84.5 percent of the tax monies collected.

The 1940s and 1950s

During World War I, Allied navy and army petroleum needs had been filled largely from producing fields and refineries in North America, especially the United States. Coordination of refining and transportation was handled by the Petroleum War Service Committee, which after the war evolved into the American Petroleum Institute. So also during World War II was the Allied war machine largely fueled by American corporations. Between Pearl Harbor and V-J Day, the Allies used 7 billion barrels of oil, the United States supplying 85 percent. Consumed during the war was an amount equal to one-quarter of all the petroleum previously produced in the United States between the development of Edwin Drake's well in Pennsylvania in 1869 to the outbreak of war in 1941.[22] For domestic consumption, gasoline was pooled and delivered from bulk plants to the nearest gasoline stations irrespective of brand or company linkages. Many bulk plants and over one-quarter of all gasoline stations were closed. Retail sales through the war years stood at less than 70 percent of 1941 levels, the result of strict gasoline rationing overseen by the Petroleum Industry War Council.

America emerged from World War II with a pent-up demand for nearly every consumer product, including automobiles and gasoline. The number of registered motor vehicles had dropped by some 4 million, down to 30 million during the war. But by 1955 registrations had redoubled. Between 1945 and 1957, the demand for all petroleum products soared some 80 percent. Nine companies manufactured automobiles in

1946 although the market was fully dominated by General Motors, Ford, and Chrysler.[23] The automatic transmission first mass-produced by GM before the war emerged as the prime mechanical innovation during the immediate postwar years.

The automobile came to epitomize American conspicuous consumption. Automobile size ballooned. The period's low-, medium-, and high-priced automobiles, the V-8s of Ford, Oldsmobile, and Cadillac, attained a wheelbase of 118, 123, and 130 inches respectively by 1959. By 1957 the "horsepower race" yielded Cadillacs and Lincolns with 300-horsepower engines (and Chryslers with 375-horsepower engines) before pressure mounted for smaller, less "high performance" automobiles. Small import cars impacted the American market beginning in the late 1950s.

Highway development was made imperative by the general malaise of traffic congestion, especially in the nation's cities. The Federal Aid Highway Act of 1944 appropriated $500 million for each of the three years thereafter and stipulated development of urban highways as well as rural feeder routes. Between 1945 and 1955, federal aid highway mileage jumped some 440,000 miles.[24] However, again no interstate system of superhighways was designated as the 1944 act and prewar discussion had suggested. Realization awaited the Federal Aid Highway Act of 1956, which funded a national system of intercity express roads. Avoiding excessive burden on any single group, most especially the trucking industry, the act's trust fund drew revenue from federal taxes on highway commodities such as fuel, tires, and tubes. It paid for 90 percent of interstate highway construction. Nearly a third of the projected 41,000-mile network was completed by the end of the 1950s.

In general, the 1950s proved to be a period of rapid expansion for most petroleum firms. Corporations scrambled to enter new marketing areas and to penetrate more effectively old territories. There came a shift to gasoline stations with larger tank capacities and thus higher potential gallonages. Bulk plants were enlarged in storage capacity and reduced in number to serve larger areas. Companies began transporting gasoline by truck directly from refineries to gasoline stations.

As the petroleum corporations expanded marketing territories— either through the construction of controlled stations or through the stations of jobbers—they increasingly came to rely on exchange agreements. The largest and most efficient refineries in a given market area supplied most of the gasoline stations in that area irrespective of brand identifications. Corporations bought one another's product. Shell might buy Tide Water's gasoline for sale in Maine, and Tide Water might buy Shell's product for sale in Oregon. Indeed, motorists in Portland, Maine, or Portland, Oregon, might find all of their gasoline originating at one or two refineries irrespective of the dozens of brand names available.

Brand differences, to the extent that they were real, were sustained through the blending of additives at terminals, at bulk plants, and even at gasoline pumps. As a whole, the industry engaged in an octane race, reflecting the needs of higher compression engines. On average, premium gasoline was pegged in 1955 at 82.5 octane, and regular at 79.1. Advertising campaigns championed the distinctive qualities of branded gasolines when in reality very little difference existed from one brand to another in given areas, all brands originating in the quality control of a relatively few regional refineries. The industry developed a stable three-tier pricing system involving the dealers of the major integrated companies, those of large independent regionals, and those of private branded independents. A price spread of two cents generally separated each tier.[25]

To protect their branded jobbers and dealers, the major corporations adopted competitive price protection plans. A company might absorb 75 percent of a retail price drop down to a certain level, then guarantee the jobber and dealer a floor or "stopout" margin. Such schemes were necessary if local dealers were to survive the price wars that raged during the 1950s, especially in the Northeast. Surplus unbranded gasolines once again flooded the market as both major and regional independent refiners sought to operate refineries at peak efficiencies. Dealer protection plans were necessary if the majors were not to undermine their own brands and the effectiveness of place-product-packaging in territorial competition. By 1970, an estimated $1 billion in competitive price supports was being paid out by the majors.[26]

Price wars spread contagiously outward from points of origin, threatening, on occasion, the wholesaling and retailing infrastructures of large regions as dealers were forced to sell below cost for sustained periods in order to remain competitive. The 1950s saw most of the large petroleum corporations expanding their trade territories in the United States on the basis of place-product-packaging. Several foreign corporations, specifically Belgium's Petrofina, France's Total, and Britain's BP, entered the North American market for the first time.

Among the most aggressive competitors for new territory was Phillips Petroleum Company. In 1956, after only three years of activity in the Southeast, the company assumed third place in Florida's gallonage race in competition with thirteen other major brands. Phillips reached fifth place in South Carolina and sixth place in North Carolina and Georgia. Over 150 jobbers were supplying some 2,700 retail outlets in a six-state area.[27] Phillips shipped gasoline by tanker from its Texas refinery to terminals along the Gulf and Atlantic coasts. The first "beachhead" was established in Tampa when the Lee and Pomeroy Oil Company switched to the Phillips brand at its fifty-five retail outlets. Phillips's "invasion" of the Southeast was driven forward by a staff of some 450 company salesmen who persuaded active jobbers to switch allegiances, or who recruited entrepreneurs willing to start new jobbing firms. About half of the Phillips jobbers in Florida started as new ventures.

The old basing-point pricing system based on Gulf of Mexico production and transportation costs was replaced by one focused on the Persian Gulf. Despite carefully controlled import quotas imposed by the Eisenhower administration, oil corporations began to turn to foreign sources of crude oil to supplement domestic supplies. American corporate involvement in crude oil production in Mexico, Venezuela, and the Middle East dated from the World War I era. For example, Standard Oil of New Jersey, Socony, Atlantic, and Gulf joined Anglo-Persian (today's BP), Royal Dutch/Shell, and the Compagnie Française des Pétroles in ownership of the Turkish Petroleum Company (later the Iraq Petroleum Company). The Red Line Agreement of 1928, which forbade any of the participating companies from operating independently of one another in the lands of the former Ottoman Empire, opened the door to other American companies to move aggressively into the Middle East. In 1936, for example, Standard Oil of California and the Texas Company joined to form Caltex, from which a flood of Saudi Arabian crude oil soon flowed. When the Red Line Agreement terminated in 1948, Standard Oil of New Jersey and Socony joined Standard Oil of California and the Texas Company in the Arabian American Oil Company (Aramco). Also in 1948, Phillips created a ten-company consortium, the American Independent Oil Company (Aminoil), to develop fields in Kuwait. Whereas eleven American companies had foreign crude oil concessions in 1945, twenty-eight companies were so positioned in 1953.

The 1960s and 1970s

Automobility's lure remained seemingly boundless, but its means for satisfaction changed somewhat in the 1960s. Motor vehicle registration grew by 31 million and with it motor fuel usage by 30 million gallons.[28] Compact cars came to the fore and, although they consumed gasoline more efficiently, they did not represent substantially new engineering. Compacts, as down-scaled versions of standard-sized models, were gradually increased in physical size. The Corvair departed more significantly toward new design but its greatest publicity came from Ralph Nader's disclosure that the car put passengers substantially at risk. When air pollution as well as safety became issues in the decade, the federal government passed the Motor Vehicle Air Pollution Act of 1965 and the Motor Vehicle Safety Act of 1966 to enforce standards.

The refining or manufacturing segment of the petroleum industry continued to drive marketing through the 1960s. To stay profitable, refineries had to process certain minimal amounts of gasoline and, accordingly, corporation marketing departments had to move that product in the marketplace. As one oil company executive observed in retrospect: "Crude that stayed in the ground earned no money. Idle plant capacity cost money. Companies that moved more gasoline and increased their

FIGURE 3.12 A Pure Oil dealer in Marietta, Ohio, engages in a "Win a Car" contest. A wide variety of marketing gimmicks drove gasoline consumption through the mid-1960s.

market share made more money. The chimera of the incremental barrel seemed the marketer's rule."[29] The more a company could produce from refinery investments, once fixed costs had been covered, the larger the profits, since only material and energy costs figured in the incremental barrels produced. Marketing territories continued to expand with the West Coast, the nation's fastest growing region, emergent as the area of most intense competition. The price of gasoline remained low even in the large eastern cities (see Table 3.5). Branded suppliers were forced to keep price protection plans in force for jobbers and dealers.

The gimmicks of gasoline retailing, driven by massive advertising budgets, made the marketing campaigns of previous decades pale in comparison (see Fig. 3.12). In 1955, the industry had spent $42 million on driveway premiums, but by the late 1960s it was spending $150 million on trading stamps alone.[30] Tide Water-Associated's "Win-a-check" campaign in northern California offered big cash prizes as well as small "instant winner" payouts and company sales jumped 57 percent in a single month. To not engage in games and gimmicks was to court permanent market loss to competitors. There were some 3 million credit cards in circulation in 1957, but ten years later Gulf, Shell, Standard Oil of Indiana, Standard Oil of New Jersey, and Texaco had outstanding about 10 million credit cards each (see Fig. 3.13).[31] Additives continued to play an important role. Shell and Continental promoted tricresol phosphate (TCP) produced by the Monsanto Chemical Company. Shell claimed that

FIGURE 3.13 By the 1950s most large oil companies had adopted credit cards as a means of stimulating sales and holding customers.

TCP gave cars up to 15 percent more power, and increased spark-plug life 150 percent. TCP was advertised nationwide in *Life* and the *Saturday Evening Post,* in 200 newspapers, and on some 50 radio and 20 television stations. Standard Oil of Indiana introduced its "de-icer" additive, and Sinclair its cold weather "Power-X" and promoted its "Supreme Gasoline with Liquid Nickel" (see Fig. 3.14).

In seeking market penetration, many corporations established retail outlets other than service-oriented gasoline stations. For example, there were some 2,000 truckstops in the United States by 1969. Pure Oil built a chain of over 300 truckstops across the Middle West, Southeast, and Southwest, with 50 located along the rapidly evolving interstate freeway system. The company's "wildwood" prototype featured large picture windows overlooking canopy-covered pump islands. A spiral staircase led up and out of the first-floor restaurant and merchandise area to motel rooms, a lounge, and a laundromat for truckers. Pure's truckstops cost upwards to $1 million each.[32] Skelly Oil also operated some 100 "full-facility" truckstops, and over 60 trucker "fuel stops" at midcontinent.

Several corporations, like Standard Oil of Ohio through its L and K subsidiary, flirted with motel construction, also primarily at interstate freeway interchanges.[33] Pure Oil developed a three-way partnership with Travelodge and the Quaker Oats Company's Aunt Jemima restaurants. Pure Oil bought freeway interchange sites, built gasoline stations, and leased adjacent tracts for motel and restaurant construction. Gulf Oil and Holiday Inns formed a partnership, Gulf supplying capital for motel construction and extending its credit card system to motel customer use in return for the inclusion of Gulf stations at motel sites.

Interstate freeway construction represented a challenge for established companies to keep their market share in an affected area, and to other companies to expand marketing territories (see Fig. 3.15). Along the Cleveland-Columbus-Cincinnati corridor in Ohio, Standard Oil of Ohio, Sun Oil, and Phillips Petroleum had moved by 1960 to enhance market

TABLE 3.5 Estimated Price Breakdown per Gallon
of Gasoline, New York, 1955

Cost of crude oil at well	6.20c
Piping to refinery	.50
Refinery labor	.67
Other refinery costs	1.00
Refinery profit	1.63
Tanker to New York terminal	1.20
Storage	.57
Delivery to retail outlet	2.20
Jobber's profit	1.33
Federal tax	1.50
State tax	4.00
Dealer's profit	5.10
Retail price	25.90

Source: Adapted from O'Connor, *The Empire of Oil,* 107.

TABLE 3.6 Brand Representation along U.S. 42
and I-71 in Ohio, Percent of Total, 1966

Brand	U.S. 42	I-71
Sohio	22	35
Shell	11	10
Sunoco	11	15
Pure	8	5
Gulf	7	—[a]
Marathon	7	—[a]
Sinclair	7	—[a]
Texaco	7	8
Mobil	3	5
Phillips	3	10
Humble	2	5
Independent	8	0

[a] Less than 2 percent

Source: "I-System Impact: Changing Pattern," *NPN* 59
(May 1967): 92.

positions through new freeway locations. Gulf, Marathon, and Sinclair,
on the other hand, had lost position (see Table 3.6). When Standard Oil of
California bought Standard Oil of Kentucky, new interstate stations were
established as a means of rebuilding the latter's corporate image. The
Standard brand across the South had been promoted primarily with
small-town jobbers and their dealers. By 1967, the company had 178
interchange stations across five states with another 150 properties owned
and awaiting development. In addition, the parent firm moved aggressively

NEW SINCLAIR GASOLINES WITH NICKEL COMPOUND REDUCE ENGINE WEAR AS MUCH AS 29%

Sinclair—and only Sinclair gasolines contain new wonder-working Nickel Compound. You get as much as 29% less engine wear when you use new Sinclair Dino or Dino Supreme Gasoline with Liquid Nickel. Less engine wear means you save on repairs and replacements. You get more miles per dollar.

While you travel, look for the sign of the Sinclair Dinosaur where you can fill your tank with new Dino gasolines.

DRIVE WITHOUT A CARE WITH A CREDIT CARD FROM *Sinclair*

In the U.S. and Canada, charge your purchases where you see these signs:

Sinclair AUTO TOUR SERVICE

FIGURE 3.14 In the 1960s Sinclair credit-card holders, most located east of the Rocky Mountains, were extended credit privileges at Richfield stations along the Pacific Coast. Sinclair customers could also obtain credit at Supertest and Irving stations across Canada.

to establish its own Chevron brand with another 130 interchange stations across eight southeastern states. Station design was the same for both chains: "the handy porcelain-and-glass box look; canopy reaching out from the office to shield islands from the elements; front bays, commonly two, left or right; red, white, and blue color scheme."[34] Parallel design anticipated the day when the Chevron brand would totally prevail.

The merchandising of tires, batteries, and accessories at gasoline stations grew into a $10-billion market during the 1960s. Corporations maintained lucrative commission arrangements with various tire manufacturers—including Atlantic (Goodyear), Shell (Firestone), and Texaco (Goodrich)—until the Federal Trade Commission ruled such marketing illegal. Some corporations introduced private tire brands to be sold exclusively through their dealers. Some companies enlarged automobile repair capabilities by adding various diagnostic tests and long-term service guarantees.

Self-service gasoline sales and gasoline retailing at convenience stores emerged in the 1960s on a large scale. Self-service was an idea that originated in the early 1930s. For example, a chain of twenty self-service filling stations had been established by the Hoosier Petroleum Company (Hoosier Pete) of Indianapolis in 1930. But the state fire marshal, contending that self-service constituted a fire hazard, had squashed the innovation before it could be popularized in Indiana. Only station personnel were legally sanctioned to attend pumps in most areas. Through the 1960s and 1970s, however, one state after another authorized self-service. Most companies designated selected pump islands at their stations as self-service, but some firms converted entire stations. By 1977, over 40 percent of the gasoline sold under the Citgo brand was self-service, as well as over 30 percent sold under the Conoco, Exxon, and Shell brands.[35] Experiments tying gasoline and grocery sales also dated to the 1930s, and even farther back to the 1910s considering the tendency of general stores in rural areas to carry gasoline at curbside pumps. In

FIGURE 3.15 At the interchange of the Pennsylvania Turnpike (I-70 and I-76) and U.S. 30 at Breezewood, Pennsylvania, a whole new "town" developed comprised largely of gasoline stations, truckstops, motels, and fast food restaurants. In these 1978 photographs, the signs of Union, Boron (Sohio), Arco, Sunoco, Shell, and Mobil compete for the motorist's attention.

the 1960s, however, pumps began to appear in front of Handy Andy, Little General, and other quick-service food stores. Southland Corporation's 1,400-unit Seven-Eleven chain was the largest. The Tenneco Corporation was the first petroleum company to link grocery and gasoline sales in outlets across the Southeast. Tenneco began by placing pumps at supermarkets.

By the late 1960s the half-century-old formula for satisfying the automobile's energy needs began to be questioned. During the 1970s motor vehicle registration increased by 49 million, second only to the fifties as the decade of largest increase.[36] Manner of fuel consumption did change, however. Petroleum shortages dictated passage in 1974 of a 55-mile-per-hour speed limit nationwide and a year later the Energy Policy of Conservation Act established a corporate average fuel economy standard of 27.5 miles per gallon by 1985. Reduced vehicle weight, smaller engine and body size, front-end drive, and lighter but stronger materials produced results with the average miles per gallon rising from 13.10 in 1973 to 15.15 by 1980.[37] With 89 percent of the interstate highway system open by 1976 and the rising costs of construction coupled with opposition from local property owner, conservation, and community action groups, emphasis on the interstate highway program shifted from new construction to maintenance and repair.

Many critics of the petroleum industry decried the nation's growing dependence on imported oil. Nonetheless, federal policy continued to emphasize holding prices to lowest possible levels in the absolute conviction that the world had an inexhaustible supply of cheap oil and that the United States would always have unfettered license to consume it. By 1972, however, refiners were beginning to put their branded jobbers and dealers on allocation and deny product to private-brand independents. Shortages ranged upwards to 400,000 barrels per day. American multinationals had begun to lose control of the world crude oil market as host governments, especially in the Middle East, began to challenge through increased royalty demands and tax assessments. The properties of some companies were seized through nationalization. American corporate share of the world crude oil market, which stood at nearly 60 percent in 1957, would be whittled down to 7 percent by 1982. The United States imported 6 million barrels per day in 1973 (about 1 million barrels coming from Arab sources). Imports supplied approximately 35 percent of the nation's petroleum needs.[38]

On October 17, 1973, the Organization of Arab Petroleum Exporting Countries (OAPEC) authorized an embargo of oil shipments to the United States in retaliation for America's military support of Israel. The next day, the Organization of Petroleum Exporting Countries (OPEC) imposed a 70 percent price increase from $3.01 to $5.12 per barrel of crude oil. By the end of the year the price had risen to $11.65, and would continue to soar as high as $40 before the end of the decade.[39] Shortages plagued American motorists now forced to queue at gasoline stations. A whole new era in gasoline marketing was born literally overnight. As a marketing strategy the quest for market share was passé. Profitability, based on price, was now fashionable. OPEC's action was quickly followed by rampant inflation, high interest rates, recession, unemployment, unfavorable American trade balances, and federal budget deficits. At first the petroleum industry profited. Exxon (formerly Standard Oil of New Jersey) posted in 1973 the highest net profit yet earned by an American corporation, some $2.4 billion. Corporations passed price inflation on to customers. From 63.07 cents a gallon in 1970, the average price of gasoline reached 87.9 cents in 1979.

New domestic producing fields were brought into production on Alaska's North Slope. The TransAlaska Pipeline System (TAPS) came to supply the United States with upward to 10 percent of its crude oil needs by the mid-1980s. With world prices inflated, domestic production increased as a result of reactivated wells in Texas, Oklahoma, California, and other states. Domestic production increased from some 2.9 billion barrels annually in 1976 to 3.1 in 1982.[40]

The OPEC price rise intensified corporate entanglement. Mergers and buyouts became epidemic. One-third of the top 100 oil firms of the mid-1950s had been merged with or been absorbed by another firm by the early 1980s. Major corporations cooperated as never before in joint ventures. For example, the Colonial Pipeline Company, one of the scores of pipeline firms in the United States, was jointly owned by Gulf, Standard Oil of Indiana, Texaco, Cities Service, Mobil, Standard Oil of Ohio, Continental, Phillips, Union, and Atlantic-Richfield (in order of their ownership share). Corporations came to be more firmly interlocked through direct and indirect directorates. For example, Exxon, Standard Oil of Indiana, and Atlantic-Richfield were interlocked through the Chase Manhattan Bank; Mobil, Shell, and Phillips through the First National City Bank; and Exxon, Continental, and Citgo through the Morgan Guaranty Bank.[41]

The OPEC price rise impacted wholesale jobbers, vastly reducing their number. Standard Oil of Indiana's total of 3,793 jobbers in 1972 was reduced to 1,963 in 1983, and Continental's 1,536 to 830.[42] Most corporations withdrew from marginal markets, canceling contracts not only with jobbers but with dealers. Protection of dealers from an arbitrary end of supply helped generate the Petroleum Marketing Practices Act of 1978.[43] Mobil withdrew from Idaho, Montana, Wyoming, and Colorado; Shell from Maine, Vermont, Arkansas, and Utah; and Standard Oil of California from Delaware, Virginia, West Virginia, North Carolina, and South Carolina. Gulf shed 3,500 retail outlets in the Middle West and Northwest through full or partial pullouts in thirteen states. In Minnesota and Wisconsin, 100 former Gulf jobbers banded together to secure an alternative gasoline supply and to market under a common "Pro" logo. Despite such holding actions the number of gasoline stations declined precipitously from 216,059 in 1970 to 158,540 in 1980 (see Table 3.1). By the end of the 1970s, 85 percent of all gasoline sold in the United States carried the brand name of a supplying refiner. Only 15 percent was sold at retail through independent private brands.[44] The majors subsidized their marketing operations from profits obtained in other segments of the industry, crude oil production and refining most specifically.

Marketing for price advantage drove most of the major firms to emphasize the secondary brands of their "concubine" subsidiaries. Tide Water developed Seaside, Conoco introduced Econo, and Phillips promoted Phil-

R-Up, among a wide diversity of brands for each firm. Among Marathon's many secondary brands were Bonded, Cheker, Gastown, Pilot, Speedway, and Superthon. OPEC-inflicted price emphasis brought an immediate end to retail gimmicks. Gone were the free gifts, the trading stamps, and, at some companies, even the credit cards. The free road map disappeared literally overnight. Publisher map sales to petroleum companies fell 50 percent in 1974 alone, forcing Rand McNally and the other publishers to market maps through vending machines at gasoline stations.

The 1970s was a time of retrenchment symbolized in landscapes across the country by abandoned and often derelict former gasoline stations. If local planning commissions had worried about the overbuilding of utilitarian gasoline stations in earlier periods, concern substantially heightened in the face of massive gasoline station redundancy. New stations continued to open, but they were invariably few in number relative to those closed. New stations tended to be larger in size, engendering higher gallonage and greater cost savings per unit.

The 1980s and 1990s

Automobile and highway technology continued on courses begun in the 1970s. Although registration of all motor vehicles increased more slowly than in the previous decade, over 181 million motor vehicles were registered by 1991, 143 million automobiles alone. Americans bought more down-sized front-drive autos as they were more fuel efficient, family-size cars achieving fuel efficiency greater than the compacts of the 1960s and 1970s. By 1990, an average of almost 21 miles per gallon was achieved by all passenger vehicles and most new vehicles ranged between 20 and 35 miles per gallon. Obviously, fuel economy remained a concern for consumers, but by the end of the decade fuel economy once again had begun to lose its significance. Only 14,000 miles of new highway were constructed between 1981 and 1985.[45]

In gasoline marketing, changes unleashed by OPEC continued little abated. Despite efforts at energy conservation, America's dependence on foreign oil continued to grow; the largest importing companies—each accounting for at least 5 percent of the total—were BP, Exxon, Arco (Atlantic-Richfield), Shell, Chevron (formerly Standard Oil of California), and Texaco. Important, however, was the fact that finished gasoline, as well as crude oil, was being imported in large quantities. Indeed, by 1985 foreign refineries, with their clear cost advantages over American plants, had come to supply upward to 10 percent of the nation's gasoline needs.[46] Consequently, there was a 16 percent reduction in American refinery capacity between 1980 and 1985 with the closing of over eighty plants. The petroleum industry continued to be dominated by a relatively few large corporations, the top twenty refiners accounting for 79 percent of the gasoline produced (see Table 3.7). Eight firms descended from various Standard Oil companies accounted for 43 percent of the total. As measured by assets, Royal Dutch/Shell and Exxon were the world's fourth and fifth largest industrial firms in 1991, following behind General Motors, Ford, and General Electric.

Self-service came of age in the 1980s with Arco stations 91 percent reoriented by 1990, Phillips 88 percent, Conoco 87 percent, and Citgo and Shell 86 percent. The industry average stood at 83 percent.[47] So-called unattended pumps (and even entire stations) had come to the fore. Customers had only to insert credit cards at pumps, an electronic processor recording the sale and issuing a receipt. Customers did not suffer the inconvenience of having to go inside to station offices to complete purchases. On the other hand, retailers lost opportunities to transact further sales. By 1991, Texaco had unattended pumps at some 14,000 branded outlets. Other companies included Citgo with 7,800, Chevron with 3,800, and Amoco with 3,100. Large "car care" centers introduced customers to the shopping-mall concept in car servicing. Clustered at one location were specialized automobile repair functions—muffler installation, brake repair, oil change, tune-up, and car-

TABLE 3.7 Company Refining Capacities in the United States, 1990

| | Capacity | |
| | Percent of | Cumulative |
Company	Industry	Percentage
Chevron[a]	10.4	10.4
Exxon[a]	7.4	17.8
Shell	6.9	24.7
Amoco[a,b]	6.6	31.3
Mobil[a]	5.3	36.6
BP America[a,c]	5.3	41.9
Texaco	4.6	46.5
Sun	4.1	50.6
Marathon[a]	4.1	54.7
Arco[a]	3.9	58.6
Conoco[a]	2.9	61.5
Unocal	2.7	64.2
Ashland	2.3	66.5
Aramco	2.3	68.7
Phillips	2.2	70.9
Petro Venezuela (Citgo)	2.0	72.9
Coastal	1.9	74.8
Total	1.4	76.2
Diamond Shamrock	1.3	77.5
Petrofina	1.2	78.7

[a] Firms derived from former Standard Oil companies.

[b] Formerly Standard Oil of Indiana.

[c] Formerly Standard Oil of Ohio.

Source: "Is Big Oil Getting Bigger?" NPN 83 (Nov. 1991): 43.

FIGURE 3.16 Convenience stores, combining the sale of gasoline, groceries, and other "convenience" items, quickly came to dominate gasoline retailing in the late 1980s. (*Source:* Photo courtesy of Texaco.)

wash facilities arrayed around a large gasoline station or convenience store.[48] There were approximately 1,700 such centers in operation in 1990.

Convenience stores became the principal new orientation in gasoline retailing (see Figs. 3.16 and 3.17). By 1984, convenience stores accounted for an estimated 12 percent of the retail gasoline market in the United States, up from 1 percent in 1974. Of the approximately 50,000 convenience stores operating in 1982, nearly 60 percent sold gasoline. Initially, gasoline was intended primarily to attract customers, thereby to boost grocery sales. The average sale per customer in 1982 varied from $2.97 at stores without gasoline pumps to an average $3.46 at stores with pumps.[49] Many convenience stores cut prices below cost at their pumps and covered losses with markups on beer, bread, milk, and other items. By the late 1980s, the petroleum corporations themselves were building and operating convenience stores. Chevron started its C-Stores, Mobil its Mobil Marts, Exxon its Exxon Stores, Sun its Stop-N-Go Stores. In 1991, Unocal, Amoco, Sun, and Marathon led the industry in convenience store outlets (see Table 3.8).

The rise of the convenience store contributed directly to the demise of the traditional gasoline station and thus to the decline in the number of places where gasoline was sold. In 1990, gasoline stations (including convenience stores and other "tie-ins" where gasoline accounted for more than 50 percent of the sales) numbered only 111,657 (see Table 3.1). Companies aggressively closed low-gallonage stations, expanding old or building new stations for high gallonage. Few companies expanded trade territories. Indeed, most corporations continued to contract into their most favored markets. Shell divested itself of 3,300 owned stations between 1975 and 1982, constructing 182 new outlets designed for high volume.[50] Many firms rethought logos and color schemes as well as station design. Texaco sought to change its image with a new red, white, black, and gray color scheme, and a new brand mark emphasizing the star and the Texaco T (see Fig. 3.16). The firm introduced a new "family-of-buildings" concept, involving separate prefabricated prototypes for convenience stores, car washes, "gas bars," and auto service

TABLE 3.8 Largest Oil Company Convenience
Store Chains, 1991

Company	Branded Outlets	Number of Stores
Unocal	2,188	13
Amoco	1,847	27
Sun	1,727	27
Emro (Marathon)	1,668	16
Shell	1,300	41
Mobil	1,167	19
Kerr-McGee	1,043	19
Chevron	1,030	25
Clark	905	12
BP America	800	15
Arco	755	5
Diamond Shamrock	703	3
Exxon	699	27
Ashland	662	17
Total	627	18

Note: Other convenience store chains selling gasoline include: Southland's "Seven-Eleven" (5,943 in 31 states), Star (5,397 in 26 states), Circle K (3,859 in 32 states), Dairy Market (1,189 in 11 states), and Cumberland Farms (1,118 in 11 states).

Source: "Convenience Store Outlets in the United States," *NPN* 83 (Sept. 1991): 51–68.

TABLE 3.9 Market Shares and Number of Branded Gasoline Outlets, 1990

Company	Percentage of Market	Number of Outlets	States with Ten or More Outlets
Shell	8.8%	9,389	38
Chevron	8.4	9,664	29
Texaco	7.8	15,111	44
Exxon	7.8	11,673	36
Amoco	7.5	9,802	30
Mobil	6.8	9,001	30
BP America	5.9	7,531	24
Citgo	5.4	9,734	42
Marathon	5.2	2,132	7
Sun	4.2	6,019	23
Phillips	3.5	7,907	29
Unocal	3.5	10,500	29
Arco	3.1	1,541	5
Conoco	2.6	4,915	32
Total	1.5	2,698	16

Source: "Shell Retains Title . . . ," *NPN* 83 (June 1991): 23; "Major Brand Retail Outlet Rankings," *NPN Factbook* 83 (Mid-June 1991): 128.

FIGURE 3.17 Bass Yager Associates of Los Angeles was hired by Exxon to develop prototypes for Exxon's service station system, including the convenience station now pervasive throughout the American landscape. Herb Rosenthal was three-dimensional design consultant on the project; Joel Davy was the principal architect, and these illustrations (*left* and *facing page, top*) represent one of his initial concepts. Exxon eventually accepted a design similar to that shown in the photograph (*facing page, bottom*). By permission of Bass Yager Associates.

centers. Texaco withdrew from marketing in all or parts of nineteen states.

The Shell Oil Company came to top the American gasoline market in the late 1980s. Shell operated 9,389 branded outlets in 38 states in 1990, and enjoyed 8.8 percent of the nation's gasoline sales (see Table 3.9). In contrast, Unocal, slower to modernize being burdened more with a jobber-oriented distribution system, marketed through 10,500 outlets in 29 states and ranked twelfth in market share with 3.5 percent of sales. Stations pumping fewer than 50,000 gallons a month were considered borderline outlets by most companies even in the early 1980s. By 1990, firms were seeking 150,000 to 250,000 gallon-per-month minimums.

Gasoline retailing was substantially impacted by the end of federal controls imposed on the oil industry. Between 1974 and 1981, crude oil and finished gasoline had been allocated across companies, supply relationships frozen, and artificial distinctions concerning allowable costs and rates of return imposed in the interest of spreading evenly across the country the effects of the OPEC-imposed "energy crisis." Through price controls, energy prices in the United States were held at artificially low levels, encouraging excessive consumption and postponing investments in new exploration and energy conservation. Many corporations became overcapitalized during the price-control era and ripe for merger or takeover. Texas oilman T. Boone Pickens figured prominently in a series of hostile takeover attempts that left Gulf, Phillips, Unocal, and other corporations substantially weakened as competitors. Gulf Oil would subse-

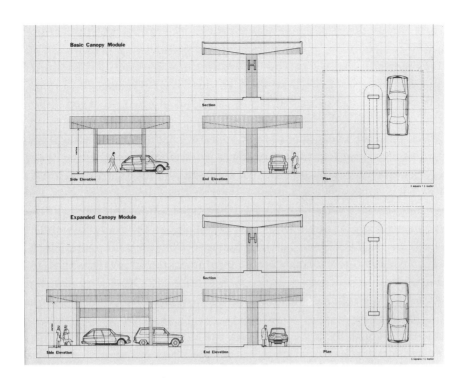

quently completely disappear as a corporation. Phillips was forced into financial restructuring, selling its coal and geothermal operations and collapsing its marketing territory substantially. In fending off attacks, corporations were left with sizable debt loads. For Phillips and Unocal that meant a much slower process of retail outlet modernization.

Place-product-packaging did not operate in isolation. It corresponded to changes in automobile and highway technology and was always integral to overall corporate business strategy. As the basis for territorial competition, place-product-packaging reflected developments in the other industry segments—production, transportation, and refining. The 1920s brought a glut of oil onto the market, a flood that only intensified through the Depression and during the post–World War II years. Place-product-packaging was essential to building customer loyalties that underlay territorially inspired market penetration. The declining position of American petroleum corporations worldwide, exacerbated by the OPEC price rises of the 1970s, drove a reworking of place-product-packaging, especially after 1981 and the lifting of industry controls. Place-product-packaging continued, but with new emphases—price as opposed to service, profitability as opposed to market share, dominated or penetrated territory as opposed to territorial expanse. Today a whole new retail apparatus is taking shape whereby the traditional gasoline station plays an ever-diminished role.

4

Corporate Territoriality

As a device of place-product-packaging, the American gasoline station cannot be understood apart from territorially based corporate marketing strategies. Companies competed with one another by establishing clear corporate identities across trade areas, chains of look-alike gasoline stations expanding and contracting along America's roadsides accordingly. Distinctive marketing geographies evolved firm to firm. For the large, vertically integrated corporations, marketing territories reflected production, transportation, and refining infrastructures, corporate marketing practices being subservient to overall corporate strategies. For the very small regional independents, however, marketing infrastructures were usually primary. Expansion and contraction of trade territories could be very rapid and very dramatic, but always a company, whether large or small, needed to create, protect, and preserve market penetration somewhere. The gasoline station and place-product-packaging were the essential mechanisms used. What follows is a set of linked vignettes descriptive of corporations predominant in American gasoline distribution through the twentieth century. We start with the Standard Oil Trust and the companies descended from it that ultimately established large retail operations. Next we turn to other major gasoline marketers that rose quickly to preeminence following the breakup of Standard Oil. Finally, we briefly treat some of the small regional independents, generally younger firms, only lately come to challenge the giants.

Companies of the Standard Oil Trust

Standard Oil, created by John D. Rockefeller and his associates in 1863 at Cleveland, Ohio, was in 1900 not a monolithic corporation but, indeed, a confederation of largely autonomous companies whose activities were coordinated to amplify overall profits. The trust was established in 1892 when a Pennsylvania suit upheld a state's right to tax all of the capital stock and dividends of a corporation operating within its boundaries.[1] Separate companies to hold properties within respective states was Standard Oil's response as it reorganized into ninety-two operating units consolidated into twenty companies. Nineteen were half owned by shareholders and half owned by Standard Oil of New Jersey which in 1899 became the parent holding company. New Jersey law, unlike New York law, enabled a corporation to own other corporations. Despite its New Jersey charter, Standard Oil continued to be administered from its office tower at 26 Broadway in New York City.

The trust was governed by committees, each committee assigned oversight of some business dimension—production, transportation, refining, cooperage, or exporting, for example. Overall, emphasis was placed on transportation (the mechanism whereby market prices were controlled) and refining. Standard Oil was content to purchase much of its crude oil from private producers and to market finished product (largely kerosene and lubricating oils) through agents. In 1900, Standard Oil produced about one-third of the nation's crude oil, but refined some 80 percent of its finished product. The latter figure would grow to 85 percent in 1911 when the trust was dissolved by the Supreme Court into thirty-four separate companies.[2]

Of the firms that emerged, the Standard Oil companies of California, Indiana, Kentucky, Louisiana, Nebraska, New Jersey, New York, and Ohio were restricted to specific trade territories in their use of the Standard Oil trademark and its derivatives (see Fig. 4.1). The Atlantic Refining Company, the Continental Oil Company, and the Waters-Pierce Oil Company were also given such territorial rights, but chose not to market under the Standard Oil name. Other firms derived from the trust included the Galena-Signal Oil Company, which specialized in railroad lubricants, and the Solar, South Penn (later Pennzoil), and Vacuum Oil companies, which produced a wide range of premium lubricating oils. The Prairie Oil and Gas Company was the largest of several pipeline companies separated out along with the Union Tank Car Company, manufacturer of much of the nation's railroad tank car fleet. The Ohio Oil Company was primarily a crude oil producer. Chesebrough (later Chesebrough-Ponds), maker of face creams, also obtained autonomy. After 1911, the Rockefellers continued to influence the management of these companies as stockholders. In 1935, John D. Rockefeller, Jr., controlled 18 percent of the stock of the combined Socony-Vacuum Company, 14 percent of Standard of California, and 10 percent of Standard Oil of New Jersey. But never again would one single interest exert direct control over the entire oil industry.

Standard Oil of New Jersey (Exxon)

The parent holding company, Standard Oil of New Jersey (now the Exxon Corporation), remained a corporate giant. Jersey Standard con-

FIGURE 4.1 Eleven companies derived from the Standard Oil Trust were given territorial rights to the use of the Standard Oil name.

trolled some 43 percent of the trust's net assets, making it, even after dissolution of the trust, the world's largest oil company and the United States's second largest company (only U.S. Steel was larger). Initially, Standard Oil of New Jersey was notoriously short of crude oil, necessitating both long-term and spot purchases from certain of its divested affiliates, especially the Ohio Oil Company. Early on, the firm emphasized the export market, developing extensive marketing territories in Europe and the Far East. Foreign expansion was a strategy calculated to avoid further antitrust litigation at home. Jersey Standard was an original partner, along with Great Britain's Anglo-Persian Oil Company Ltd. (now British Petroleum), in the Turkish Oil Company, which established crude oil production in Iraq, Saudi Arabia, and other countries derived from the former Ottoman Empire. By 1930 Jersey Standard had its own producing fields in Canada, Mexico, Venezuela, Colombia, Romania, and Russia. Domestic production was handled by two subsidiaries: the Carter Oil Company, which operated initially in West Virginia and Pennsylvania and later in the Far West, and the Humble Oil and Refining Company, which operated in the Southwest, especially Texas. Jersey Standard's refineries were located at Bayonne, New Jersey, and Baytown, Texas, and the company maintained an extensive tanker fleet to tie together its diverse worldwide operations.

The Supreme Court had assigned Jersey Standard a marketing territory of six states—New Jersey, Maryland (including the District of Columbia), Virginia, West Virginia, North Carolina, and South Carolina (see Fig. 4.1). By 1930 the company had extended its Esso brand into Delaware, Pennsylvania, and New York through a newly created affiliate, Standard Oil of Pennsylvania. It also acquired the Beacon Oil Company in

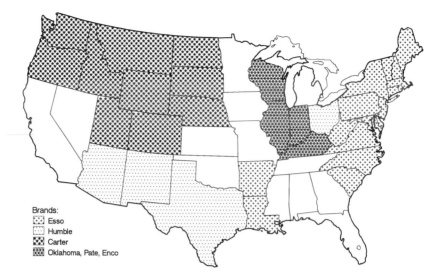

FIGURE 4.2 Standard Oil of New Jersey marketed under the Esso, Humble, Carter, Oklahoma, Pate, and Enco signs in 1960.

FIGURE 4.3 The switch from "Esso" to "Exxon" used Jersey Standard's "Put a Tiger in Your Tank" advertising promotion to symbolize continuity.

THE GAS STATION IN AMERICA

New England. But initially nearly half of its gasoline production was sold to Standard Oil of New York for distribution in New York. Jersey Standard did not expand into retailing rapidly. Fearing additional antitrust litigation, the company did not adopt the leasing policies that drove other firms to quickly build large gasoline station chains. Even so, by 1926 the company controlled some 5 percent of the U.S. gasoline market.

Whereas Standard Oil of New York and the Atlantic Refining Company had not disputed Jersey Standard's use of the Esso brand in their court-assigned territories, such was not the case elsewhere in the country. When in 1935 Jersey Standard sought to introduce Esso stations in Missouri, Standard Oil of Indiana took court action, successfully charging that use of the red, white, and blue color scheme in combination with a Standard Oil–derived brand name close to its own S.O. trademark constituted an illegal taking. Jersey Standard was seen to "appropriate, without expense, fraudulently and unfairly, the good will and reputation, celebrity, and public confidence" which the plaintiff had built up.[3] Again in the 1960s Indiana Standard blocked Jersey Standard's use of the Esso brand in its fourteen midwestern-state marketing territory. Unsuccessfully, Jersey Standard maintained that its Chicago rival had not used either S.O. or Soco in its marketing, and that it was utilizing court protection of these trademarks "solely for the purpose . . . of wrongfully and unlawfully preventing and restraining effective competition."[4] Similarly was Jersey Standard later prevented from marketing under the Esso brand in the territory of Standard of Kentucky. However, the Esso logo was successfully introduced in Louisiana and Arkansas—a small victory.

Jersey Standard was left with no other recourse than to invade the territories of its former affiliates through the brands of subsidiaries. By 1960 gasoline station chains had been built around the following trademarks: In Ohio, Texas, New Mexico, and Arizona, Standard Oil of New Jersey marketed under the Humble brand, named for the lucrative Humble Oil Field near Beaumont, Texas (see Fig. 4.2). In ten states from the northern Great Plains to the Pacific Northwest, the corporation marketed Carter gasoline provided by a refinery in Billings, Montana, tied to the company's producing fields through the Yellowstone Pipeline. In Kentucky, Indiana, Illinois, and Wisconsin, Jersey Standard experimented with a number of brands. Purchase of Chicago's and Milwaukee's largest independent marketers brought, respectively, the Oklahoma and Pate brands into the Jersey Standard fold. Into the Oklahoma operation was dovetailed the Bonded stations of the Gasteria Oil Company. Later, the Oklahoma, Pate, and even the Carter and Humble brands were replaced by Enco. The word "Enco," which reflected the fact that Standard Oil of New Jersey was still the world's largest "energy company," looked like the word "Esso" when printed in rounded red letters and placed on a white elliptical disc with blue border.

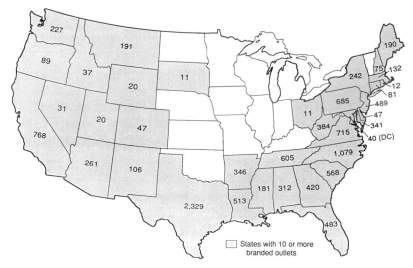

FIGURE 4.4 States with ten or more Exxon outlets in 1990. (*Source:* "Branded Outlets," *National Petroleum News Factbook* 82 [Mid-June, 1990]: 44-51.)

Although Jersey Standard was prevented from taking its original logo nationwide, it was not discouraged from adopting common advertising, thus generating a single corporate identity. One of the most popular and effective advertising schemes originated with Oklahoma, was adopted by Carter, and then spread across the entire corporation by stages. The "Put a Tiger in Your Tank" promotion swept the country. Gasoline pumps were turned into tigers with cardboard heads and striped hoses. Tiger paw prints were painted on driveways. Children prodded parents to stop for tiger whips, tiger jump ropes, and tiger masks. The company's tiger would be used again in the 1970s when the diversity of separate brands was abandoned for the single Exxon trademark used domestically by the company thereafter (see Fig. 4.3).

In 1960 Jersey Standard began a successful market penetration of California, the fastest growing area in the United States. It bought, only to have the purchase overturned by the Department of Justice on anti-trust grounds, 3,900 West Coast Flying A, Seaside, and Pathfinder gasoline stations from the Tide Water-Associated Oil Company. Why do companies merge? asked the *National Petroleum News*. Some regional companies sought, it concluded, larger scale operations. However, the article warned, "sheer geography isn't the controlling factor; big volume and real growth potential are what count."[5] Clearly, merger was the quickest means of achieving these ends. Stymied with the Tide Water-Associated purchase, Jersey Standard bought the 1,500 outlets of Standard Oil of California's Signal Division. The Signal Gas and Oil Company had sold the chain to California Standard in 1947 in order to concentrate on crude oil production at Signal Hill and in other California fields. In converting the chain to Enco in 1967, the Signal brand reverted to the

THE GAS STATION IN AMERICA

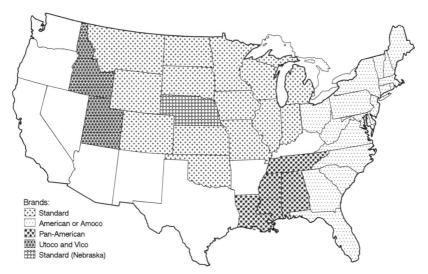

FIGURE 4.5 Standard Oil of Indiana marketed under the Standard, American, Amoco, Pan American, Utoco, and Vico signs in 1935.

original company, which then renamed its Hancock and Norwalk stations in creating a second Signal chain.

The Enco brand created little excitement and in 1971 Standard Oil of New Jersey took the unprecedented step of selecting a new identity for its product and itself. After substantial market research and extended testing in various parts of the United States, the Exxon brand was adopted for the company's American operations, Esso still appearing elsewhere in the world (see Fig. 4.3). Although the OPEC-generated price inflation proved the company noncompetitive in certain states, it still markets through some 11,600 branded outlets in forty states (see Fig. 4.4).[6] Exxon has ceased operations in Vermont, much of upstate New York, and Kentucky, Indiana, Illinois, Wisconsin, North Dakota, and Nebraska. In addition to the West Coast, the firm has expanded in recent years into Tennessee, Georgia, Alabama, Mississippi, and Florida. The gap in Exxon's nationwide marketing strategy is the original territory of its old nemesis, Standard Oil of Indiana (now Amoco).

Standard Oil of Indiana (Amoco)

The breakup of the trust left Standard Oil of Indiana with a large trade area, fourteen states from Michigan and Indiana in the east to Oklahoma and Montana on the southwest and northwest respectively (see Fig. 4.1). The company was also left with the world's largest oil refinery at Whiting in Indiana just across the state line from Chicago, and much smaller refineries at Wood River, Illinois, across the Mississippi River from St. Louis, Sugar Creek near Kansas City, Missouri, and Casper, Wyoming. Producing fields were located in Wyoming and Louisiana. It was at Whiting in 1913 that company chemists William Burton and Rob-

FIGURE 4.6 Road map advertising illustrated the extent of American Oil's territory in the 1950s, and related that company to the other subsidiaries of parent Standard Oil of Indiana.

ert Humphrey revolutionized gasoline refining, producing a synthetic product by cracking high boiling-point oil under high temperature and high pressure. The Burton Patent, adopted by many other companies, greatly enhanced Indiana Standard's prestige if not profitability.

In 1929, Standard Oil of Indiana took control of the Pan American Petroleum and Transport Company and its producing fields in Mexico and Venezuela. Purchased also were the Pan American refineries in Mexico, Aruba, Germany, and the United States, the last located at New Orleans, Savannah, and Baltimore. With Pan American came 50 percent control of the American Oil Company of Baltimore and its subsidiary, Lord Baltimore Service Stations, Inc. In 1935 Pan American Oil marketed under the Pan-Am logo in the mid-South and American Oil marketed under the American logo down the East Coast from Maine to Florida (see Fig. 4.5). Indiana Standard also purchased Standard Oil of Nebraska, consolidating its Standard brand at midcontinent, and the Utah Refining

Company of Salt Lake City, giving it dominance in Utah and Idaho with the Vico and, later, the Utoco brand (see Fig. 4.5). Indiana Standard (or Stanolind, as it was often called) sold its foreign investments to Standard Oil of New Jersey. Five years later properties in Mexico were nationalized, leaving Jersey Standard and not Indiana Standard with substantial losses.

The Indiana Standard story is substantially that of its American Oil affiliate (see Fig. 4.6). Louis Blaustein had worked for Standard Oil for eighteen years when in 1910, turning down a company transfer to a European post, he invested his savings in an old stable, a horse, and a tank wagon in Baltimore to sell kerosene and gasoline. Having constructed a chain of gasoline stations to boost gasoline sales, the small company achieved a technical breakthrough when it produced an antiknock gasoline by mixing in benzol, a volatile byproduct of steel-mill coke ovens. He called the new gasoline Amoco.[7] His first tank wagon had been painted bright green, with the company's name in white letters trimmed in red. The red, white, and green color scheme was soon adopted in gasoline station decor and signage. Starting in New Orleans, Pan American also built a chain of stations under a red, white, and green color scheme, pushing Panamoc and Panolene gasoline brands at the pumps. At the same time, Standard Oil of Indiana, the parent firm, adopted red, white, and blue, pushing its Red Crown and White Crown gasolines into prominence under the Standard Oil Products sign.

The trade territories of Standard Oil of Indiana and its various subsidiaries were underpinned by a distinctive geography of producing, transporting, and refining facilities. In 1950 the bulk of the company's producing fields were in Texas, Oklahoma, Kansas, Colorado, and Wyoming (see Fig. 4.7). Crude oil pipelines connected these fields with refineries. Product lines and river barge and ocean tanker fleets connected refineries to bulk terminals. Gasoline was distributed to jobbers and dealers primarily by truck.

In 1954 and 1960, respectively, Pan American and Utah Refining were merged into American Oil, which became Standard of Indiana's sole operating company. Indiana Standard's original territory continued to be served by a Standard division of American Oil. Corporate reorganization was not easy. Indiana Standard had marketed at midcontinent primarily through some 3,800 commission agents. It had only 119 jobbers. American Oil, on the other hand, had been largely jobber-oriented, especially in the South where some 85 percent of its products were sold through jobbers.[8] In the Middle West some confusion reigned. Station signs read "Standard," but the pumps were labeled "American." In the 1970s, the word "American" was replaced by "Amoco." The name had been used on American Oil's stations starting in the 1930s, but had been phased out in many locations. Now it was brought back to dominate in the belief that in high-speed driving a five-letter word was easier to distinguish than one

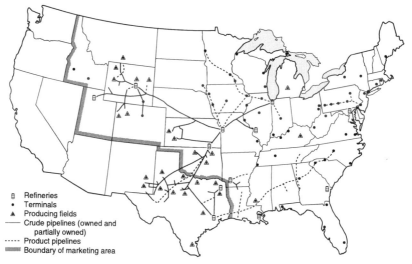

FIGURE 4.7 Underlying each company's marketing strategy was an infrastructure of producing, refining, and transporting facilities. The map portrays Standard Oil of Indiana's infrastructure of the 1950s.

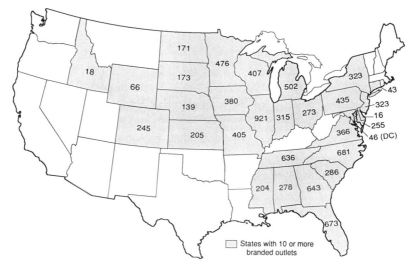

FIGURE 4.8 States with ten or more Amoco outlets in 1990. (*Source:* "Branded Outlets," *National Petroleum News Factbook* 82 [Mid-June, 1990]: 44-51.)

of eight letters. In the 1980s the word "Standard" lapsed, except in parts of the Middle West and the corporation changed its name to Amoco Corporation. Adopted were the Indiana Standard colors (augmented by black) with the company's familiar oval with torch as sign.

Amoco is today an international corporation with production in the Middle East and elsewhere in the world. The firm markets in Europe and in Australia among other locations. But domestically the firm is limited to the more successful market areas where it traditionally enjoyed significant market penetration (see Fig. 4.8). The company withdrew from marginal markets in northern New England, West Virginia, Louisiana, Oklahoma, and Montana after OPEC's price increases. During the 1960s it launched an unsuccessful attempt to penetrate the California market. In its competition with Standard Oil of New Jersey (later Exxon), Amoco was able to totally defend the heart of its market in the Middle West while advancing more successfully into the very core of Exxon's territory. Nonetheless, Exxon proved the winner in penetrating the lucrative West Coast market from which Amoco is now removed.

Atlantic-Richfield (Arco) and Sinclair

When the Atlantic Refining Company was divorced from the Standard Oil Trust it had three refineries (Philadelphia, Pittsburgh, and Franklin, Pennsylvania). All of its domestic marketing apparatus was restricted to Pennsylvania and Delaware where it had the right to use the Standard brand (see Fig. 4.1). However, nearly 60 percent of its kerosene and lubricating oils were exported. It had no crude oil production, no pipelines, and no tankers. Most of its foreign business, oriented to the Far East, was handled through a commission house, that of Warden, Frew, and Company. Much of its lubricating oil went to the Galena-Signal Oil Company. Beginning in 1915, the company reoriented to the gasoline trade by building a chain of gasoline stations focused on Philadelphia and Pittsburgh. It began developing crude oil production in Kansas, Oklahoma, Texas, and New Mexico, the crude sent by pipeline to the Gulf Coast and on by tanker to its Philadelphia refinery. A product line was constructed from Philadelphia to Pittsburgh and the western Pennsylvania refineries closed. The company expanded into New England under its Atlantic trademark and expanded vigorously southward through Virginia, the Carolinas, Georgia, and Florida. To serve the Southeast, a refinery was constructed at Brunswick, Georgia.

The Sinclair Consolidated Oil Company, headed by Harry Sinclair, was an amalgam of several predecessor firms with extensive crude oil production and numerous small refineries in Kansas, Oklahoma, and Texas. The company developed an extensive chain of gasoline stations in the Middle West from Kansas, Nebraska, and the Dakotas to Michigan and Ohio. Its largest refinery, constructed at East Chicago, Indiana, was served by one of the first long-distance trunk pipelines. When in 1930 the firm purchased the assets of the Pierce Petroleum Corporation (the St. Louis–based descendant of Waters-Pierce, the ex–Standard Oil company that marketed in Texas and Mexico), another refinery in Oklahoma and one at Tampico, Mexico, were added. The merged gasoline station chains overlapped very little, giving Sinclair even market coverage southward across Texas and as far into Mexico as the Yucatan. The Mexican holdings became the principal foundation for the Pemex gasoline brand after Mexico's nationalization of its oil industry in the 1930s.

In 1932 Sinclair Consolidated merged with both the Prairie Oil and Gas Company and the Prairie Pipe Line Company to form simply the Consolidated Oil Corporation, although the new firm continued to market under the Sinclair brand. Prairie had been a major supplier and transporter of crude oil for Standard Oil of New Jersey. With pipeline overcapacity, Consolidated sold the old Sinclair Pipeline to Standard of Indiana, giving the latter firm greater access to Texas producing fields. In 1941 Consolidated operated three large refineries at East Chicago, Marcus Hook, Pennsylvania, and Houston along with six smaller facilities in New York, Wyoming, Oklahoma, and Texas. It operated tanker fleets tying the Gulf and Atlantic coasts, and serving the Great Lakes. It also supplied 9,600 dealer-operated stations and 17,521 commission service stations.[9] It marketed under a red, white, and green disc with the letters "H.C." (high compression) emphasized. Its most widely recognized logo, however, was the green dinosaur.

The Richfield Oil Company of California was built on crude oil production and refinery capacity located in California and, after receivership in 1935, was jointly controlled by Consolidated and another of the new major independents, Cities Service. In 1940 Richfield's market was confined to California, Oregon, and Washington, although by the 1960s it had expanded into all of the states west to the Rocky Mountains. Richfield Oil of New York began as the eastern outlet for Richfield of California, but was bought outright by Consolidated in 1935. As a Sinclair subsidiary, it continued to market under the Richfield blue and yellow colors and flying eagle logo from Maine to South Carolina. The New York firm was the largest all-jobber company in 1964 when it finally was merged with Consolidated, by that time renamed the Sinclair Oil Company. At an average cost of $3,000 per station, Sinclair converted Richfield's outlets to its own colors and resupplied stations with Sinclair packaged goods, road maps, credit-card applications, and all the other paraphernalia of place-product-packaging.

In 1965 Atlantic and Richfield merged to form Atlantic-Richfield (a name later changed to Arco). Atlantic's 8,300 stations and Richfield's 4,400 gave the firm strong East Coast and West Coast market positions. Arco then moved in 1969 to purchase Sinclair, adding another 22,000 outlets between the East Coast and the Rocky Mountains (see Fig. 4.9).[10] To avoid antitrust litigation, the contracts on 4,500 Sinclair and Atlantic outlets in eleven northeastern states were sold to British Petroleum along with 31 terminals, 135 bulk plants, and 2 refineries, including Sinclair's Marcus Hook facility and Atlantic's Port Arthur, Texas, plant.[11] With the Department of Justice still moving to invalidate the Atlantic-Richfield merger on restriction of trade grounds, some 9,700 Sinclair outlets were actually disposed of, giving BP a chain of stations from Maine all the way to Florida. Arco agreed to use the Sinclair brand on former Sinclair stations in twenty-one central states. But still the De-

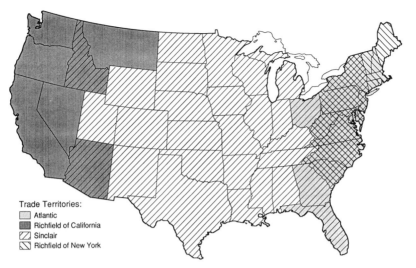

FIGURE 4.9 Companies aggregated as the Atlantic-Richfield Company in 1969. The name of the firm was later changed to Arco.

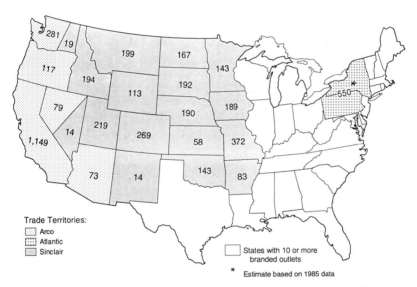

FIGURE 4.10 States with ten or more Arco, Atlantic, or Sinclair outlets in 1990. (*Source:* "Branded Outlets," *National Petroleum News Factbook* 82 [Mid-June, 1990]: 44-51.)

partment of Justice was not satisfied, ordering divestiture of all Sinclair stations in fourteen midcontinent states, some 2,500 in number. A new Sinclair Oil Company would ultimately emerge from this action to serve those outlets.

Arco's fortunes soared when it pioneered crude oil production on Alaska's North Slope. With completion of the TransAlaska Pipeline the company was well positioned to dominate the West Coast market. Suddenly, its East Coast marketing facilities were redundant. In 1985, with deregulation of the oil industry under the Reagan administration, Arco sold its Philadelphia refinery to a newly created company called, logically enough, Atlantic Oil. Financing came from a Dutch-controlled Bermuda-based transporter of crude oil, Trans-World Oil. Some 576 Arco stations were converted to a new Atlantic brand, and the remaining 430 stations sold to Shell Oil. Thus in 1990 the Atlantic brand still survived at the core of the old Atlantic Refining Company's original marketing area (see Fig. 4.10). And the Sinclair brand still thrived in the heart of what was once the old Consolidated Oil Company's heartland. Brand identity, and the customer loyalties that it engenders, has a market value in and of itself which drives brand persistence even when originating corporations disappear. Only the Richfield trademark is gone, but in its traditional marketing region there thrives the much-mutated Arco.

Standard Oil of California (Chevron) and Gulf Oil

Standard Oil of California, formed in 1906, was an amalgam of earlier firms with names such as California Star Oil Works, Pacific Coast Oil Company, and Standard Oil of Iowa, some with roots dating back as early as 1873. Primarily a producer of crude oil and a refiner of kerosene and lubricants, California Standard (or Socal, as it was frequently called) came slowly to gasoline retailing. At first its gasolines were sold through agents, for example, the National Supply Stations, Inc. National Supply was established in 1912 when California Standard was denied permission by the City of Los Angeles to establish a chain of stations on the grounds that they would be hazardous and unsightly and reduce property values in the city.[12] The purchase of National Supply in 1914 brought to Standard Oil of California clusters of stations not only in greater Los Angeles, but also in the San Diego, San Francisco, and Oakland areas. Stations, simple twelve- by fifteen-foot wooden houses walled in glass with canopies extending over pumps on graveled drives, were painted red, white, and blue. The chain grew to 288 in 1919, with stations in Oregon and Washington as well as in California, and to 2,200 in 1925 (725 company-owned and 1,475 dealer-owned).[13] All stations sported the company's distinctive chevron logo.

With California Standard's principal producing fields in central California and its refineries in the San Francisco area, the company's primary market remained, through the 1930s, those five West Coast states where it owned the Standard Oil name (see Fig. 4.1). The firm ventured overseas in search of new crude oil, becoming a partner with the Texas Company (Texaco) in the California Texas Oil Company. Caltex, the latter company's popular name, established major fields in the Middle East and began marketing gasoline in Europe and Africa. After World War II Standard Oil of California pushed its marketing apparatus eastward into the Rocky Mountains and the Southwest through two subsidiaries, the Cali-

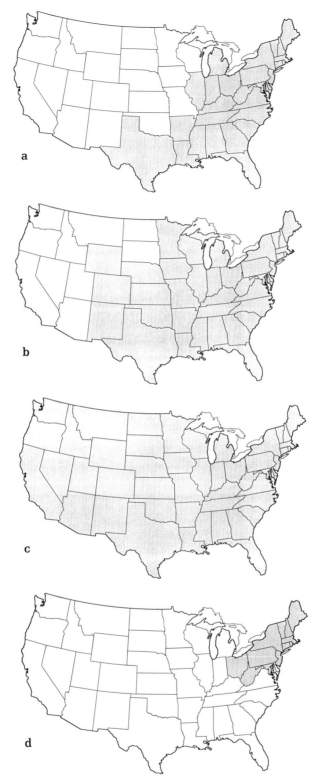

FIGURE 4.11 Marketing territories for the Gulf Oil brand: (a) 1930, (b) 1960, (c) 1970, and (d) 1990.

fornia Company and Standard Oil of Texas, all under the Calso and Chevron brands. Also established was the California Oil Company to market in the Northeast under the Calso trademark.

In 1961, California Standard bought Standard Oil of Kentucky, another former trust company (see Fig. 4.1).[14] Kentucky Standard (or Kyso) was a marketing company that bought its product primarily from Jersey Standard's Pascagoula, Mississippi, refinery. With 8,700 branded outlets it had neither crude oil supplies nor refineries of its own. Jersey Standard, which, indeed, had supplied Kentucky Standard with 98 percent of its gasoline needs between 1911 and 1948 (and some 76 percent thereafter), immediately launched an unsuccessful attempt to extend its own Esso brand into California Standard's newly purchased territory. Although it defended its trademark rights, California Standard abandoned the Standard Oil name altogether in the 1970s. With $5 billion in assets, 20,000 employees, twelve refineries, and 16,000 branded outlets in thirty-nine states, the company consolidated all of its operating units into a new firm, Chevron USA, thus giving itself a single marketing identity across the United States.[15]

The Gulf Oil Company had its beginnings in 1901 with the discovery of oil in the Spindletop Field of Texas. Financed by and ultimately controlled by Andrew Mellon of Pittsburgh, the company would evolve primarily as an exploration and production company which, despite its extraordinary successes aboard, remained crude-short in the United States. With lucrative fields already tapped in Mexico, Venezuela, and the Persian Gulf, Gulf obtained interests in the Turkish Petroleum Company and shared in the development of the oil industry in Iraq. But after World War II its lead in tapping Kuwait's massive oil reserves gave it resources five times larger than its domestic base. In the United States Gulf was well established only in West Texas although it had producing wells scattered across Oklahoma, Louisiana, and Kansas. Overall, the company's strategy was to find and produce crude oil and then integrate downstream through the development of refinery and marketing facilities.

In 1930 Gulf's marketing territory extended from Texas across the Southeast and northward into the Middle West and Northeast (see Fig. 4.11a). By 1960 the company had expanded north from Texas into the Rocky Mountain states and by 1970 was marketing in all of the coterminous forty-eight states (see Figs. 4.11b and c). Numerous jobbing companies and several small regional refiners were absorbed in the process. In 1930 the Paragon Refining Company of Cleveland added 400 gasoline stations to the Gulf chain in Ohio and Michigan. A pipeline laid from Tulsa to Toledo and on to Pittsburgh solidified this move. In 1960 Gulf purchased the Wilshire Oil Company of California, thus adding a refinery and 600 outlets with some 4 percent of the West Coast market.

With a glut of foreign oil on its hands, Gulf sought not only rapid expansion of its domestic gasoline station chain, but to compete through

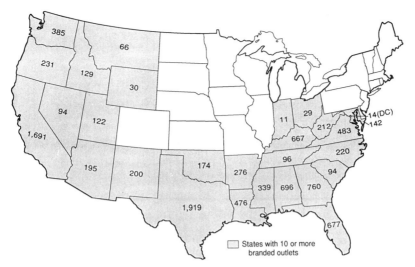

FIGURE 4.12 States with ten or more Chevron outlets in 1990. (*Source:* "Branded Outlets," *National Petroleum News Factbook* 82 [Mid-June, 1990]: 44-51.)

lower prices as well. In 1961 it brought to the market a subregular grade Gulftane gasoline designed to sell for several cents below the price of regular grade gasoline. But cheap oil was not to be. The OPEC price rises, complicated, perhaps, by mismanagement, hit Gulf hard. Substantially reliant on now high-priced foreign supplies, the company began to abandon marketing territory as vigorously as previously it had sought to expand. First Gulf withdrew from the Middle West and then from the hard-won ground of the Far West. From 31,000 stations in 1968 the company's total fell to 21,000 in 1974, and to 14,500 in 1982.[16] Finally, in 1984 Gulf agreed to a merger with Chevron following an unfriendly takeover attempt launched by T. Boone Pickens, Jr., chairman of the small Mesa Petroleum Company.

The merger with Chevron splintered Gulf. Contracts for over 5,600 branded outlets in eight southeastern states were sold to Standard Oil of Ohio (Sohio), a company in the process of being absorbed by British Petroleum. Sohio obtained permission to market under the Gulf orange disc for five years (with options to renew) and when conversion came it was not to the red, white, and blue of the former Standard Oil company, but to the yellow and green of BP America. Along with the chain of stations went bulk terminals and a refinery in Louisiana. Chevron, for its part, began to convert to its colors some 2,700 stations across Texas, Louisiana, Arkansas, and Oklahoma. Finally, Chevron sold the former Gulf stations in the northeastern states to Cumberland Farms, a Massachusetts operator of convenience stores. Only in the Northeast is the Gulf brand still found, another case of brand persistence (see Fig. 4.11d). Today Chevron markets in the Far West (its traditional territory) and across the Southeast (its gleanings from Standard Oil of Kentucky). Its inheritance from Gulf serves to tie these two areas together, primarily across Texas, giving the company a coast-to-coast spread (see Fig. 4.12).

British Petroleum (BP) and Standard Oil of Ohio

Standard Oil of Ohio dates from 1870 and was the first of the various Standard Oil companies to be formed. Specializing in kerosene and lubricating oils the company operated a refinery at Cleveland, obtaining its crude oil initially from Pennsylvania and later from Ohio producing fields. When the company began to expand beyond Cleveland it did not acquire new properties in its own name. Rather, ownership and control was placed in the hands of various stockholders. In 1879 ownership was conveyed to trustees as a matter of consolidating ownership and coordinating management. It was these trustees who transferred control of the myriad Standard Oil interests to Standard Oil of New Jersey, a process not completed until 1900. Ohio Standard remained merely one of the several regional derivatives of the trust (see Fig. 4.1). The firm marketed solely in Ohio, although it did move with vigor into exploration and crude oil production in Texas, Oklahoma, Louisiana, and Illinois. By 1950 refineries had been built at Toledo and Lima in Ohio, and across the Ohio River from Cincinnati in Kentucky. A wholly owned pipeline stretched into southern Illinois and shared ownership of other lines gave access to Oklahoma, Texas, and Louisiana. So dominant in Ohio was the Sohio brand (the name introduced in 1928) that the company maintained subsidiaries to market under other trademarks such as Fleetwing, White Rose, and Enarco.

Ohio Standard, like Jersey Standard, found itself with a popular brand that it could not use to colonize beyond its original trade area. Attempts to do so were beaten back by Standard Oil of Indiana and Standard Oil of Kentucky. And yet it could not expand in Ohio for fear of government antitrust action. Thus the Boron trademark was developed in the 1960s and used to invade markets in Michigan, Kentucky, and Pennsylvania conveniently served by the company's refineries. With domestic crude oil reserves dwindling in the 1970s, Sohio began to view its future with alarm. Not only was the company "land-locked" territorially, but it was desperately crude-short, producing only some 16 percent of its needs in 1969.[17]

British Petroleum originated in 1909 as the Anglo-Persian Oil Company Ltd. with capital supplied by British government–owned Burmah Oil. British Petroleum would maintain a long and often intimate relationship with the British government in founding the Middle Eastern oil industry. In 1928 Anglo-Persian sold half of its share in Turkish Petroleum to Jersey Standard, Gulf, and other American firms and established the Red Line Agreement. BP Oil (the corporate name adopted in 1954) expanded its marketing activities across Europe and began to look longingly at North America. Its first foothold across the Atlantic came in 1958 when it

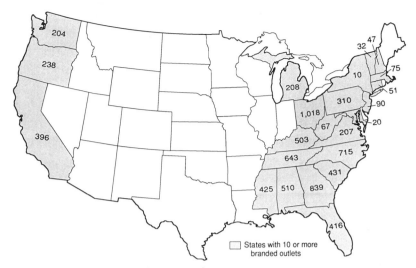

FIGURE 4.13 States with ten or more BP America outlets in 1990. (*Source:* "Branded Outlets," *National Petroleum News Factbook* 82 [Mid-June, 1990]: 44-51.)

established some 400 Canadian outlets in Quebec and Ontario. A refinery built at Montreal was supplied with crude oil from the Persian Gulf. But 1969 was the key year in BP's North American conquest. First the company acquired 9,700 Sinclair and Atlantic outlets in sixteen states from Maine to Florida. This was a mixed blessing. The Sinclair portion of the purchase was predominantly jobber-supplied and Sinclair had not been able to achieve market penetration any higher than 5 percent in any state save Rhode Island.[18] Second, the company acquired what would become a controlling interest in Standard Oil of Ohio.

BP Oil had scored outstanding successes in crude oil exploration, first in the North Sea off Scotland and then on Alaska's North Slope, giving it control of one-quarter of the world's reserves. What it lacked in North America was refinery capacity and a deeply penetrated trade territory from which to vigorously expand its marketing operations. BP bought an immediate 25 percent interest in Sohio in exchange for Alaskan crude oil reserves. However, a BP subsidiary was established to develop those reserves under contract to Sohio. An exchange of stock was arranged such that with production reaching 600,000 barrels a day BP would take a 54 percent ownership of Ohio Standard. The Department of Justice approved the merger on condition that Sohio's 1,500 Boron stations in Pennsylvania and one-third of its approximately 3,100 outlets in Ohio be divested. In 1984, in anticipation of BP's takeover, Ohio Standard acquired 5,600 Gulf outlets in eight southeastern states. Thus Sohio expanded its marketing to twenty-one states before merger.

In 1987 BP Oil bought the remaining 45 percent of Sohio and became through a subsidiary BP America, Ohio Standard's successor. Conversion of the former Atlantic, Sinclair, Gulf, Boron, and Sohio stations had been held in abeyance. Laws both in Great Britain and in the United States barred the company from engaging in any promotional activities so long as stock sales were pending.[19] BP America's entry into North America did not end with Standard of Ohio. In 1988 the firm acquired Mobil's Ferndale, Washington, refinery and swapped Mobil's California, Oregon, and Washington gasoline stations for BP stations in the Southeast. BP was a $59-billion entity with operations in seventy countries, BP America representing about 35 percent of the company's global assets.[20] Today BP America markets in the Northeast (except Maine and Rhode Island), in the eastern Middle West, the Southeast, and along the West Coast (see Fig. 4.13).

Standard Oil of New York (Mobil)

The Standard Oil Company of New York (Socony) inherited the New York and New England states as trade territories in 1911, what the company would call Soconyland (see Figs. 4.1 and 4.14). However, the company had been primarily an exporter of kerosene, especially to India, China, and Japan. Its motto "Oil for the Lamps of China" was known worldwide. Gasoline sales exceeded kerosene sales in 1912, but most of the gasoline was obtained from Jersey Standard and Atlantic refineries. At first, the company sold through jobbers who were allowed to establish their own brand identities, the Metro stations in New York City being the largest such chain. After its territory had been invaded by Atlantic, Jersey Standard, and various of the new independents such as Sun Oil and Tide Water, Standard of New York moved to establish its own Socony brand through aggressive gasoline station chain development, which in turn led to purchase or establishment of producing and refining subsidiaries elsewhere in the country, each with their own chains.

The Magnolia Petroleum Company was organized in 1894 at Corsicana where oil was first discovered in Texas. As a Socony affiliate Magnolia controlled some 18 percent of the Texas gasoline market in 1926. With refineries at Corsicana and Beaumont the company spread its stations into Louisiana, Arkansas, Oklahoma, and New Mexico (see Fig. 4.15). The General Petroleum Company of California operated refineries at Vernon and Torrance near Los Angeles and marketed fuel oil along the West Coast as far north as Alaska and as far south as Chile. Gasoline sales began in 1923 with a chain of some 1,500 outlets established in over 400 West Coast communities by 1925.[21] In 1934 the firm was marketing in five western states. The White Eagle Oil and Refining Company, with refineries in Kansas and Wyoming, established a chain of stations across eleven states from Iowa and Minnesota on the east to Utah and Idaho on the west. With a refinery at Detroit, the White Star Refining Company operated exclusively in Michigan. The Wadhams Oil Company operated exclusively in Wisconsin although its refinery was located at East Chicago, Indiana. The Lubrite Refining Company, with a refinery in East St.

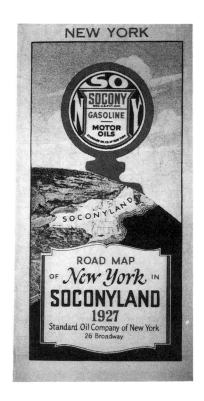

FIGURE 4.14 Cover of 1927 Standard Oil of New York road map depicting "Soconyland."

Louis, Illinois, dominated Socony's business in Indiana, Illinois, and Missouri.

Several of these subsidiaries had actually come with the Vacuum Oil Company, which merged with Socony to form Socony-Vacuum in 1931. Vacuum Oil had been the Standard Oil Trust's leading exporter of premium lubricating oils and had patented the Gargoyle and Pegasus trademarks as well as the Mobiloil brand name. It operated two refineries in western New York. The new combined company supplied some 37,000 branded outlets in twenty-nine states. It controlled 34 percent of the market in New York, and from 7 to 19 percent in the other states served. Socony-Vacuum joined with Jersey Standard in Stanvac to undertake crude oil exploration and production in Indonesia. This subsidiary marketed across the Far East and built refineries in Romania and Italy to serve the European market. In 1940 Socony-Vacuum joined Aramco in the Middle East. Critics saw in Socony-Vacuum a company as hyphenated as its name. "It was a company of pieces, decentralized into geographical and functional fiefdoms."[22] The company went through several name changes: Socony-Mobil, Mobil, and finally the Mobil Corporation as it reoriented its identity toward its most popular brand.

In 1960 Mobil Oil marketed in forty-two of the original forty-eight states. It was not represented in Kentucky, Mississippi, Alabama, Georgia, South Carolina, or Florida. By 1990 the company's marketing territory essentially had collapsed into thirty states. Mobil had withdrawn from the Pacific Northwest, the Rocky Mountain states, and the Plains states save for eastern North Dakota. In the South it had achieved a permanent place only in Florida and adjacent Alabama (see Fig. 4.16). Clearly, the heart of its territory remained New York and its adjacent states. The attempt to create a national distribution system failed and, like many of the other major petroleum companies, it had to be content to serve selected regional markets, prime among them the region of its origins.

Ohio Oil (Marathon)

The Ohio Oil Company was bought by the Standard Oil Trust in 1889 in order to give access to new oil fields in western Ohio. Until 1911 the

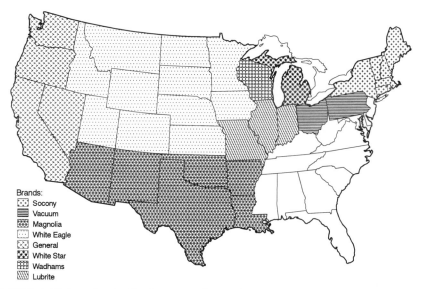

Brands:
- Socony
- Vacuum
- Magnolia
- White Eagle
- General
- White Star
- Wadhams
- Lubrite

FIGURE 4.15 Standard Oil of New York marketed under a variety of different brands in 1934. All stations, however, displayed Pegasus, the company's "Flying Red Horse."

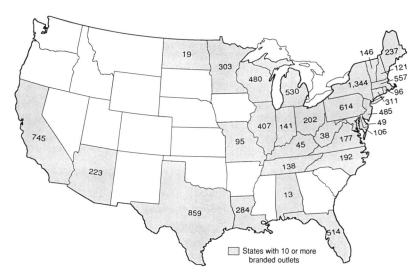

States with 10 or more branded outlets

FIGURE 4.16 States with ten or more Mobil outlets in 1990. (*Source:* "Branded Outlets," *National Petroleum News Factbook* 82 [Mid-June, 1990]: 44-51.)

firm remained the principal supplier of crude oil to Standard Oil of New Jersey through the Buckeye Pipeline. To reduce this dependency Jersey Standard formed its Carter and Humble subsidiaries. Ohio moved into the southern Illinois producing fields, establishing a refinery at Robinson. Other fields were tapped in Wyoming, Oklahoma, Texas, Louisiana, and California, as the company settled into a primary role as crude oil producer, often selling its oil to other companies at or near the originat-

FIGURE 4.17 The Ohio Oil Company in the 1930s marketed gasoline under the Linco brand in the area outlined on the map cover.

ing wells. In 1936 Ohio Oil merged with the Transcontinental Oil Company, which added small refineries in Kansas, Oklahoma, and Texas. Transcontinental also brought a chain of 350 gasoline stations spread from Louisiana and Arkansas to Colorado and Wyoming, marketing under the Marathon brand. In order to integrate downstream, Ohio Oil had bought in 1924 the Lincoln Oil and Refining Company from which a chain of several hundred Linco stations had been created which spread from western Ohio across Indiana into Illinois. By World War II the western stations had been abandoned and the Marathon brand brought east to serve a revitalized midwestern chain (see Fig. 4.17). After World War II Ohio Oil continued its emphasis on crude oil production through successful foreign investment, especially in Libya. It participated in the Conorado Petroleum Corporation, a worldwide exploration company jointly owned with Conoco and Amerada.

Ohio Oil purchased the Aurora Gasoline Company in 1959, adding another 600 Speedway 79 outlets in Michigan to its total of 2,700 gasoline stations across the Middle West. In 1962, the company changed its name to the Marathon Oil Company, enabling customers to associate the visible brand in its trade territory with a corporate entity. In the same year the company strengthened its position as a gasoline supplier through purchase of the Plymouth Oil Company, a refiner, pipeline operator, and wholesaler of gasoline to small independent jobbers, especially in the Southeast. Marathon also extended its branded chain into the Southeast (unsuccessfully, it would prove) with stations oriented to interchanges on I-75, the principal axis connecting the cities of the Middle West with Florida. In the 1970s Marathon began to experiment with numerous secondary brands, prime among them a rejuvenated Speedway. In 1990 the Emro Marketing subsidiary operated some 1,600 of the firm's 3,700 outlets. In the South, Marathon was represented entirely by Emro, primarily through convenience store outlets (see Fig. 4.18).

To make itself less vulnerable to takeover, Marathon sought to buy

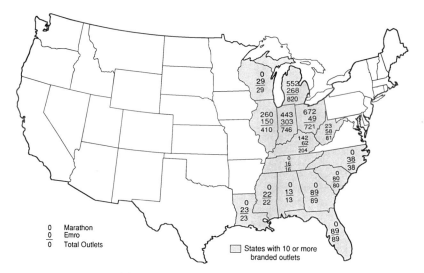

FIGURE 4.18 States with ten or more Marathon outlets in 1991. (*Source:* "Branded Retail Outlets," *National Petroleum News Factbook* 83 [Mid-June, 1991]: 44-51.)

the American subsidiary of Canada's Husky Oil Ltd., only to have the Department of Justice reject the plan. What made Marathon desirable to suitors was its large domestic oil reserves. In 1980 Marathon operated in every major American oil field and had proven reserves of 683 million barrels of crude oil and 2,100 billion cubic feet of natural gas.[23] Its refineries in Ohio, Illinois, and Louisiana were among the nation's most modern. Following a bid of Mobil, Marathon agreed to a takeover by the U.S. Steel Corporation. U.S. Steel's purchase saved the steel manufacturer about $500 million in taxes in the first year, and stood to save some $1 billion more over the productive life of Marathon's Yates Field alone since the tax laws let the field be valued for tax purchases at a higher cost than the property represented on Marathon's books. Economist Robert Reich observed, "Because U.S. Steel can take new depletion deductions against this high-valued property, the Yates reserves are worth far more to it than they were to Marathon, which had already extracted what it could of the oil fields tax-deduction potential."[24] The field's tax benefits were renewable through transfer. Following the merger, U.S. Steel changed its name to USX, its Marathon Division becoming its most profitable unit.

Continental Oil

The Continental Oil Company was Standard Oil's Rocky Mountain representative. The 1911 court decree gave it rights to the Standard Oil name in six states from Montana and Idaho south to New Mexico (see Fig. 4.1). Actually, the modern company was an amalgam of Continental and

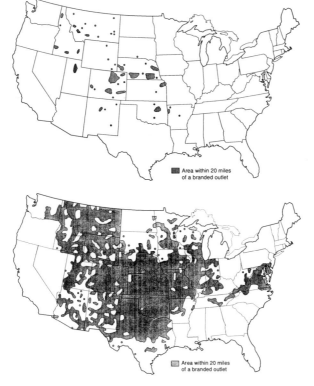

FIGURE 4.19 Areas within twenty miles of a Conoco outlet in 1926 (*top*) and 1940 (*bottom*).

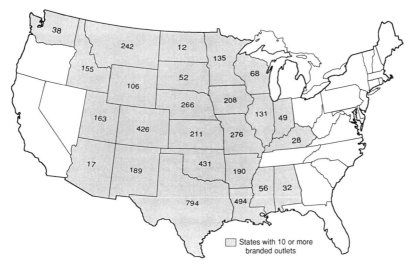

FIGURE 4.20 States with ten or more Conoco outlets in 1990. (*Source:* "Branded Outlets," *National Petroleum News Factbook* 82 [Mid-June, 1990]: 44-51.)

numerous other midcontinent firms, a consolidation arranged by J. P. Morgan and Company for diverse investors including Dutch interests. The Mutual Oil Company, the Texhoma Oil Company, and the Marland Oil Company (all early industry pioneers) were absorbed in the 1920s. The power of capital to drive territorial growth in retail marketing is vividly illustrated when Continental's distribution pattern for 1926 is compared with that of 1940 (see Fig. 4.19). From a scattering of isolated marketing operations (the largest around Denver and in southern Nebraska), the company expanded vigorously across all of the Rocky Mountain states, into the Southwest, and into the Middle West. Marland's purchase of the Prudential Refining Corporation of Baltimore, shortly before its merger with Continental, provided an eastern outlier. (In 1949 Continental withdrew from the eastern seaboard, selling the contracts for its outlets to Cities Service.) The firm operated refineries in or near its principal producing fields: Billings, Montana; Glenrock, Wyoming; Denver, Colorado; Ponca City, Oklahoma; Artesia, New Mexico; and Wichita Falls and Lake Charles, Texas. Continental, through its Conoco brand, has long represented itself as a western company. In 1951 the company purchased the Douglas Oil Company in what proved to be an unsuccessful attempt to extend its trade territory westward to the Pacific Coast.

Most of the major oil companies invested in coal, both as an alternative energy in and of itself and as a potential source of gasoline through conversion. Continental's purchase of the Consolidated Coal Company in 1965 represented such a diversification. Thus in 1981 Conoco had 1.7 billion barrels of oil, 3.8 trillion cubic feet of natural gas, and 14.3 billion tons of coal, making it a target for takeover.[25] Following an unfriendly approach by Mobil, Continental merged with the Dupont Corporation in 1982. As a Dupont division, the company withdrew from its attempted penetration of the California market, but continued expansion into the Central South (see Fig. 4.20). Today's marketing territory looks strikingly similar to that of fifty years ago.

The Major Independent Companies

We have already dealt with several of the major oil companies that evolved outside the Standard Oil Trust: Richfield, Sinclair, Gulf, and BP America. These firms, of course, either absorbed or were absorbed by one or another of the Standard Oil companies. Among the remaining major players were foreign firms such as Shell, Petrofina, and Total which discovered the necessity of having a North American involvement in order to remain competitive in the increasingly integrated world petroleum market. But, for the most part, the other majors were totally homegrown: Texaco, Skelly, Tide Water, Cities Service, Sunoco, Mid-Continent, Union, and Pure. These firms were able to rise to prominence because they emphasized gasoline marketing. The former Standard Oil companies had their capital tied up in antiquated refineries that produced kerosene and lubricants. They were also saddled with outmoded distribution networks regarding gasoline and motor oils. But the new players were able to equip themselves quickly with specialized refineries and gasoline station chains to garner large slices of the rapidly evolving gasoline market. They were successful players at place-product-packaging.

Shell Oil

Royal Dutch-Shell was established in 1907, a merger between the Royal Dutch Petroleum Company and the Shell Transport and Trading Company Ltd. of Great Britain. Before World War II the firm operated in every major producing area in the world—Indonesia, Romania, Mexico, Venezuela, and the United States, among other countries. (Unfortunately for Shell, the company did not participate in developments in the Middle East, choosing instead to purchase surplus crude oil from such companies as Gulf Oil.) Its early strategy was to match crude production with refineries in nearby regional markets. This philosophy contrasted with that of Standard Oil, which sought to serve world markets totally by exporting from the United States. Shell's first involvement in North America was to supply Sumatran crude to Standard Oil of California. But as the latter company established its own production Shell's contracts were withdrawn. Shell required foothold in the United States for one very important reason. The Standard Oil interests set world oil prices before World War I. With a near monopoly in the United States, they could set U.S. prices high, take exaggerated profits at home, and use these profits to offset deficit pricing abroad to undercut competition there. Shell required an American presence from which to counter Standard Oil in its sanctuary.[26]

Shell established a marketing subsidiary in 1912, the American Gasoline Company of Seattle (the first company to sell gasoline and motor oil exclusively). Soon California Standard dropped its price for gasoline from eighteen cents to ten cents a gallon. Unable to sell its imported product profitably, Shell turned to establishing its own producing fields in California through another subsidiary, California Oil Fields Ltd. The Valley Pipeline was constructed to carry crude oil from Coalinga and other fields to the firm's refinery at Martinez, east of Oakland. Standard Oil of California had marketed gasoline primarily through private garages served by agents such as National Supply. Shell took the offensive by building a chain of gasoline stations starting in the San Francisco area, and then in Portland and Seattle. Shell purchased the Puente Oil Company in Los Angeles, adding hundreds of outlets in the process. By 1922, 44 percent of Shell's sales were through gasoline stations as opposed to only 14 percent for California Standard. By 1925, Shell had

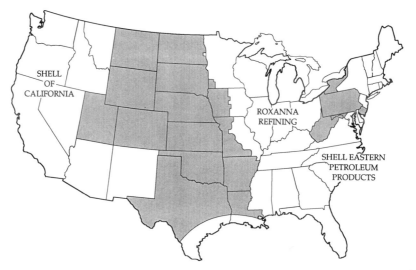

FIGURE 4.21 The Shell Oil Company withdrew from extensive portions of its American marketing territory during the Depression years of the 1930s.

nearly 3,000 gasoline stations throughout California, Oregon, and Washington.[27]

Shell also established the Roxanna Petroleum Company with crude oil production centered around Cushing, Oklahoma, and a pipeline connecting with a large refinery at Wood River, Illinois, near St. Louis. Initially, Roxanna marketed through jobbers, prime among them the Automobile Gasoline Company of St. Louis, which in 1905 had established the nation's first gasoline station. Roxanna purchased the latter firm in 1922 when it also bought the Union Oil Company of Delaware and a 26 percent interest in the Union Oil Company of California, the latter remaining a separate company. Shell-Union, a holding company, was formed and work begun to build a nationwide Shell marketing area through three operating companies: Shell of California, Roxanna, and the newly formed Shell Eastern Petroleum Products, Inc. As the 1920s had brought an excess of gasoline onto the market with very narrow profit margins, companies sought to increase profits by increasing sales volumes, which meant expanding trade territories by opening ever larger numbers of outlets each year. Companies sought to offset smaller and smaller per-unit profits at the retail level by increasing volume at the refinery level, thus to enjoy economies of scale in refining.

The onslaught of the Depression spelled disaster for Shell's grand design for nationwide retailing. Between 1930 and 1934 Shell lost more money than any other oil company. Emphasis on volume quickly gave way to cost competitiveness. For each area, Shell either brought its costs in line with those of its most favorably situated competitor or abandoned the market. Competition was intense. In the Middle West, for example, Standard Oil of Indiana enjoyed a 2.6 cents per gallon profit margin, but

FIGURE 4.22 States with ten or more Shell outlets in 1990. (*Source:* "Branded Outlets," *National Petroleum News Factbook* 82 [Mid-June, 1990]: 44-51.)

Shell only a 1 cent margin. Indiana Standard could lower its price by 2.5 cents and make a profit, but Shell in following suit would incur an outright 1.5 cent loss.[28] Gasoline consumption decreased a billion gallons a year in both 1932 and 1933 and in the furious scramble for the residual business prices dropped nationwide on average from 18 cents to 13 cents a gallon. Shell withdrew completely from Wyoming, Utah, Colorado, South Dakota, Nebraska, Kansas, Oklahoma, Arkansas, West Virginia, and Pennsylvania. It withdrew from the larger parts of Montana, North Dakota, Iowa, Missouri, Texas, Louisiana, New Jersey, and New York (see Fig. 4.21). The company closed unprofitable stations in trade areas retained, replacing them with larger, more modern facilities. A larger gasoline station prototype with enclosed service bays was introduced with the art-modern design, borrowed from Shell's new headquarters building in San Francisco. Bright yellow façades with vivid red trim were dropped in favor of subdued cream with subtle red and yellow striping. Shell also introduced a cheap, subregular gasoline and established subsidiaries such as the Guardian Oil Company to sell secondary brands.

After World War II Shell concentrated on achieving the increased penetration of selected markets. It upgraded its gasoline stations by introducing new prototypes and by consistently moving to higher and higher per-unit volumes. In 1990 the company supplied approximately 9,300 branded outlets in some forty-one states, including Hawaii. Its trade area is bimodal, the western and eastern halves tied only in coastal Texas (see Fig. 4.22). With far fewer outlets than rivals Texaco, Exxon, or Unocal, in 1990 Shell nonetheless held the largest share of the American gasoline market. The lessons learned during the Depression, especially emphasis on lowered per-unit costs, came to serve the company well.

Shell's successes have not been scored with benefit of sizable new sources of crude oil. Shell has tended over the decades to price its gasolines higher than other brands. Rather, Shell has emphasized quality and a wide menu of services at its traditional stations, including light engine repair, lubrication, and washing.

Texaco, Skelly, and Tide Water-Associated (Getty)

Texaco originated in 1902 with the discovery of oil in the Spindletop Field of Texas. The company early emphasized gasoline and motor oils exclusively in establishing some 229 wholesale terminals nationwide with the exception of five far-western states. Initially, terminals were supplied by ocean tanker and railroad tank-car fleets from a single refinery at Port Arthur, Texas. Other small refineries were either purchased or built oriented to intended markets. A distinctive Texaco marketing strategy evolved. Rather than penetrate any single region as a major base of operation (as the ex–Standard Oil companies did in their respective heartlands) Texaco was intent on being second (or at least third) best. Thus the company was the leading marketer hardly anywhere, but did succeed in capturing 8 to 10 percent of market share nearly everywhere. By 1926 the Texaco chain of approximately 4,000 gasoline stations spread across forty-six states, although 56 percent of the sales did come from eight states: Texas, New York, Florida, North Carolina, Illinois, Virginia, New Jersey, and Pennsylvania.[29] Between 1935 and 1977, Texaco was the nation's leading gasoline marketer and the only company to operate in every state. Texaco's nationwide marketing territory reflected in no small measure the firm's early desire to avoid vulnerability to local price cutting as practiced by the Standard Oil Trust, the very incentive that had brought Shell to the United States.

In 1928 Texaco, officially the Texas Company, acquired the Galena-Signal Oil Company and the California Petroleum Company. The latter purchase added refineries in California and helped to solidify the company's western operations. In 1931 Texaco acquired the Indian Oil Refining Company and much of its chain of stations in the eastern United States as well as its respected Havolene brand of motor oil. With some 40,000 outlets nationwide in 1932, Texaco was well positioned to advertise on national radio as no network listener was ever far from a Texaco station. In 1932, the year the company introduced its Fire Chief gasoline, it began radio sponsorship of comic Ed Wynn. In 1940, it began sponsorship of Metropolitan Opera broadcasts from New York City, presently the longest continuous sponsorship in broadcast history. Later, Texaco used television to advantage, sponsoring the Texaco Star Theatre with Milton Berle and comedy specials with Bob Hope.

Texaco continued to expand its domestic marketing in both the 1950s and 1960s largely by purchasing jobbers. In 1959, it bought the Paragon Oil Company of Long Island City, New York, and solidified its position in

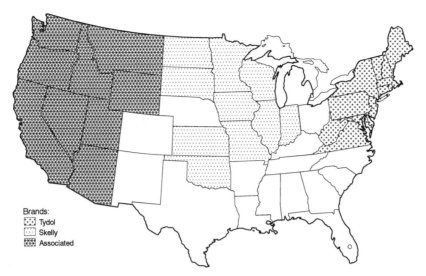

Brands:
Tydol
Skelly
Associated

FIGURE 4.23 Companies controlled by J. Paul Getty marketed under the Tide Water, Flying A (Associated), and Skelly brands in 1950.

the New York City metropolitan area. But Texaco was poorly positioned to face the OPEC price rises in the 1970s. Its refineries were small and relatively inefficient, being designed to serve local markets. Consequently, its cost structure was high. Texaco stations, although numerous, tended to be small and low in gallonage. In 1975, Texaco served 7.5 percent of the U.S. gasoline market with 30,000 stations, whereas Shell served the same sized market with only 18,000 stations.[30] Texaco closed refineries and withdrew from Montana, North Dakota, Kansas, Minnesota, Iowa, Wisconsin, Michigan, Indiana, and Ohio. With its crude oil reserves dwindling, Texaco sought a crude-oil-rich merger partner. Besting Pennzoil (later to be saddled with a court-imposed $4-billion settlement for interfering with a Pennzoil-Getty agreement), Texaco bought the Getty Oil Company.

J. Paul Getty, reportedly at one time the world's wealthiest person, began as a wildcatter in the Southwest and finished as a major player in the Middle East. By 1950, Getty controlled two oil companies with domestic marketing, the recently merged Tide Water-Associated Oil Company (which marketed in the Northeast under the Tydol brand and in the Far West under the Flying A brand) and the Skelly Oil Company at mid-continent (see Fig. 4.23). In 1966, the western manufacturing and marketing properties of Tide Water-Associated were sold to the Phillips Oil Company and the residual eastern facilities reorganized into the Getty Oil Company, marketing under the Getty brand. In 1977, Skelly was merged into Getty. Getty Oil had owned 89 percent of the Mission Oil Company—a holding company—which in turn had owned 73 percent of Skelly. Getty Oil also owned 7 percent of Skelly directly in what for many years stood as one of the industry's more complicated ownerships, a legacy of a short

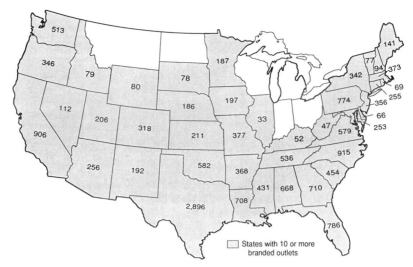

FIGURE 4.24 States with ten or more Texaco outlets in 1990. (*Source:* "Branded Outlets," *National Petroleum News Factbook* 82 [Mid-June, 1990]: 44-51.)

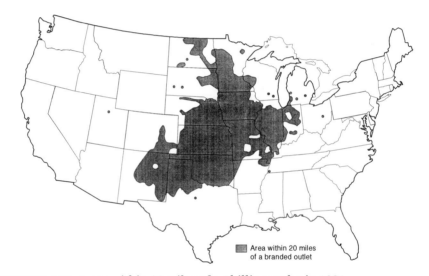

FIGURE 4.25 Areas within 20 miles of a Phillips outlet in 1931.

period during the Depression when Standard Oil of New Jersey actually controlled Skelly.[31] In 1980 Getty returned to the West Coast with the purchase of the small regional Reserve Oil and Gas Company.

Following its absorption of Getty Oil, under Department of Justice mandate Texaco sold the former Getty chain of some 1,900 outlets in eleven northeastern states. Today a new Getty Petroleum Company operates from Maine to Virginia as one of the nation's largest regional independents, still marketing under the Getty sign. The former Skelly chain was converted to Texaco, returning the company to trade areas in Kan-

FIGURE 4.26 The Phillips Petroleum Company adopted its "Phillips 66" brand borrowing on the popular transcontinental U.S. 66 that formed an axis diagonally across the firm's trade territory.

sas, Iowa, and Minnesota vacated only a few years before. Texaco's difficulties in the late 1980s were complicated by a takeover attempt that left the company slimmed down and emphasizing modern, high-gallonage stations in select markets. Today Texaco sells in forty-four states through some 15,000 outlets (see Fig. 4.24). A substantial proportion of the company's stations in the eastern United States, as well as substantial refinery capacity, is today owned by Saudi Arabian interests.

Phillips

Initially a producer of crude oil in Oklahoma, the Phillips Oil Company began to refine and market gasoline in 1927. The company had huge holdings of natural gas from Kansas through the Texas Panhandle, making it the leading producer of natural gasoline (squeezed from natural gas), liquefied petroleum gas (bottled gas), and carbonblack. The Phillips 66 brand was very quickly established through jobbers across a trade territory stretching from New Mexico on the southwest to Minnesota on the north to Indiana in the east (see Figs. 4.25 and 4.26). In 1947, purchase of the Wasatch Oil Company extended Phillips's marketing from Utah to Montana and Washington. Thus began a very aggressive expansion policy that saw Phillips spread across the South and Middle West to the East Coast. In the early 1960s the firm was opening some 3,000 stations a year largely by diverting jobbers from other companies. Attempting to operate in all of the coterminous forty-eight states, Phillips bought Getty's former Flying A chain in the Far West only to have the purchase voided by the U.S. District Court on grounds that it violated antitrust laws. The Flying A chain then passed to the Oil and Shale Corporation (Tosco), owner of both the Signal Oil Company in California and the Lion Oil Company in the Central South. Fending off a takeover attempt by T. Boone Pickens in the 1980s, Phillips was forced to withdraw from its weaker markets as the company reorganized. Today it retails in twenty-

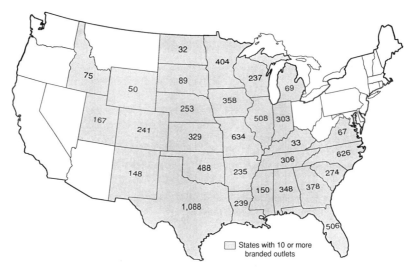

FIGURE 4.27 States with ten or more Phillips outlets in 1990. (*Source:* "Branded Outlets," *National Petroleum News Factbook* 82 [Mid-June, 1990]: 44-51.)

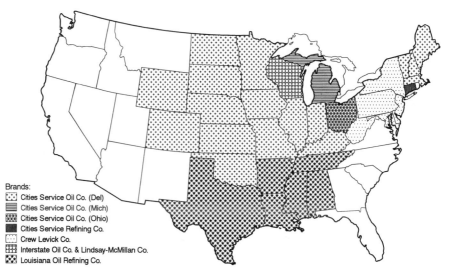

FIGURE 4.28 Cities Service operated through numerous subsidiaries in 1930. All but the Louisiana Oil Refining Company ("Loreco") marketed under the Cities Service sign.

nine states with some 7,900 branded outlets. It is noticeably missing from the West Coast and the Northeast (see Fig. 4.27).

Cities Service (Citgo)

Cities Service was an amalgam of companies interlocked through ownership, with all eventually marketing under the Cities Service sign (see Fig. 4.28). Cities Service grew out of a public service company that provided natural gas to customers in several northeastern metropolitan

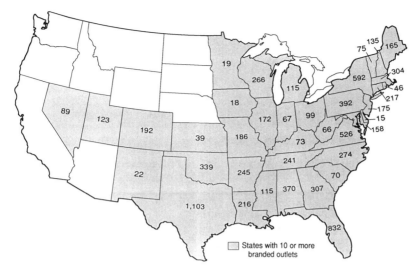

FIGURE 4.29 States with ten or more Citgo outlets in 1990. (*Source:* "Branded Outlets," *National Petroleum News Factbook* 82 [Mid-June, 1990]: 44-51.)

areas. In search of its own sources of natural gas, it generated large crude oil reserves and, consequently, determined to enter the gasoline business. Activities quickly extended to Oklahoma, Texas, and Louisiana. By 1930, the combined companies operated refineries in Massachusetts, Pennsylvania, Indiana, Louisiana, Oklahoma, and Texas. Along with Sinclair, Cities Service controlled Richfield of California. Its largest foreign involvements were in Venezuela and Colombia. In 1965, the various Cities Service companies combined under the name Citgo ("Cit" for Cities Service; "go" for "power, energy, and progressive nature").[32] Other names considered included Citco, Cisco, and Citex. The chain bought the 450-outlet Jenney Oil Company, the stalwart New England refiner and marketer whose origins went back to 1812 and the sale of whale oil. For Citgo it was not all growth. In 1968, the company sold its rights to 2,300 outlets in nine middle-western states to Gulf, and rights to its western Pennsylvania outlets to Standard of Ohio for its new Boron chain. In 1983, following purchase by the Occidental Petroleum Company, a leading crude oil and natural gas producer, Citgo was sold to the Southland Corporation, then the nation's largest convenience store retailer. In 1986 Southland, in turn, sold 50 percent of Citgo to Petroleos de Venezuela, giving another foreign oil company access to the American market. Citgo, for its part, gained access once again to a plentiful supply of crude oil. Today Citgo markets in thirty-six states through some 9,700 branded outlets (see Fig. 4.29).

Sun Oil and Sunray Mid-Continent (DX)

The Sun Oil Company was the creation of the Pew family, longtime oil people who persisted in their opposition to the Standard Oil Trust. Organized in Ohio in 1890 on the foundations of several preceding firms, including the Sun Oil Line Company, Sun Oil quickly became a fully integrated firm with producing wells, pipelines, and a refinery at Toledo. But it would be the firm's successful prospecting in Texas and its securing of lucrative contracts from the United Gas Improvement Company, a Philadelphia utility, that would drive the company's geographical structuring in the twentieth century. A refinery was built at Marcus Hook and a shipbuilding subsidiary established at Chester, both in Pennsylvania, where a tanker fleet was built to carry crude oil from the Gulf of Mexico to the Delaware River. The company's first gasoline station was built in 1920, and by 1928 a chain of some 500 stations had evolved across Pennsylvania, New York, Ohio, and Michigan. In 1940, the firm's products were available at some 9,000 outlets, 1,500 of them owned by the company.[33]

Sun Oil specialized in a single premium gasoline called Blue Sunoco, derived from a company-patented catalytic cracking process (the Houdry Process) developed at Marcus Hook. High in octane, its use reduced engine knocking without the addition of tetraethyl lead. Sunoco could advertise that its gasoline was "poison free" as no harmful lead oxides gummed up spark plugs and valves. "The High Powered Knockless Fuel at no Extra Price," Sunoco advertisements boasted.[34] Sun Oil could not meet demand totally from its own cracking plants and thus bought gasoline supplies from Jersey Standard, Atlantic, and California Standard to blend with its own product, retaining, in the process, adequate octane levels. The company defended its claims and its trademarks in the courts, defeating, for example, Continental Oil's attempted use of the Blue Conoco gasoline brand.

The company's marketing strategy—based on the price and quality of one grade of gasoline—proved vulnerable in the 1950s when American automakers began introducing high-compression engines in their cars, thus inaugurating an octane race. Sunoco's response was to introduce custom blending at its pumps, thereby making available to its customers a variety of gasoline grades. Overseas expansion after World War II involved crude oil production in Argentina, Australia, Iran, Libya, and Venezuela, among other countries, as well as production in the North Sea off Scotland. The firm pioneered oil recovery from the Athabasca tar sands of northern Alberta in Canada. Surplus refinery output encouraged Sun Oil to service small regional marketers perhaps more so than any other major company. In addition, the firm sought to expand its own branded chain into Florida. But Sunoco also grew through merger. In 1972, the company bought the Sunray Mid-Continent Oil Company.

The Sunray Oil Company was incorporated in 1929 to engage primarily in the acquisition of producing leases across Kansas, Oklahoma, Texas, and Louisiana. It became a fully integrated petroleum company in 1953, through merger with the Mid-Continent Petroleum Corporation. Sunray brought to the new combine a surplus of crude oil and Mid-

FIGURE 4.30 States with ten or more Sunoco and/or DX outlets in 1991. (*Source:* "Branded Retail Outlets," *National Petroleum News Factbook* 83 [Mid-June, 1991]: 44-51.)

Continent brought a surplus of refinery capacity. With refineries at Corpus Christi in Texas and at Duncan and Tulsa in Oklahoma, the firm expanded a chain of D-X (later DX) stations from Oklahoma north through Kansas, Nebraska, and the Dakotas, and northeast through Missouri, Iowa, Minnesota, Wisconsin, Illinois, and Indiana. Of the some 6,000 branded outlets, approximately half were jobber-oriented.[35] The firm expanded in the 1960s into Louisiana, Mississippi, and Tennessee. The purchase of Sunray Mid-Continent by Sun Oil in 1972 created a thirty-four-state marketing operation with some 15,000 outlets. However, with the OPEC crisis at hand the actual merger brought a wholesale abandonment of stations carrying both the Sunoco and DX brands. Two marketing divisions were formed, thus preserving the DX name in the West, although most of the surviving DX stations east of the Mississippi River were converted to Sunoco. In 1990, the Sun Refining and Marketing Company served some 6,000 branded outlets in a much reduced twenty-eight-state marketing territory (see Fig. 4.30).

Union Oil (Unocal) and Pure Oil

The Union Oil Company of California was organized in 1890 through merger of several predecessor firms. From twenty-two producing wells and a small refinery a West Coast corporate empire quickly evolved. The company was involved in every major California producing field and ultimately built four refineries in that state. Gasoline retailing began in the Los Angeles area, which remained the company's stronghold in contrast to archcompetitor Standard Oil of California, which was San Francisco–oriented. By 1940, a chain of gasoline stations spread across California, Arizona, Nevada, Oregon, Washington, and Idaho. Although

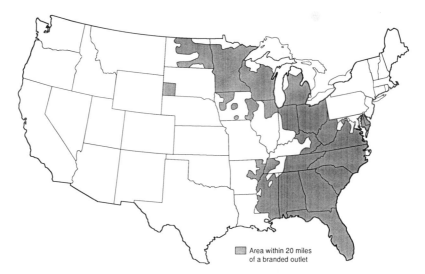

FIGURE 4.31 In 1949 the Pure Oil Company's trade territory sprawled irregularly from North Dakota and Minnesota on the north to Florida on the south. Northern and southern marketing areas were weakly linked in the Great Lakes area.

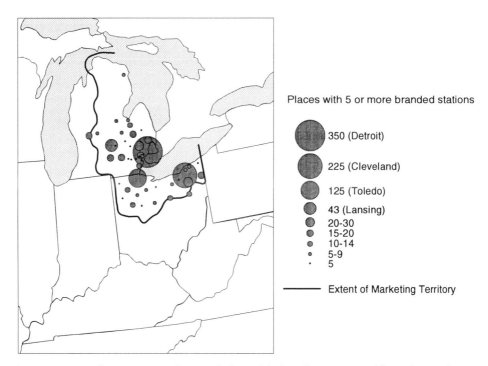

Places with 5 or more branded stations

350 (Detroit)

225 (Cleveland)

125 (Toledo)

43 (Lansing)
20-30
15-20
10-14
5-9
5

——— Extent of Marketing Territory

FIGURE 4.32 The 1952 purchase of the Hickok Oil Company (the Hi-Speed brand), which centered on Detroit, Toledo, and Cleveland, enabled Pure Oil to strengthen ties between its northern and southern trade areas. Buyout of regional independents and local jobbers was an expedient means of enhancing market penetration.

THE GAS STATION IN AMERICA

FIGURE 4.33 States with ten or more Unocal outlets in 1990. (*Source:* "Branded Outlets," *National Petroleum News Factbook* 81 [Mid-June, 1989]: 44-51.)

the firm marketed in British Columbia, and in Central and South America as well, its foreign operations were limited. It was very much a regional oil company, conservatively managed through the Depression years but reactivated through refinery modernization and the pioneering of crude oil production in the Gulf of Mexico off the coast of Louisiana after World War II. In the mid-1960s Union Oil enjoyed a surplus of crude oil but operated in a geographically confined West Coast market. It was a company looking for a merger partner and that partner proved to be the much larger Pure Oil Company.

The Pure Oil Company evolved in 1920 out of the reorganized Ohio Cities Gas Company, the natural gas utility for Columbus, Springfield, and Dayton. Like the Cities Service companies, it entered the gasoline business on the basis of crude oil discoveries tied to natural gas exploration. From its initial successes in West Virginia the firm helped pioneer in Oklahoma, buying several producing companies in the process. Major refineries were located in Oklahoma and in Pennsylvania with smaller natural gasoline plants in West Virginia, Oklahoma, and Texas. The company first marketed gasoline in Ohio and then began purchasing small jobbing companies and expanded its chain of outlets into Pennsylvania, New York, and Indiana. In 1920, the Pure Oil Company of Minnesota was purchased with a chain of stations in Minnesota, North Dakota, and Wisconsin. The company then worked to tie separated middle-western trade areas together through the Chicago metropolitan market, moving the corporate headquarters to that city (see Fig. 4.31).

Next Pure Oil emphasized the Southeast, acquiring through the 1920s and 1930s controlling interests in a host of jobbing companies including Wofford Oil, Seaboard Oil, and Colonial Oil, which nonetheless kept their separate corporate identities. In 1938 Pure Oil supplied, primarily through jobbers both owned and independent, some 17,000 branded outlets.[36] A year later Pure Oil sold to the Gulf Oil Company rights to its stations in Pennsylvania and New York. In 1952, Pure Oil purchased the Hickok Oil Corporation, which added a refinery at Toledo and 1,600 Hi-Speed stations in Michigan and Ohio, all quickly rebranded to Pure (see Fig. 4.32). The 1965 merger of Union Oil and Pure Oil created a 20,000-outlet chain, the Pure stations converted to the Union brand over a period of years. The challenge was to tie together another set of geographically separate trade areas. Today's slimmed down and modernized chain of some 7,400 outlets remains clearly divided east and west (see Fig. 4.33)

The Small Regional Independents

The line between the major independents, all of which displayed regional orientations, and the regional independents, many of which had pretensions to national market, is definitely arbitrarily drawn. We have already dealt with many once-independent regionals absorbed by larger companies: Signal by Jersey Standard, American by Indiana Standard, Wilshire by Gulf, White Eagle by Socony-Vacuum. We have also discussed the merger of regional firms to form major companies: Richfield by Atlantic, Sunray Mid-Continent by Sun, Pure by Union. What remains is a brief description of the lesser firms that today individually control 1.5 percent or less of the American market but which, as corporations, remain important operatives in the American economy.

American Petrofina (Fina) and Total

Although totally separate, these two companies are appropriately treated together. As subsidiaries of foreign corporations their involvement in the North American market stems from a shared impulse—the same impulse that brought the much larger Shell and British Petroleum operations to fruition in the United States. Belgian-owned American Petrofina (a subsidiary of the Compagnie Financière Belge des Pétroles, SA) established its American operation in 1954 by buying several small refining and marketing companies in the Southeast and Middle West, including the American Liberty Oil Company (Amlico), the Panhandle Oil Company, and the Atlas Corporation's El Dorado Refining Company (see Fig. 4.34). The last firm had built and sold several gasoline station chains over the years, including in the 1930s that of the Sovereign brand in conjunction with several other small refiners, and the El Reco brand after World War II. Upgrading, remodeling, repainting, and resigning quickly established an 830-outlet Fina chain across Oklahoma, Texas, New Mexico, Louisiana, and Arkansas. Nearly all stations were dealer-operated and jobber-supplied. In the 1960s American Petro-

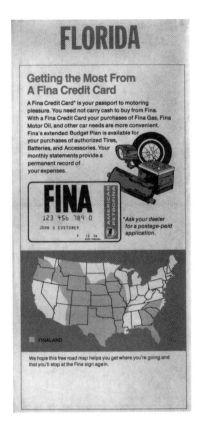

FIGURE 4.34 In 1974, American Petrofina proudly displayed "Finaland" in its advertising, a hard-won trade territory constructed in only two decades.

fina purchased Tenneco's 380 outlets in ten Rocky Mountain states, bringing Fina's total to 3,400 branded outlets.[37] The intended purchase of the Sinclair chain from Arco in the 1970s was blocked by the Department of Justice, although purchase of 1,000 BP stations in Florida, Georgia, and the Carolinas was approved. In the 1980s the Belgian firm acquired from the liquidated Champlin Oil Company stations scattered from Minnesota to Texas. In 1990, the company operated 3,100 branded outlets in twenty-five states (see Fig. 4.35).

French-owned Total (a subsidiary of the Compagnie Française des Pétroles) entered the U.S. market in 1971 through purchase of the Leonard Refining Company, a small company with crude oil production and a refinery in central Michigan, and outlets in Michigan and Wisconsin selling under both the Leonard and Citrin brands. Apco, a Kansas-based refiner and marketer, was added in 1978 and Vickers, an Oklahoma refiner and marketer, in 1980, giving Total some 2,700 outlets in less than a decade.[38] In 1990 the firm operated across twenty-two states (see Fig. 4.36). In order to compete worldwide, both Petrofina's and Total's parent companies recognized the importance of the world's largest gasoline market—the United States. To influence world prices the large internationals seek to operate in one another's backyards. No firm or set of national firms can be allowed a territorial sanctuary from which to set prices and profits in order to undermine competition elsewhere.

Ashland

Larger railroad tank cars and new methods of financing them were instrumental in launching many of the small independent refiners and jobbers who established regional gasoline chains. Especially important were the car trust notes and firms such as the General American Transportation Company which sold them. Important also were barge and tanker fleets and the technologies of water-oriented terminals. All of these devices enabled small refiners to integrate downstream into mar-

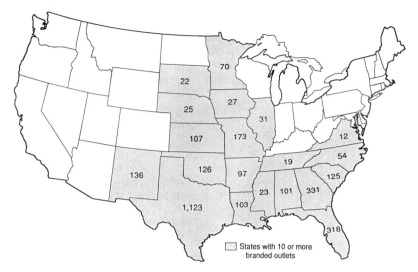

FIGURE 4.35 States with ten or more Fina outlets in 1990. (*Source:* "Branded Outlets," *National Petroleum News Factbook* 82 [Mid-June, 1990]: 44-51.)

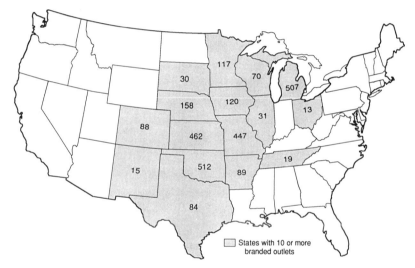

FIGURE 4.36 States with ten or more Total outlets in 1990. (*Source:* "Branded Outlets," *National Petroleum News Factbook* 82 [Mid-June, 1990]: 44-51.)

keting, as they enabled marketers to obtain a cheap product through reduced transportation costs. One such company was Ashland Oil.

Like the Quaker State, South Penn (Pennzoil), and Kendall companies, Ashland was a producer of lubricants, its principal motor oil being Valvolene. But unlike the other firms mentioned, Ashland moved into gasoline retailing in the 1930s. With production in the mountains of West Virginia and Kentucky, Ashland found itself in a territorial niche sandwiched between several major companies, specifically Jersey Standard, Ohio Standard, and Kentucky Standard. With navigation improvements on the Ohio River, Ashland established a barge fleet and began moving

FIGURE 4.37 States with ten or more Ashland Oil Company* outlets in 1990. (*Source:* "Branded Outlets," *National Petroleum News* 82 [Mid-June, 1990]: 44-51.)

gasoline from its refinery at Ashland, Kentucky, introducing the Ashland brand across the eastern Ohio Valley. By 1950 the company had absorbed numerous small refineries and their associated gasoline station chains: the National Refining Company (a former Sohio subsidiary with the White Rose brand), the Frontier Oil Refining Company (Frontier), the Aetna Oil Company (Aetna), and the Allied Oil Company (Allied). Not only did Ashland Oil find a territorial niche into which it could unobtrusively slip with its various brands, but it became an important supplier of gasolines to other independent marketers in the Middle West and Upper South. During the 1950s its brands were sold in eleven states from New York, Pennsylvania, and Virginia on the east to Wisconsin and Illinois on the west. The company has since withdrawn from New York, but has expanded south and west largely through its Super America branded convenience stores (see Fig. 4.37).

Kerr-McGee, Murphy, and Clark

Cursory acknowledgment of other regional independents provides a sense of completion to the story told here. Kerr-McGee Oil Industries, originally a crude oil producer and refiner, entered marketing with the purchase of the Deep Rock Oil Corporation in 1955. In 1960 the Kerr-McGee and Deep Rock brands were used by jobbers and dealers across seventeen states from Wisconsin, Minnesota, and North Dakota to New Mexico, Texas, Arkansas, and Mississippi—the approximate dimensions of today's marketing territory. Here is a conservative company that remains primarily a producer and a refiner.

The Murphy Oil Company originated in Arkansas as a producer of crude oil and a refiner, only later integrating downstream through pur-

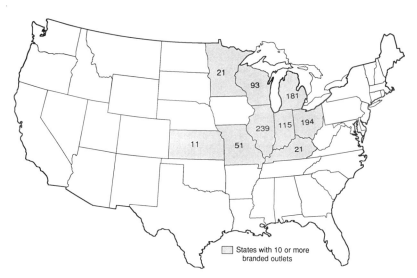

FIGURE 4.38 States with ten or more Clark Oil Company outlets in 1990. (*Source:* "Branded Outlets," *National Petroleum News Factbook* 82 [Mid-June, 1990]: 44-51.)

chase of Spur Oil of Nashville, a regional marketer. The company expanded with the following strategy: 1) establish a beachhead in a regional market; 2) supply that market by custom-refining crude either owned or purchased; 3) acquire a refinery; and 4) replace purchased crude with company production.[39] Placing strong emphasis on crude oil production, the company scored successes in Canada, Venezuela, and the Persian Gulf, becoming a "mini-international." By 1970, it was marketing through some 1,200 Spur stations from Minnesota, Wisconsin, Michigan, and Ohio in the Middle West through most of the southeastern states to Florida. Today's marketing territory extends across Louisiana, Texas, and Oklahoma as well. Here is a progressive firm that has become a balanced, integrated company.

The Clark brand originated in 1932 with Emory Clark and his one-pump service station in Milwaukee. By 1963, his original $14 investment had grown into a refining and jobbing business with 1,000 branded outlets spread across ten middle-western states. Like Kerr-McGee and Murphy, Clark Oil Company stations were small, prefabricated structures set on large driveways fringed by bulk tanks and billboards. Fast service and gasoline priced one to two cents cheaper than the majors were the sales ploys. Clark built its first refinery in 1943 near Chicago and began its own exploration and production in 1957. In 1967, the firm purchased the Sinclair refinery at Wood River, Illinois. Hit by the OPEC price increases, the company's ownership changed several times through the 1980s, but always a separate Clark chain persisted. Today there are some 900 outlets in twelve middle-western states (see Fig. 4.38). Here is a marketing firm that integrated upstream into refining and producing, perhaps a route less successful than the reverse path taken by Kerr-McGee and Murphy.

Although one might like to treat the remaining independents that operate with their own brands today (Amerada Hess, Burmah, Cenex, Diamond-Shamrock, Martin, Pennzoil, and Ultramar, for example) and even those companies recently absorbed into other corporations and still fresh in memory (Bay, Billups, and Husky, among others), the story of corporate territoriality in gasoline marketing has been outlined. The picture is one of diverse corporations, each pursuing a different mix of strategies based in part on the accidents of corporate origins and subsequent abilities to anticipate technological and other changes. Critical for each company, however, was a secure territorial base where branded products were well known and, accordingly, degrees of market penetration achieved. Access to crude oil and the geographical inertia of refinery and pipeline locations strongly dictated where territorial emphases were placed. Clearly, corporate territorial behaviors changed over time largely as a function of the price of crude oil. Through the 1910s and 1920s successful companies pushed gallonage by spreading branded outlets over the widest possible geographical areas. The Depression caused most firms to stabilize trade areas but some others to withdraw from extensive territory. The post–World War II years saw another aggressive burst of territorial expansion halted only by the OPEC price increases and the soaring cost of crude oil. Since 1973, most companies have sought to reinforce only those markets of deepest penetration and marketing territories, for most firms have substantially diminished.

Of course, the Department of Justice and the federal courts have played an important role in keeping the playing field even such that the territorial contests could play out with the game not overly dominated by the very few. Place-product-packaging, therefore, should be viewed as a promotional strategy contained within and subordinate to overarching territorial impulses pitting corporation against corporation in the quest for market—territorial aggressions mediated by a surveillant government. As automobility became central in American life, gasoline, the great energizing product of the petroleum industry, was simply too important not to regulate. Prevented was an overly limited vested interest taking control of the nation's mobility. Thus it is from the perspectives of place-product-packaging and corporate territoriality that we are now positioned to treat the gasoline station as a landscape element symbolic of the gasoline-driven American mania for movement.

5

The Gas Station as Form

Having explored the American gas station from more historical and geographical perspectives, we will now look more closely at its design. Gasoline stations are commonly viewed from behind the wheel of a car as one seeks service. Step out from behind the wheel—putting off one's second skin, as the car has been called—and look closely at the gasoline station as a type of place. Elements emerge: driveways, pumps, sign stanchions, sometimes foliage plots, and, of course, the station buildings. Station buildings draw maximum attention and are easily sorted into categories for analysis. But the other elements are variously related to fit as ensembles, the whole relating variously to context, fitting either easily or with difficulty, as the case might be, into surrounding landscape.

We concentrate in this chapter on the visual epicenter of the ensemble, the gasoline station building, emphasizing form as it relates to function. Our thinking is rooted in the work of cultural geographers who have focused on building morphologies, especially house types.[1] Although the emphasis in folk-housing studies has been on diffusion of material culture outward from cultural hearths, gasoline stations have appeared everywhere almost simultaneously. They were spread through the media of an organized commercial industry. Thus we turn to petroleum industry trade journals to trace changes in gasoline station form. What was it that drove the simultaneous evolution of succeeding types nearly everywhere? Of course, place-product-packaging and corporate territoriality supply the answers.

How was it then that the gasoline station evolved as a distinctive physical form on American roadsides? Aside from the economics of station location, social scientists have paid little attention to gasoline stations as landscape phenomenon.[2] Humanists have taken more interest in that various works have sketched in outline the history of this roadside form, although emphasis has been placed more on the unique and the unusual than on the typical.[3] Herein we describe the structural evolution of the gasoline station between 1920 and 1990, noting the relative popularity of different building types through time, a study based substantially on materials gleaned from the pages of the *National Petroleum News*, the petroleum industry's leading trade journal.

The Gasoline Station

Let us offer a concise definition for the gasoline station. Gasoline stations (filling stations or service stations, as they also have been called) are roadside facilities specially designed to sell gasoline and other closely related products, such as lubricants, tires, and batteries, for the automobile. Many gasoline stations also offer minor repair services, such as motor tuning and tire alignment. Largely excluded from emphasis here are the establishments that tie gasoline sales into other dominant product lines. Such places—convenience stores, car washes, truckstops, and the like—fully dominate gasoline retailing today. Our focus is on the traditional gasoline station now numbering fewer than 100,000 in the United States, down from 236,000 as late as 1969.[4] Between 1920 and 1970 traditional stations accounted for approximately 40 percent of the total gasoline sales outlets in the nation. But even though they comprised a minority of the total outlets, they produced a majority of sales and the image of the gasoline station dominated the American public's conceptualization of gasoline retailing accordingly. Gasoline stations were especially designed to promote corporate identities. We would argue that they were the primary place-product-packaging device essential to corporate territoriality.

In 1911, as previously discussed, the Standard Oil Trust was divided into separate companies. The trust owned some 90 percent of the nation's refinery capacity and controlled some 85 percent of the total petroleum market, much of it oriented to kerosene and other petroleum products, such as candles, household lubricating oils, oils for harnesses and belts, and floor dressings. With the increasing popularity of the automobile after 1915, the Standard Oil companies experienced difficulty expanding rapidly enough to serve the new gasoline market, with capital being invested in other product lines. Independent oil producers made substantial gains by orienting initial refinery and marketing facility toward fueling America's new motorcars. The gasoline station became the prime weapon in this competition.

Where and when the first gasoline station appeared is difficult to establish since various kinds of "stations" appeared on the American scene between 1907 and 1913. Standard Oil of California opened a station in Seattle in 1907. A feedline from a main storage tank led to a smaller tank equipped with a glass gauge and valve-controlled hose. In 1909 the American Gasoline Company of St. Louis, a Shell agent, built the first "drive-in" station to be located apart from bulk plant facilities.[5] The

FIGURE 5.1 Standard Oil of Ohio's first station located in Columbus, Ohio, circa 1910. (*Source:* Photo courtesy of BP America, formerly known as Standard Oil of Ohio.)

station comprised a small tin shed housing barrels of oil and two converted hot-water tanks sporting short lengths of garden hose. In 1910 the Central Oil Company of Flint, Michigan, built the first structure specially designed for gasoline distribution: a large canopy supported by posts covering two driveways separated by a single hand-operated pump.[6] Standard Oil of Ohio's first station, like the initial contrivances of most companies, was an ad hoc creation totally without design pretense (see Fig. 5.1). It was Gulf Oil that built the first architect-designed station in Pittsburgh in 1913. The hexagonal building included a roof cantilevered outward on all sides to cover thirteen electrically operated gasoline pumps. Here the company distributed the first free commercial road maps in the United States.[7]

Standard of California launched its chain of look-alike gasoline stations in 1914, largely in response to competition from Shell.[8] All thirty-four stations were standardized: small houses with attached canopies, each building uniformly painted and identified by common signs (see Fig. 5.2). Located on fenced, landscaped sites they cost from $500 to $1500 to build. By 1920 there were approximately 15,000 service stations in the United States—an increase of approximately 1,200 stations per year. In 1920 most stations were dealer-owned (owners contracting for the products of one or several oil companies), but company-owned and -operated stations were rapidly increasing in number. Companies sought to control retail profits by owning stations while at the same time adopting carefully contrived gasoline station designs calculated to improve company image. In 1922 Shell Oil supplied 1,841 retail outlets in California, Ore-

THE GAS STATION IN AMERICA

FIGURE 5.2 Standard Oil of California was one of the first companies to create a chain of look-alike stations from a single design prototype. (*Source:* Photo courtesy Chevron Corporate Library.)

gon, and Washington. Only 204 stations (or 11 percent) were company-owned, but they accounted for 44 percent of Shell's gasoline sales in the region.[9] By 1930 most companies had leased their stations to dealers in the face of legislation in Iowa and other states heavily taxing chain-store profits. Standardization of building types and uniform color schemes and signage continued through lease agreement.

Through the 1960s the United States enjoyed a surplus of petroleum, forcing gasoline prices down to consistently low levels. Price was unimportant in industry competition, the principal producer and refiner setting the price of gasoline in each marketing region. Gasoline was freely exchanged between companies to reduce transportation costs and to promote the cheapest and most efficient distribution of gasoline from refinery to pump. The gasoline of a dozen or more companies (each championing the unique qualities of its own brand) might actually originate at a single regional refinery. Companies did compete, of course, through territorial marketing strategies based on the development of brand consciousness through advertising. And gasoline station design was a critical element in a company's quest for visibility. The standardized station was a most important advertising device by which companies sought to develop sales territories.

Gasoline Station Design and the *National Petroleum News*

The *National Petroleum News* was founded in 1909 to serve the independent oil producers by promoting open competition in an industry

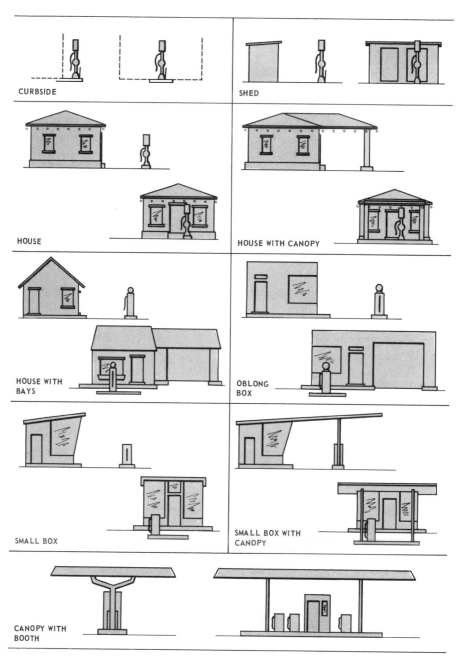

FIGURE 5.3 Gasoline station types identified in an analysis of illustrations in *National Petroleum News,* 1910 through 1990.

dominated by the Standard Oil Trust.[10] During the 1920s and 1930s the journal provided an important price-reporting service. Although the majority of articles concerned exploration and production, considerable emphasis was given to reporting gasoline station innovation. Indeed, the journal sponsored annual gasoline station design contests. After World War II the journal developed as a general news magazine for the oil industry with spin-off publications, including *Petroleum Processing* and

FIGURE 5.4 A "curbside" station. (*Source:* Advertisement of Dayton Pump and Manufacturing Company in *NPN* 7 [September 1915]. Courtesy *NPN.*)

Petroleum Week, concerned with production and marketing, respectively. Purchased by McGraw-Hill Publishing Company in 1953, the *National Petroleum News* switched from a weekly to a monthly format and became exclusively a marketing journal. Today it is independently published. Despite these changes, the journal has consistently carried advertising and articles oriented to gasoline station owners and operators.

Illustrations in the *National Petroleum News* depicting gasoline stations were systematically sampled across the magazine's entire run to determine prevailing structural types. Nine types were identified: the curbside, the shed, the house, the house with canopy, the house with bays, the oblong box (with and without modifications), the small box, the small box with canopy, and the canopy with booth (see Fig. 5.3). These gasoline station types were named for the principal structural features following nomenclature used in the journal.

The Curbside

The term *filling station* first applied to the curbside pumps and related underground storage tanks developed by a host of manufacturers about 1915 (see Figs. 5.3 and 5.4). These "stations" were installed along streets in front of grocery, hardware, and other stores that had expanded from carrying household petroleum products into gasoline sales as well. In the beginning, gasoline, like kerosene, was dispensed in tin cans. Pumped from small storage barrels, gasoline was poured by hand into automobile tanks. Gasoline was distributed by wholesale jobbers who ran horse-drawn tank wagons refilling the barrels kept in commercial car storage garages and automobile repair shops (see Fig. 5.5). The curbside station was an important innovation. Automobiles were filled mechanically and thus more efficiently, and centralized distribution reduced the threat of fire across a community.

After 1920, fire safety ordinances forced curbside stations to close in the larger cities. In 1923 the New York Supreme Court upheld a City of Buffalo zoning ordinance that not only forbade curbside stations, but also restricted the locations of other types of gasoline stations. The action forced Standard Oil of New York to organize a real estate department to acquire gasoline station sites in Buffalo and in other cit-

FIGURE 5.5 An example of the tank wagons employed by agents of Standard Oil of Indiana in the opening decades of the twentieth century across the Middle West.

FIGURE 5.6 A curbside pump stands before a vacant general store in Kent, Illinois, 1974.

ies where similar ordinances were expected. Of the approximately 700 gasoline stations then operating in New York State, 600 were curbside stations.[11] Curbside pumps continued to thrive only in rural areas in conjunction with general stores and other roadside businesses (see Fig. 5.6).

FIGURE 5.7 A "shed" station in Pittsburg, Kansas, circa 1910. (*Source: Stanolind Record* 2 [July 1921]: 14.)

The Shed

The first off-street, drive-in gasoline stations brought a number of structural innovations. Small sheds were built to house lubricating oils, greases, and equipment (see Fig. 5.3). Before 1915 few motorists drove their automobiles in inclement weather as automobiles were not enclosed. In winter in the North cars were stored during the cold months. Thus the sale of gasoline was a "fair weather" activity and little effort was made initially to protect either the station operator or his customers. Sheds came in a variety of shapes and sizes (see Fig. 5.7). Driveways were usually of dirt or, if improved, of gravel. Some stations were surrounded by board fences to hide the utilitarian metal, clapboard, or tarpaper sheds and the clutter of the unimproved driveways. Visually, these early stations had much in common with the buildings of lumber and coal yards or petroleum tank yards. The sheds themselves were storage buildings common to a host of businesses involved in the handling of bulk commodities.

The House

In urban places the early curbside and the shed-type "filling stations" were generally located in and around the central business districts. After 1920 the oil companies invested heavily in neighborhood "service stations." These stations often intruded first upon the best residential streets where large houses on big lots faced wide, paved thoroughfares. The oil companies sought the large corner lots capable of accommodating the necessary driveways, and accessible to motorists from two streets. Before 1930, stations not only had to attract customers, but they had to be attractive as well. Resistance to the destruction of old houses and the disruption of residential neighborhoods lent support to zoning and other land use controls generally feared by gasoline interests. The oil companies sought to build stations that blended into residential neighborhoods, thus to reduce opposition to their real estate practices.

The neighborhood service station was made to look like a small house, the most popular styles sporting low hip roofs (see Fig. 5.8). Most stations contained small offices, one or two small storage rooms, and public restrooms, as in Pure Oil's "English cottage" (see Figs. 5.9 and 5.10). Entrance to a men's room was usually inside the station houses as a convenience to employees as well as customers. Entrance to a women's room was usually discreetly hidden behind or alongside the building. Handcranked oil dispensers were located at the center of the office opposite the front door: a desk, chairs, and a stove completed the basic furnishings. Customers who entered the station came face to face with the oil pumps, a reminder to change oil or, in other instances, a soft drink cooler or racks of cigarettes or candy (see Fig. 5.9).

Many of these buildings were prefabricated. An oil company could select one of several standardized buildings listed in a manufacturer's catalogue, or a custom-designed prefabricated building could be developed for the company's exclusive use. Manufacturers of prefabricated buildings pointed to various cost savings. Buildings were of structural steel construction; sections could be easily bolted together, saving labor costs. A prefabricated building could be salvaged and reassembled at another site should an initial location prove unprofitable. "Prefabs" were faced in brick, stucco, zinc, or heavy galvanized steel, surfaces easy to clean and maintain. Tile (either clay or metal), copper, zinc, or galvanized steel was used for roofing. In 1923 the Arthur B. Shepard Company advertised its "Type-G" station as sixteen feet wide, fourteen feet deep, and ten feet high. The building, constructed with a heavy structural steel frame, white enameled steel siding, metal roof, and plate glass windows set in steel sash, cost about $2,200.[12]

Most prefabricators used a variety of architectural adornments to decorate their buildings. The use of pilasters to simulate pillars at the corners of buildings was common. One company offered several Classical Revival buildings including a station with an entablature in a front facing gable (highly reminiscent of the Casey, Illinois, station that initially launched the two authors on their respective explorations of the gasoline station phenomena). The lower cost of prefabricated buildings enabled oil companies to erect more buildings and thus develop larger trade territories more quickly. Shell Oil's rapid deployment throughout California took advantage of prefabricated station structures.

Some corporations pursued traditional architectural styles as a

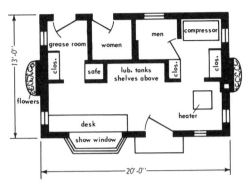

FIGURE 5.8 A Standard Oil of New Jersey station prototype, as depicted on its 1920s road maps, was a rectangular house with red tiled, hip roof. The roof was echoed by a small tiled canopy over the pump island.

FIGURE 5.9 Diagram of a "house" station. The English Cottage style was adopted by the Pure Oil Company. (*Source:* Halbert, "Merchandise Display Window Features Pure Oil Co.'s New Stations." Courtesy *NPN.*)

FIGURE 5.10 Model of Pure Oil's English Cottage station. (*Source: Pure Oil News* 12 [June 1929]: 21.)

FIGURE 5.11 A postcard view of a Jenney Oil Company gasoline station sporting the firm's "colonial" decor. The canopy attached to but did not integrate with the roofline of the station house, anticipating the evolution of the house with canopy station prototype.

means of establishing company identities. In New England the Jenney Manufacturing Company sought to "blend its stations into the regional landscape" (see Fig. 5.11). The company developed a "cottage" with steeped high roof and cupola, trimmed with shuttered windows and cornice to simulate a Federal-style house. Unfortunately, the result was termed "Colonial architecture," an early instance of Georgian, Federal, and Classical Revival styles being confused under the "Colonial" rubric. The Beacon Oil Company, also of Massachusetts, launched another chain of Colonial stations. The Pure Oil Company refined its "English cottage" style (see chapter 6).[13] At Pure Oil the steep, end-gabled roof was blue tile and the walls were white stucco placed either on hollow tile or on wood lathe. Presumably, the use of tall end chimneys and front bay windows with flower boxes made these buildings distinctly English.

Notable with the rising concern for image in gasoline station design was increased attention to the pump. Although Gilbert and Barker Manufacturing Company, an early pump manufacturer, advertised the globe surmounting the pump as a place for retailer labeling in 1912, the suggestion seems not to have been widely adopted until the late teens and early twenties.[14] Corporation logos silk-screened to the inside of glass globes for protection from weathering, however, became common by the mid-1920s. About 200 gasoline pump manufacturers were in business by 1925. By then the "visible pump" was standard with a glass cylinder atop the pump as guarantor of honest marketing. Fuel pumped into the cylinder with gallon indicator was held in place for customer viewing before being released into the customer's fuel tank. Fuel grades also began to be distinguished according to color and enhanced the visual display at the point of sale.[15]

The House with Canopy

The addition of a canopy integrated into the roof of the small house or cottage produced another distinctive type of gasoline station (see Fig. 5.12). Standard Oil of Ohio pioneered a prefabricated prototype in 1916.[16] The station building was fifteen feet square with the canopy supported in front by a single post covering a similar area (see Fig. 5.13).[17] In 1918 the Gulf Oil Company adopted a brick and tile roofed station with canopy supported by four brick columns covering two front driveways and Standard of Indiana a very similar building with small, globelike light fixtures (see Fig. 5.14). Standard Oil of New York added canopies to its colonial stations in 1923 which carried iron balustrades to simulate porches.[18]

The use of tile for roofing and stucco for wall facings invited use of Spanish architectural styles. The Ventura Refining Company in Los Angeles adopted "mission type" buildings. In 1917 the Texas Company in-

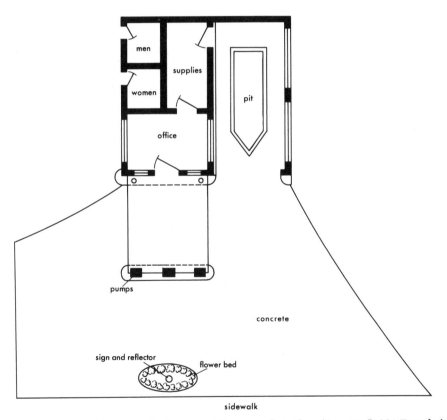

FIGURE 5.12 Diagram of a "house with canopy" station. (*Source:* "1931 Trends in Station Design," *NPN* 23 [March 4, 1931]: 93. Courtesy *NPN*.)

FIGURE 5.13 A prefabricated "house with canopy" station on old U.S. 66 at Wilmington, Illinois, in 1974. This and similar buildings were used extensively by Standard Oil of Ohio and Standard Oil of Kentucky (Kyso) among other companies.

troduced stations constructed with hollow tile and brick walls with stucco finish, a red tile roof, and double arched covered driveways.[19] Standard Oil of California's white stuccoed house and canopy station sported red and blue paint trim (see Fig. 5.15).

The House with Bays

By 1925 most gasoline stations were equipped with grease pits and car-washing floors. As car washing required a solid, well-drained surface, concrete aprons were built. Grease pits, open trenches with walls of poured concrete or masonry, were usually located immediately beside a station house. Cars were elevated slightly above a pit on ramps that straddled the trench. The term *grease monkey* applied to the mechanic who worked below. After 1925 rotary lifts operated by air compressors gradually replaced the grease pits. Where winter weather interfered with outdoor car maintenance, prefabricated steel and glass washing parlors and lubritoriums appeared.[20] More common, however, was the addition of one or more covered bays to existing station houses or the construction of new stations with two or more bays covering the washing and lubricating floors (see Fig. 5.16).[21] Before 1935, building additions usually adopted the architecture of the original structure. For example, the Pure Oil Company carried the steep gabled roofs of its English cottage stations across appended service bays. After 1935, additions were usually simplified, flat-roofed boxes. The very large gasoline stations with

THE GAS STATION IN AMERICA

FIGURE 5.14 A Standard Oil of Indiana station at Macomb, Illinois, in the 1920s. Note how the station has been inserted into a previously all-residential neighborhood.

FIGURE 5.15 A Standard Oil of California house with canopy station on the Pacific Coast Highway at Huntington Beach, California, circa 1930. (*Source:* Photo courtesy of Chevron Corporate Library.)

FIGURE 5.16 A Texaco "house with bays" station at Springfield, Illinois, originally built as a Phillips station.

three or more bays (sometimes in separate buildings) were often called "super service stations." These facilities advertised "one-stop" automotive service. In addition to washing and lubricating, engine, brake, muffler, and other repair services were usually available.

The Oblong Box

The economic depression of the 1930s brought many changes to gasoline station design. To counter deteriorating gasoline sales, many companies expanded auxiliary product lines requiring larger display rooms and larger storage spaces. The sale of tires, batteries, and accessories (the so-called TBA line) was universally adopted by the major firms. At the same time, companies began to emphasize automobile repair, which required more and larger bays. In addition, the Depression encouraged a few companies to expand territorially since construction of new stations in new areas did not divert customers from a company's established outlets, but could attract trade from one's competitors. To develop these new territories, the oil companies built stations that were distinctly different. Most companies also used new stations to reinforce territorial cores in the drive to increase gallonage and market penetration.

Hip and gable roofs were replaced by flat roofs. Offices were enlarged and integrated with the service bays. The whole was integrated as an "oblong box" with rectangular perimeter dimensions (see Fig. 5.17). The amount of plate glass was increased with a corresponding reduction in

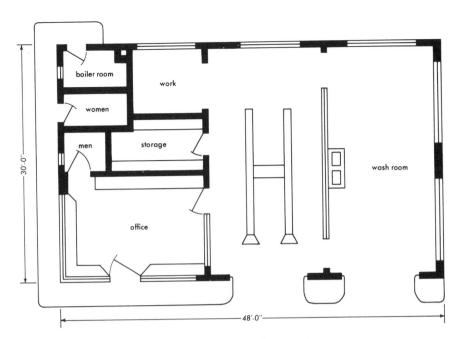

FIGURE 5.17 Diagram of a typical oblong box station.

FIGURE 5.18 An oblong box station. The simple lines of the box and the extensive use of glass on the steel frame follow closely the edicts of "modern architecture" as practiced in Germany in the 1930s.

FIGURE 5.19 The Ohio Oil Company produced some of the most successful International-style stations, placing great emphasis on glazing across building façades.

exterior decoration. Walls of stucco or brick were painted using colors appropriate to a company's signage. Terra cotta was a popular facing material in the 1930s while porcelain enamel predominated in the 1940s and 1950s. This new gasoline station design followed loosely the edicts of the new "International" style of architecture championed by the Bauhaus school in Germany (see Figs. 5.18 and 5.19). Marketing engineers (as most companies called their architect-designers) took pride in introducing streamlined, modern stations. "Modern architecture," however, was certainly a misnomer. More correctly, they had introduced "Depression architecture," a stripped down, functional design to put a new, optimistic face on hard economic times.

Several of the nation's leading industrial designers were challenged with raising gasoline station architecture to a higher plane. Industrial design was a newly emergent profession charged by American manufacturers with configuring products with maximum sales appeal. Walter Dorwin Teague, hired by Texaco in 1934, created a new look for the company: white "streamlined" boxes that were thought to give impressions of speed, modernity, and progress (see Figs. 1.3 [p. 3] and 5.20). Some 10,000 of these stations were ultimately constructed.[22] Norman Bel Geddes likewise created for Socony-Vacuum an exciting new prototype clearly influenced by the European-inspired International style. However, it proved too avant garde and none were built. Instead, the firm turned to Frederick Frost, a consulting architect, who, with project manager David Dodge, produced an oblong box with a rounded "drum-like" office section very similar to Texaco's new entry.[23] In this way, a new standard format was born—thoroughly functional, and thoroughly bland in its functionality.

Most oil companies modified the oblong box thus to facilitate customer recognition. The roof of the office section might be constructed slightly higher than the bays (Mid-Continent D-X stations in the 1930s), or it might be lower (Atlantic stations in the 1960s). One corner of the office might be curved to contain the front door (Standard Oil of Indiana in the

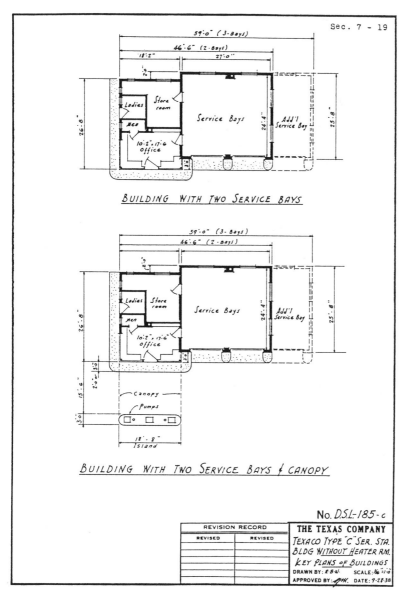

BUILDING WITH TWO SERVICE BAYS

BUILDING WITH TWO SERVICE BAYS & CANOPY

No. DSL-185-c

REVISION RECORD		THE TEXAS COMPANY
REVISED	REVISED	Texaco Type "C" Ser. Sta.
		Bldg Without Heater Rm.
		Key Plans of Buildings
		DRAWN BY: R.B.U. SCALE: 1/16"=1'-0
		APPROVED BY: J.H.K. DATE: 9-28-38

FIGURE 5.20 Texaco's oblong box, two plans for which are shown here, was sheathed in porcelain enamel to visually contrast sharply with its surroundings. It was to stand alone in the landscape to speak loudly of the firm's modernity. (*Source:* Plan courtesy of Texaco.)

1940s). An office façade might be extended forward (Texaco in the late 1940s) or recessed relative to the bays (Sinclair in the early 1940s). Some companies, such as Standard Oil of California, retained the canopy as a form of trademark. Others, such as Shell in the 1950s, adopted towers or pylons (see Fig. 5.21). Texaco used both but placed canopies only on its stations across the Southwest, the canopies serving as sunshades (see Fig. 5.22). Reintroduction of the Colonial style brought flat gable and

FIGURE 5.21 The Shell Oil Company's S20B station was an early example of a modified oblong box. By introducing modest deviations, each company sought to set its stations apart—the practice of "difference in sameness."

FIGURE 5.22 A 1968 Texaco station at El Reno, Oklahoma, on U.S. 66 sports the canopy that Texaco reserved for outlets across the southern states.

THE GAS STATION IN AMERICA

multiple gable roofs with cupolas (Atlantic stations in the 1960s). Despite these modifications, however, the prime characteristic of the oblong box was its distinctive shape based on a rectangular floor plan and rectangular silhouette.

The Mid-Continent Petroleum Corporation appears to have been the first to adopt the oblong box as a standard design.[24] Its first station was opened at Sapulpa, Oklahoma, in 1931 at a cost of $11,000. The exterior of the building featured large expanses of plate glass set in unpainted aluminum window and door frames. The walls were covered with black vitrolite, which gave the appearance of highly polished glass.

Before 1950 most oblong boxes were prefabricated.[25] Steel I-beam frames were shop-assembled in sections and then bolted together at a construction site. Structures were usually covered with porcelain enamel sheets and plate glass.[26] In 1958 the Shell Oil Company's prefabricated "S20B" stations ranged in price from $19,000 to $22,000 (see Figs. 2.11 [p. 44] and 5.21). After 1950 cinder- and concrete-block construction replaced prefabricated steel and by 1960 acrylic-vinyl and translucent plexiglas (including sheets backed by fluorescent tubes for night lighting) had become popular. After 1960 plastic was used to simulate other building materials such as wood, stone, and brick.[27]

Exemplifying marketing's press of every advantage during the De-

FIGURE 5.23 The new Tokeheim pumps figure prominently beneath the canopy of this Standard Oil of California station in San Francisco, 1949. (*Source:* Photo courtesy of Chevron Corporate Library.)

FIGURE 5.24 The results of "face-lifting" and "top-hatting": an oblong box modified in the Shell's "ranch" style.

pression was the successive redesign of fuel pumps to augment the sales experience through sound as well as sight. Flashing pump panels, clock-face meters, and a bell that sounded after each gallon sold were added for visual and auditory confirmation of an honest sale. Tokeheim Oil Tank and Pump Company took advantage of the pure display value inherent in these devices and assumed leadership in the pump manufacturing field in the 1930s. Walter Teague's streamlined new stations for Texaco also set a standard for Tokeheim, which then designed streamlined pump housings fully integrable with the new stations.[28] Stations thus grew to be even more memorable examples of place-product-packaging in the hands of the decade's industrial designers (see Fig. 5.23).

In the 1920s the oil companies had worked to soften the intrusion of the gasoline station in the American landscape, but in the 1930s they sought to maximize gasoline station visibility. The new oblong boxes contrasted (even clashed) sharply with their surroundings, the better to attract attention. The use of porcelain enamel invited adoption of vivid colors. The glistening porcelain and glass façades were more easily lit at night, offering a potential "twenty-four hour sales appeal." The new oblong boxes enjoyed other advantages according to advertisers. Prefabricated buildings could be erected quickly; as well, they could be salvaged should a station prove unprofitable on a given site. (Actually, relatively few failed stations were ever moved.) They could be easily maintained for the new façade materials did not require constant painting.[29] Oblong boxes were larger and contained little wasted space. The large expanses of glass facilitated selling through point of purchase display. The new stations were "bigger, better, and brighter."

By 1960 the gaudy porcelain and plastic oblongs had met with disfavor from planning and zoning commissions and had suffered enough

FIGURE 5.25 The "Matawan" style station, named by Texaco for the town in New Jersey where it was introduced in 1964. (*Source:* Photo courtesy of Texaco.)

FIGURE 5.26 An oblong box that has been "colonialized" by Sun Oil.

criticism from the public at large that several oil companies began to explore design modifications to "blend" gasoline stations into new suburban landscapes. Shell introduced the "ranch style" in 1960 at Millbrae, California. The *National Petroleum News* praised the station: "It very definitely does not gloss, glitter, or glare. The so-called 'ice box' look is out. While most of the designs still use a basic metal building, they mustn't look like metal. Rustic features like cedar shakes, used brick, roof overhang, and darker colors are common." By 1966 Shell had 3,500 of the new stations in operation. The average cost for a totally new building was $65,000.[30] Older oblongs could be easily adapted to the new style by replacing the porcelain enamel and other wall facings, by adding a flat, front gable roof, and by extending the eave on one end of the building to form a porch (usually to shelter vending machines and protect the entrances to the restrooms). The ranch style was essentially the old oblong without its glitter and without its flat roof, updated through "face-lifting" and "top-hatting" (see Fig. 5.24).[31] The new stations were called "blend-ins."

By 1970 several companies had developed distinctive styles. Texaco introduced the mansard roof in 1964 on a new station built at Matawan, New Jersey.[32] The station featured hexagonal roof sections (repeating the shape of Texaco's new signs) and side-entry bays with the front of the building finished with stone (plastic, simulating stone, was used in later buildings) (see Fig. 5.25). The Teague years were clearly over. The American Oil Company and Sunoco "colonialized" their stations in the Northeast by adding rafters to the old flat roofs to form hip roofs, adding cupolas, reducing the size of the window areas, and resurfacing buildings with used red brick (see Fig. 5.26).[33]

FIGURE 5.27 A Clark Oil small box on University Avenue in Urbana, Illinois, 1978.

THE GAS STATION IN AMERICA

FIGURE 5.28 The Derby Oil Company, a middle-western refiner and retailer, used the small box exclusively in the 1950s.

The Small Box

The rise of the new "independents" (the localized jobbers and small regional distributing companies) led to the development of a new station type: the "small box." Most independent stations sold only gasoline and oil, along with sundry lines of merchandise such as cigarettes and soft drinks. The independents tended to shun the premiums, credit cards, and other promotional gimmicks used by the major oil companies and to emphasize lower gasoline prices by one or more cents per gallon. "Bulk stations" early typified the independent retailers; the above-ground storage tanks dominated station grounds and symbolized the lower retail prices of wholesale jobbing.[34] This form of gasoline sales imposed few building requirements. Stations needed only small offices, storage rooms, and restrooms (see Figs. 5.27 and 5.28). Small prefabricated, glass and enamel-plated structures served quite adequately.[35] Large billboards lining the driveways were also common.

The Small Box with Canopy

Canopies had gone out of style in the Northeast and the Middle West with the adoption of the oblong box. Severe winter weather added to canopy upkeep and canopies interfered with nighttime lighting. Covered drives were thought to be confining. Inexperienced drivers tended to shun canopied stations.[36] Only along the Pacific Coast, in the Southwest, and in the Southeast did the canopy survive, popular as a shade against the sun. Many national companies (such as Texaco and Sinclair) built canopied stations in those areas to compete with the regional companies (such as Standard Oil of California in the Far West).[37] After 1960 the large canopies were adopted widely by independents, but as an advertising gimmick. Canopies carried large signs and engendered a sense of presence—a sense of place—which the small office buildings alone could not achieve. Several canopy styles became popular. The "butterfly" canopy was attached to the station building and swept upward and out over the drive with its pumps. The "standard" flat-roofed variety was self standing over a portion of the driveway. Most canopies tended to measure around thirty by forty feet, equal to covering two driveways and a single pump island.

The Canopy and Booth

By 1970 many new stations had appeared which were little more than canopies.[38] Station offices were reduced to small booths located on one of the pump islands (see Fig. 5.29). Booths contained an attendant, a cash register, and little else. Restrooms and vending machines were housed in separate shedlike buildings located at one edge of the driveway. Canopies and buildings were prefabricated with canopies large enough to cover two or more driveways. These stations, a return by the major companies to the strict "filling station" idea, were a direct result of OPEC's higher gasoline prices and resultant gasoline shortages.[39] The American motorist was more aware of price to the potential advantage of the independent retailers who had always sought to keep prices low. The major oil companies emphasized their own "independents," the "concubine companies" with their own identities that emphasized value and economy.[40]

Convenience Stores with Canopies and Unattended Pumps with Canopies

The past two decades have brought the convenience store to the forefront of gasoline retailing. Most convenience stores are modest, single-story, rectangular structures of masonry or metal construction, the front façade opened up in large windows before which stand gasoline pumps covered by a large, self-standing canopy (see Fig. 5.30). Convenience store chains, such as the Southland Corporation's Seven-Eleven Stores, added gasoline as a "loss-leader" attraction, inclining gasoline corporations to establish their own convenience store chains as a means of protecting regional gasoline markets. Although convenience stores are the latest fashion in gasoline retailing, they are not, in the strictest sense, gasoline stations, but a new form of tie-in. Only the isolated, unattended pumps (most covered by canopies) pretend a new form of station fully divorced from other activities. Fully automated, these latter stations represent a complete return to the "filling station" idea. Negated is any sense of service. Since isolated, unattended pumps have only recently appeared on the American scene, it is too early to speculate as to their impact on gasoline retailing.

The Popularity of Station Types by Period

Volumes of the *National Petroleum News* published at decade intervals were analyzed to determine the relative popularity of the various

FIGURE 5.29 A canopy and booth station viewed from beneath the canopy.

FIGURE 5.30 In the 1990s convenience stores rapidly replaced gasoline stations.
A Jet-24 "C-Store" in Lafayette, Louisiana, 1993.

gasoline station types by period.[41] It was assumed that the various gasoline station types appeared in the illustrations of this journal in approximate correspondence to their actual appearance in the American landscape. (A test of this proposition appears in chapter 8.) Stations depicted in both advertising and nonadvertising materials were categorized for 1920, 1940, 1950, 1960, 1970, 1980, and 1990 respectively (see Table 5.1). Only the nonadvertising illustrations were available for analysis for 1930.

"Curbside" stations were depicted in over one-third of the total illustrations in 1920, but were nearly absent thereafter. The shed-type station, which accounted for 9 percent of the illustrations in 1920, had practically disappeared by 1940. The house, which also accounted for 9 percent of the total in 1920, maintained a small popularity through 1940 with a residual appearance thereafter. After the curbside station, the house with canopy was the first significant new station type to appear. Accounting for nearly one-third of the total illustrations in 1920, its popularity decreased steadily after 1930. The house with bays station appears to have been a transitory type of the 1930s, involving enlargement of house and house with canopy stations to handle TBA and light repair functions. No gasoline station type dominated as completely or for as long a period as the oblong box. Over half of the stations illustrated in 1940 and 1950 were of this type, and nearly two-thirds in 1960 and

TABLE 5.1 The Changing Popularity of Gasoline Station Types by Decade Intervals, 1920 to 1990

Type	Percentage of Stations							
	1920	1930[a]	1940	1950	1960	1970	1980	1990
Curbside	37%	0%	0%	0%	0%	0%	0%	2%
Shed	9	0	1	1	0	0	0	0
House	9	8	8	2	1	1	0	0
House with canopy	31	29	8	2	1	0	0	3
House with bays	1	12	6	2	0	0	0	0
Oblong box	0	3	54	57	63	62	34	13
Small box	1	0	4	19	9	1	0	3
Small box with canopy	0	0	0	1	8	12	7	0
Canopy with booth	0	0	0	0	1	8	23	1
Other designs	12	48	19	16	17	16	20	20
Convenience store with canopy	0	0	0	0	0	0	16	51
Canopy with unattended pumps	0	0	0	0	0	0	0	7

[a] Illustrations in advertisements were not analyzed for 1930. The authors were unable to obtain complete copies of Volume 22. Advertising was commonly omitted from bound periodicals in libraries during the 1930s.

Source: Author content analysis of *NPN* for respective years.

THE GAS STATION IN AMERICA

FIGURE 5.31 The Atlantic Refining Company's "Greek Temple" in Philadelphia. (*Source: Architectural Terra Cotta Brochure Series,* Vol. 5: *The Garage* [New York: National Terra Cotta Society, 1915].)

1970. The small box reached its peak of popularity in 1950, declining thereafter. The small box with canopy, on the other hand, appears to have grown in popularity in direct proportion to the small box's decline. Only a trace of the canopy and booth type was evident in the illustrations of 1960, but 8 percent were so classified in 1970. Canopies, combined with either the small glass box or the attendant's booth, appeared in 20 percent of the total illustrations in 1970. They were evident, combined with small glass boxes, booths, convenience stores, or unattended pumps, in 46 percent in 1980 and 63 percent in 1990. Canopies were clearly in the ascendancy and have become, irrespective of region, a major signifier of gasoline retailing. The canopy has become an effective means of updating older station types, especially oblong boxes. The convenience store is the latest fashion in retailing along with automated, unattended pumps covered by the increasingly ubiquitous canopy.

Unique Designs before World War II

The late 1920s and the early 1930s saw many unique gasoline station designs appear. Only 54 percent of the stations illustrated in 1930 could be classified as opposed to an average of 83 percent for the other years. Filling stations were constructed to simulate windmills, pyramids, pagodas, castles, mosques, wigwams, and a host of other romantic landscape features.[42] Gasoline stations in at least two places, in Lancaster, Pennsylvania, and Maryville, Missouri, were constructed in the form of giant gasoline pumps. One type of novelty station, a lighthouse, was prefabricated. Perhaps the most elaborate gasoline station ever con-

FIGURE 5.32 Mission Revival styling played out across much of the Standard Oil of California chain as in this station at Malibu Beach, California. (*Source:* Photo courtesy of Chevron Corporate Library.)

structed was built by the Atlantic Refining Company in Philadelphia in 1918. The central building and the extensive colonnades that surrounded the large driveway were faced in white terra cotta tile. The entire complex was styled after a Classical Greek temple (see Fig. 5.31).[43] The "seashell" stations of the Quality Oil Company of Winston-Salem, North Carolina, a Shell jobber, are treated in chapter 7. Few novelty stations were replicated in great numbers. Most of the unusual stations were experimental: costly experiments that did not produce the substantially higher sales necessary to keep them profitable. They violated the basic idea behind place-product-packaging.

Regional Designs before World War II

The 1920s and 1930s were decades that saw distinctive regional designs come to the fore in certain parts of the country, promulgated both by large national and small regional firms. For example, in the Southwest and Far West "old mission" themes came repeatedly to the fore (see Fig. 5.32). Texaco introduced a mission style as early as 1917 with walls constructed of hollow tile and brick covered with a stucco finish and roofs of tile. Union Oil followed with canopied stations stuccoed and tiled throughout California. That state's smaller Ventura Oil Company also adopted a mission style, but with a very strong "pueblo" look with flat roofs and adobe-appearing walls penetrated by decorative vigas.[44] Stations were faced with stucco to give the appearance of adobe and had flat roofs with prominent belfries (the mission bell being the company's

FIGURE 5.33 Former Beacon Oil station at Jamaica Plain, Massachusetts, in the livery of Standard Oil of New Jersey's "Colonial Beacon." (*Source:* Photo courtesy of Exxon.)

trademark). Gasoline pumps were hidden inside the supporting canopy pillars. These stations were configured using a design vocabulary loosely based on Spanish and Mexican Colonial architecture, inspiration coming from Spanish themes employed at various world's fairs held in the years before World War I in San Diego, San Francisco, and Portland.

New England was another area where oil companies large and small sought design inspiration from idealized Colonial pasts. Socony-Vacuum variously combined Georgian Revival and Classical Revival ornamentation including pillars and pilasters, balustrades, and even Palladian windows. The Jenney Manufacturing Company built in Boston a chain of Colonial stations with hip roofs and dormers, bay windows, and arched doorways. A Bostonian, it was claimed, could purchase gasoline and not offend his or her aesthetic sense.[45]

Another Boston-centered chain, the Beacon Oil Company formed in 1919, also rooted its identity in New England's colonial past.[46] In a ferociously competitive retail market, Beacon and other firms scrambled for choice filling station sites, each firm attiring its stations in memorable architecture to heighten brand loyalty. In 1922 the architectural office of Coolidge and Carlson designed Beacon's prototype station, called the "Watertown." The building's prominent columns, balustrade, dome, and lantern were copied from Charles Bulfinch's Massachusetts State House, one of Boston's premier landmarks located on Beacon Hill. A globe, banded to denote latitude and longitude, was piled atop the already prominent dome and lantern, the whole to signify Boston's claim to be "The Hub." The "Watertown"'s all-white exterior, true of the State House only after 1917, reinforced the then-popular conception of things colonial. Light fixtures above the balustrade accentuated the dome's height by day and combined with the light atop the lantern at night to offer a striking light display (see Fig. 5.33). The design's broad hint of a beacon effected by the night lighting was an unmistakable play on the company's name.[47] Thus in several ways was an advertising appeal generated from an architectural base.

With its copper dome soon weathered green, each Beacon station seemed like a splendid "monument," in the words of one former company executive.[48] Thirty-five to fifty examples of the style were built, all within forty miles of Boston's center. Altogether Beacon owned or leased by 1929 some 350 stations throughout New England (except Vermont) and New York.[49] The chain comprised many dissimilar buildings acquired from previous operators and another company prototype, the "Fitchburg." But the distinctive Watertown silhouette was the major corporate logo to appear on the cover of Beacon's regional tour guides and road maps. Standard Oil of New Jersey took control of Beacon Oil in 1929, renaming the new subsidiary Colonial Beacon.[50] Thus Jersey Standard bought for itself a period of transition where regional loyalties, rooted in an idealized colonial past, continued to engender brand loyalty. But in the 1950s the Colonial logos finally came down and the Esso signs went up.

Architecture in any society is fluid, constantly changing. This is especially true of commercial architecture, where buildings are part of continuing advertising campaigns to establish marketing territories, clearly illustrated in American gasoline distribution where places—gasoline stations—were deliberately packaged around product and service lines. Although stations have had to look like gasoline stations, each company has tried to make its stations distinctive. Nonetheless, deviations could not depart substantially from norms as they evolved. The challenge has been to find that rare quality of "difference in sameness" that would attract customers but also reassure them. This need prompted a constant drift to new color schemes, signage, and decoration, but always within a narrow range of building types in any one time period. On the other hand, major changes in marketing strategy have always prompted the development of new station prototypes. The house with canopy prevailed until the expansion of TBA retailing, and the introduction of automobile repair encouraged rapid adoption of the oblong box during the Depression. Oblong boxes prevailed until the recent period of high gasoline prices. Today the canopy dominates, but in new forms, reminiscent of some of the earliest filling stations, and in conjunction with the convenience store.

In the early years the oil companies used traditional building and architectural ideas. House, house and canopy, and house and bay stations retained the scale and adopted the materials and styles of American domestic architecture. When gasoline retailing was in its infancy, the oil companies trod carefully in introducing the gasoline station to the American roadside, especially in residential neighborhoods. Gasoline stations were designed to blend into their surroundings. With the automobile permanently entrenched in American life, the industry more recklessly impacted the American scene. Faced with a slow growth market after 1930, the oil companies evolved the oblong box as a truly distinctive form of architecture. Oblong boxes, especially those covered with porcelain enamel, stood apart from surrounding features to disrupt and, in many instances, to blight the landscape. In recent decades a more mature industry has begun to recognize its responsibility for quality architectural and landscape design. If the evolution of gasoline stations is typical of other forms of commercial architecture in the United States, significant changes in building types can be expected when industry-wide dislocations in supply, demand, and related price of product occur.

Unlike building types associated with folk architectural traditions, gasoline stations did not spread across the landscape diffused from clearly defined culture hearths. Prototypes were developed through experimentation in many places and then adopted almost universally across the country aided by such mechanisms of communication as industry trade journals. The *National Petroleum News* was the leading journal serving the American petroleum industry and, as such, played a leading role in encouraging gasoline station change through annual design contests and the weekly and later monthly reporting of design innovations and individual company adoptions. It seems imperative that the study of twentieth-century commercial architecture include content analyses of appropriate trade journals. Journal illustrations (both of an advertising and nonadvertising nature) as well as descriptive textual materials offer a resource little tapped by geographers and historians interested in the evolution of commercial building types.

Like other aspects of landscape, the roadside is a transitory thing. Its various forms and its various elements, whether of good, bad, or indifferent taste, ought to be recorded and understood as a part of our changing American culture. Also pressing are the immediate concerns of preservation. Perhaps, good examples of roadside architecture from the early part of this century will be preserved for future generations. Questions need to be answered. What was typical in the landscape in different places at different times? What was atypical? What should be valued? What should be preserved? We hope that the oil companies will promote selected retention of older gasoline stations typical of past periods, and that local communities will encourage such preservation in order to ensure greater diversity and interest in the American landscape.

How much of the nation's early gasoline station heritage has survived? Clearly, roadside architecture, including gasoline stations, has proven very ephemeral indeed. Even the ubiquitous oblong boxes, buildings that Americans in the 1950s and 1960s assumed would be around forever, are very rapidly being torn down or remodeled beyond recognition. Of the more exotic station types even fewer survive. For example, of Beacon Oil's Watertown stations only four have survived. One building housed at the end of the 1980s a fruit market, another a pizzeria, and another an ice cream store. Only one functioned as a gasoline station.

6

Gas Station Design – The Large Corporation

From an overview of changing gasoline station form over time, we now examine the design process through the architectural engineering of one firm—the Pure Oil Company—which we take to be representative of the industry from the 1920s through to the 1960s, when Pure Oil merged with Union Oil. Gasoline marketing was structured as much by entrepreneurial drive as by consumer demand.[1] Place-product-packaging's architectural components along the American roadside emerged at the juncture of consumer and entrepreneurial interests. After 1915, oil company executives employed designers to consciously style gasoline stations. In the 1920s, competitive companies contrived and managed bold images for their stations in order to enhance themselves territorially in the emergent national market for gasoline. Sought was design sophistication that hinged on calculating the attractive if not the tasteful. Gasoline station design was not merely an accommodating of mechanical systems useful in dispensing petroleum products. Rather, companies staked their reputation on the images created.

At first, market segmentation was not carefully considered. Sought was the widest possible appeal in winning patronage from those wealthy enough to own automobiles. The images of the upper classes appealed to middle-class aspirations for moving up the social ladder. Promise of consumer self-realization was not new to advertising when the oil industry adapted it to place-product-packaging.[2] The images appropriated for gasoline stations carried suburban upper-class residential overtures, especially in decorative details derived from colonial American and English architectural traditions. Pure Oil's corporate image initially hinged on its "English cottage" station designed by corporate architect C. A. Petersen.

History roots understanding in the details of specific and relevant sets of design decisions. Although specific examples of gasoline station architecture have been analyzed from the geographer's perspective, which emphasizes the aggregate consequences of corporate action yielding one or another form, the deeds of specific individuals within corporations offer a complementary view.[3] The English cottage type of station (of which Petersen's was one of the best) merits a detailed history. It is a widely remembered image of a large oil corporation and has been labeled "among the most successful" of the suburban-style stations.[4] It is perhaps unrepresentative only in the fact that the English cottage has been more memorable than images designed for other early, large petroleum companies.

Pure Oil's Search for Identity

The Pure Oil Company evolved in response to emerging opportunities in the petroleum trade. Founded in 1914 as the Ohio Cities Gas Company, it was principally a public utilities holding company with a few natural gas– and oil-producing properties. At the end of its first year, however, the company opened such a lucrative oil field that its oil production, refinement, and sales eventually became more profitable than its original utilities. The company's first gasoline stations were opened in Dayton, Ohio, in 1918. To correctly reflect the shifting emphasis toward oil, the company was renamed the Pure Oil Company in 1920.[5]

The stations from which Pure distributed its oil products were a heterogeneous-looking aggregation comprised both of the buildings it constructed and those of the companies it bought to expand its network.[6] For the sake of easier corporate recognition along the roadside, Pure decided to build its new stations in a single style. Thus, in March 1923 E. C. Miller, an architect in Columbus, Ohio, drew the design for Pure's stations and the Edwards Manufacturing Company of Cincinnati used Miller's design to produce prefabricated kits for what became known inside Pure Oil as the "Edwards type" station (see Fig. 6.1).[7]

In December 1924, Henry M. Dawes resigned as U.S. comptroller of the currency in the Coolidge administration to become president of the Pure Oil Company. Dawes had also been a member of the Federal Reserve Board and several private companies.[8] His mission was to apply his big business experience to a rational restructuring of all aspects of the company that had grown by opportunistic increments in retailing gasoline across the eastern United States.

Dawes's attempted rationalization of Pure naturally required an examination of its retail outlets. They presented many problems, beginning with authority. Opinions differed widely between personnel within and without the company's engineering division, which built its stations, regarding appropriate construction techniques and building styles. A second issue was economy. It was appreciated that if Pure had a single station type for all its outlets, rather than a collection of different ones, savings in money and time could be achieved from purchase of a standardized set of materials and equipment. The third issue was style. Pure's

FIGURE 6.1 Pure Oil's Edwards-type station was depicted on the company's road maps through 1926.

polyglot collection of buildings encompassed its own stations stretched across eight states and the stations of its major affiliates in six other states. Although the largest number of Pure's stations were the Edwards type, they did not dominate Pure's network. A striking example was in Pure's early headquarters city, Columbus, where the firm's nineteen stations included eight of the Edwards type, five of the affiliated Moore Oil Company, two of the affiliated Colonial Oil Company, and four additional stations, each of varied appearance.[9] As Carlos B. Dawes, Henry's nephew, complained, "The Advertising Department is considerably handicapped in fashioning the various architectural types to one distinguishable Pure Oil. The repitition [sic] of an architectural design has the same advertising value as the repitition [sic] of a trademark."[10] A single station style would provide a badly needed territorial marker. Carlos was charged with studying every aspect of service station design in order to recommend adoption of the single design best suited to the company's requirements. His study was certainly underway by April 1925 and the first word in its eventual title, "Standardization of Service Stations: Report," underscores the general objective of the design process.

The young Dawes reviewed other factors in addition to architectural style. "Layout" or plan was taken up first in "Standardization." Dawes presented numerous drawings of the ideal arrangements of driveway, gasoline pumps, station building, grease pit, curbs, and streets in relation to each other; he included air pump, grass, and pedestrian sidewalks in some plans. Correspondence with various suppliers of electrical and lighting equipment and machinery and roofing material was provided in respective sections on each category to substantiate Dawes's final recommendation.

Other sections of the report included proposals for landscaping, painting, fencing, signs, and pump canopies. Each of these factors was intended individually and orchestrated as an ensemble to achieve just the effect Pure wanted in the consumer's eye. Aesthetics and economy

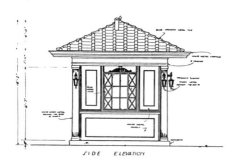

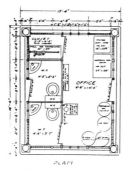

FIGURE 6.2 Edwards-type station as modified by Carlos B. Dawes in 1925. (*Source:* Dawes Arboretum, Newark, Ohio.)

together governed the search for the proper Pure image. As Dawes explained to bidders on the landscaping element,

> the object of the sales force of any institution operating for commercial profit is to increase the demand for the products of the organization without materially augmenting the unit cost of distribution. We are interested, therefore, in a system for landscaping our service stations, in adding to the attractiveness of the stations at not too great an initial cost, at the same time increasing the efficiency of service, and enhancing the advertising value of the station which unity, beauty and distinctive dignity will afford.[11]

Architectural style of the station building itself, the centerpiece of Pure's layout ensemble, remained a prime question. Indeed, it comprised a second chapter in Carlos Dawes's final report. Adhering closely to the practices prevailing in the family-managed business, Dawes recommended an Edwards-type station adapted only slightly by his aesthetics and the practical advice gleaned from Pure's station employees. Hence, the fluted columns on the corner of the Edwards type were extended to the ground, its eaves were lowered, and cove lighting was added to make Pure's stations look better according to Dawes. Windows were lowered and cross muntins were used only on the side windows to overcome the employees' complaint that it was hard to clean the windows otherwise. Also, total floor space was increased to provide separate storage for tools and clothes and a separate office more easily accessed and kept clean.

The five variations Dawes finally presented on the adapted Edwards type were distinguishable only by their shape and size. Designated Type

A through Type E, these stations were either small or large in size and rectangular or hexagonal in floor plan (although one had a small square floor plan). Each could be built of metal on a wooden frame, steel, cast stone, stucco, or brick. Despite Dawes's adaptations, the impression of his prototypes remained that of the Edwards type's peculiar combination of classical embellishments on an otherwise plain little box, hardly more than a shed. Postcards and photographs of stations were gathered in another section of Dawes's report without a reference in any text. Entitled "Rejected Designs," they included other severely utilitarian stations with a minimum of applied decoration, stately stations with decorative allusions to current suburban styles, and what we have termed the unique.

By May 1925, Carlos Dawes proceeded toward construction of a Type B, the small rectangular variety of proposed station (see Fig. 6.2), although his final report, dated October 12, 1925, would advise selection of the best after testing all five variations in practice. Clearly, Carlos Dawes had a favorite variation on the image of prestige by which one roadside authority has categorized the Edwards type.[12]

The Dawes patriarchy remained unimpressed with the tinkered Edwards type that their younger family member produced. The patriarchs wanted to send a dramatic signal along the roadside that a new era had dawned at Pure.[13] Simultaneous with Carlos's completion of "Standardization," Henry M. Dawes hired C. A. Petersen, a gasoline station architect active since the start of the industry, to head the new marketing construction department. His first order of business was the search for Pure's proper architectural image. Petersen, a self-certain designer, soon clashed with the president's nephew on the turf Carlos Dawes had heretofore controlled. Petersen coveted a different image for Pure's stations than the staid classicism of Dawes's adapted Edwards type. As a consequence, Beaman Dawes, chairman of the Pure board of directors, removed his son Carlos from control of the design process in order to give unchallenged authority to the newly employed Petersen.[14]

Emergence of the English Cottage

Image was the essence of Petersen's riddle. Pure's new station type had to be cheap in labor and materials, yet project a distinctive impression. Petersen intended to solve the problem of cost by aiming for a structure most of whose materials could be supplied by the average lumberyard from materials otherwise used in house construction.[15] Petersen's solution also was required to display prominently Pure's corporate livery of blue and white, yet be welcome in the very residential neighborhoods that resisted gasoline stations in their midst because of garish colors and other characteristics considered unsightly. Noise and the potential for fire and even explosion were additional deterrents

FIGURE 6.3 Carl Petersen's Kenmore gasoline station, 1923.

FIGURE 6.4 Pure Oil Company's first English Cottage.

FIGURE 6.5 Pure Oil's English Cottage was depicted on the company's road maps through the 1930s.

to neighborhood gasoline stations. Nonetheless, Pure wanted its stations ensconced amid the homes of the middle- and upper-middle-class families who would form the core of Pure's market. Therefore, as part of a general trend in petroleum retailing, Petersen sought remedy in a residential style of gasoline station to be placed, as often as not, in residential areas.

Petersen's prototype for Pure was a station he had designed in 1923 for the Kenmore Oil Company in Pittsburgh (see Fig. 6.3). He assumed that this earlier design would be a safe point of departure chiefly because it had overcome neighborhood resistance in Pittsburgh. It took Petersen about a month to redesign the Kenmore model and emerge with the creation he called the "English cottage" (see Figs. 6.4 and 6.5).[16]

The English cottage functioned as a sign with two messages, one corporate and one cultural. The corporate message was the unmistakable signal to the motorist that the building was a Pure Oil Company station and that of no other firm. The station was comprised of virtually two vertical planes, one for each of Pure's colors, a blue roof and a white ground floor. Carlos Dawes's search for a nonfading blue roofing tile closest to Pure's blue led to a single supplier, the Ludowici-Celadon Company. Pure accepted Ludowici-Celadon as its sole supplier of the tile, despite the high cost that violated Petersen's order to design a distinctive yet economical building.[17] The roof with this tile was a broad glistening plane, uninterrupted by any other architectural feature, faced outward toward traffic, and inclined so steeply that it was practically another wall atop the wall enclosing the office beneath. The deep blue roof of the cottage juxtaposed to its white walls could be detected by approaching motorists up to 200 feet before other stations, Petersen speculated.[18]

The station's second message was domestic. Pure Oil's stations sought to convey the soothing reassurances of a private home, in part belying the company's profit-making motive. Customers were to feel comfortable in a homelike environment that had implications of class and status rooted in domestic tradition.

The ideal was a middle-class aspiration, with other ideals and realities in competition, including communal housing for utopian socialists.

While many Americans lived in densely populated urban neighborhoods of boarding houses, apartment buildings, and row houses with a minimum of space and landscaping, the hegemonic cultural goal was different. It was a free-standing, owner-occupied shelter for the nuclear family, traditional in style, surrounded by generous open spaces of grass, shrubs, and trees, and removed from the urban core in a community of similar homes. Ideal suburban developments entailed a centrally located open space and took advantage of the natural topography especially by including curvilinear streets. Communities embodying this ideal found their precursor in Llewellen Park, New Jersey, begun in 1853. However, with the later coincidence of more widely diffused wealth, a public more generally educated in allusions to past English gentry, and—most of all—to easy access to the automobile, the suburban ideal mushroomed outside every American city in the 1920s. These residential reserves were thought to combine the best of city life with country life. On the one hand, they were close to the rich financial and educational opportunities of the city which were imagined impossible in the unsophisticated, rural countryside. Yet, on the other hand, these suburbs were believed to retain the wholesome tranquility associated with rural life by prohibiting the noise, traffic, dirt, racial diversity, and resulting tension associated with the city. Suburbs were places to escape, relax, and raise children.[19]

Revivalism achieved principally through the external application of historical decoration on houses was the prevailing architectural mode in the suburbs of the 1920s. Stuccoed walls with half-timbered gables, elaborate chimney pots atop steeply pitched roofs, some with roof ridges raised at the ends to simulate age and to conjure the sense of a venerable estate, spawned the most numerous suburban homes. Often labeled Tudor Revival, more recently the name Tudorbeathan has been coined to convey the quality of these homes' historically inaccurate admixture. Spanish haciendas, Dutch Colonial homes, French Norman farmhouses, as well as less common ethnic architecture, inspired a smaller number of other essentially picturesque houses. A few elements of this tradition were occasionally selected for decoration in the less wealthy bungalow suburbs. In the more affluent settings, however, fully stated, picturesque styles stood compatibly beside the otherwise rival classicism inherent in Colonial Revival residences. Whichever the tradition selected, suburbanites were clearly striving with residential iconography to convince themselves and others of having achieved the gentry classification that they perceived as a higher plane of existence.[20]

A key question in popular domestic architecture of the 1920s concerned which Revival style was best suited for the exterior. Although architects and developers debated the issue without resolve, general agreement arose that the interior of homes should function as the playground for individualized expression. Arbiters of popular taste advised women to make their homes reflect their unique personalities. Preference for the open floor plan became general in the nation in the 1920s and style no longer dictated plan. Thus, the external and internal design elements of earlier residential styles were selected for combination into whatever pattern most satisfied the individual owner's preference. A new freedom was proclaimed in these individualized residential creations.[21]

Beneath the suburb's apparent individualism, however, lay a conservatism rooted in anxiety. Suburbanites essentially valued the norm and abhorred eccentricity. Hence, they readily bought the less-creative house designs sold by suburban developers and their communities looked remarkably alike despite the willful mixture of various Revival façades. Suburbanites also attempted rigid maintenance of their elitist residential retreats through covenants and zoning. Adoption of a relatively few Revival styles almost everywhere in suburban America bespeaks something of the rigidity of the suburban movement.[22]

Picturesque houses with their complementary settings comprised an ensemble that has been termed the "Romantic Suburb."[23] As a domestic retreat, everything was made to look tranquil, tucked away, in order. Not only was every family enveloped in a house whose exterior architecture proclaimed stability but the house was covered with vines, surrounded with flowers and shrubs, and protected by stately trees on a manicured lawn. Each of these settings was a self-sufficient landscape unit separated by a generous distance from the other nearly identical units. The whole was swathed in sentimentalism. As one scholar has noted, "Offices in each American city turned out house after house, which, if the architects had the right touch, looked like soft-pencil sketches or watercolors rather than houses." The shimmering vision produced by this technique was in keeping with the nature of the suburban dream. Its verbal attributions were equally appropriate. "Quaint" was the word suburbanites often preferred for their idealized landscape. Later observers have used "painterly" and "picturesque."[24]

The Romantic Suburb was the controlling image behind C. A. Petersen's English cottage. Despite its name, however, it was not conditioned by exacting references to historical antecedents. Although Petersen referred to the English cottage as an expression of an English building tradition, he understood that tradition to mean an exemplary craftsmanship and restriction to the use of brown and green. "Any one-story building can be called a cottage," he stated. Petersen doubtless was acquainted with some of the Cotswold cottages (which popularly connoted "cottage" in the 1920s) by the Tuileries Brochures advertising the products of Ludowici-Celadon.[25] But Petersen was exposed more frequently to the nationally homogeneous suburbs that sprang up at the very time he was traveling through the major eastern cities for the Gulf Oil Company before he came to Pure. Petersen's design replicated no historical cottage. Instead, it was a creative adaption of his Kenmore station into a Cotswold-like cottage for the Romantic Suburb.

FIGURE 6.6 An English Cottage in Monroe, Wisconsin.

Pure had not specified the type of residential neighborhood into which the company's new sign was to be accepted. Petersen himself assumed the Romantic Suburb definition. He had in mind neither of the two Indianapolis neighborhoods where Pure built the first English cottage prototypes in 1927. Both of those neighborhoods were comprised of simple frame houses with neoclassical details built around the turn of the century. Each filled its lot almost completely. The English cottage stood out boldly in these landscapes (see Fig. 6.6).[26]

The place Petersen did have in mind was the Minneapolis suburb of Wayzata, whose character he described at the time as a place of "natural beauty" populated by "the wealthier class of people from Minneapolis who were building handsome mansions." He confirmed the propriety of his design for such a neighborhood by the fact that a new oil bulk plant masked by an English cottage theme was well received there.[27]

Petersen not only articulated the often unspoken upper-middle-class assumptions of Romantic Suburbs, but he also masterfully tapped the domestic urges beneath them. His descriptions for the English cottage were nearly the same as those used by proponents of suburban housing: "quaint charm," "warmth," and a "homey appearance."[28] He decoded the

THE GAS STATION IN AMERICA

FIGURE 6.7 Detailed line drawing by C. A. Petersen.

FIGURE 6.9 Detailed line drawing by
C. A. Petersen.

FIGURE 6.8 Detailed line drawing by
C. A. Petersen.

elements of the romantic suburban house and, in support of his ideas, represented them in drawings with legends. Doorways made attractive with steps, handrails, bracket-supported hoods, picture windows, and even shuttered windows with flower boxes cued domesticity, according to Petersen. His legends candidly disclosed the commercial advantages for Pure Oil (see Figs. 6.7, 6.8, and 6.9).

According to folklorist Henry Glassie, the tendency for expressions of popular culture to become national norms can be attributed to "efficient synchronization" of society's arbiters of taste, its economic, religious, and governmental institutions. In the case of the English cottage, the synchronization was the product of honest aesthetic preference. Petersen said he chose the English tradition for Pure's station not only because that tradition's ubiquity in America would help ensure the station's acceptance throughout the nation, but also because that tradition was the most beautiful and the oldest, given America's origins. The Romantic Suburb was an *idée fixe* with Petersen. The endless search for Revival architecture embodied in what he labeled an "exclusive suburban area" jealously guarded by village fathers were conditions for which Petersen admitted a preference even fifty years after he designed the English cottage.[29]

Petersen and Henry Dawes were in total agreement in their profit calculations as well as personal sentiment for the Romantic Suburb. Petersen made no changes in his original design before presenting it to Henry Dawes, the sole judge. In keeping with the practice of the time, Petersen painted his design in watercolors for presentation to his boss. "When I showed my cottage design to President Dawes, his first words were 'This is exactly what I had in mind.'" He awarded Petersen a $750 check and, to underscore his personal approval, noted that the check was against his personal account, not the company's. In August 1927, Pure publicly announced adoption of the English cottage for its corporate sign along the roadside.[30]

Henry Dawes's reverence of the Romantic Suburb was demonstrated not only by his instant and vigorous approval of the English cottage. The attributes of that idealized landscape were present in the house and city in which he had chosen to live. Dawes's Evanston, Illinois, house was a massive two-story neoclassical mansion created for him in 1913 by Ernest Mayo, who specialized in residential architecture for Chicago's North Shore elite.[31] Evanston's staunch defense of the freestanding home for the suburban nuclear family against the perceived threat of multifamily apartments resulted in 1921 in the passage of Illinois's first municipal zoning ordinance and generated self-assigned accolades as the "gem suburb" and the "City of Homes."[32]

Dawes's aesthetic preference was an expression of his personality. Leonard K. Eaton's description of the average client of conservative architecture in contrast with the average client of innovative architecture in the early twentieth century coincides remarkably with the personality of Henry M. Dawes. Like other aesthetic conservatives, Dawes was an extrovert, not deeply contemplative yet quite clever, especially in business. Indeed, restructuring Pure Oil to win greater profit was Dawes's driving ambition for the last forty years of his life. This ardently competitive business ambition nonetheless was to increase existing consumption patterns. Like other aesthetic conservatives he was born to wealth and college educated. His family's distinguished achievements in public offices, however, marked Dawes as exceptional among his fellow conservatives. He did more than vote Republican and give money to the Grand Old Party. Not only did Henry hold an important financial appointment in the Harding administration, but his brother, Charles G. Dawes, was vice-president in the Coolidge administration. Leisure was social, not private, for aesthetic conservatives. Dawes's membership in several clubs and golfing fit the elite pattern as did his singular disregard for highly individualized forms of expression, such as music or poetry. His conservative taste did not run to the desire for contemporary art.[33]

Development of the English Cottage

Once conceived and approved, implementation of Pure's new gasoline station style was comparatively effortless. Petersen directed assistants in the creation of plans for the necessary stations of different sizes, which utilized different building materials.[34] Meanwhile, he labored alone on the three drawings of the stations to ensure that the precious essence of the adopted building-as-sign was rendered perfectly in the

FIGURE 6.10 In the late 1930s with the adoption of larger, flat-roofed buildings, Pure Oil designers used various devices to simulate the steeply pitched roof of the English Cottage.

FIGURE 6.11 Providing shade, canopies typified Pure Oil stations across the South. (*Source: Pure Oil News* 21 [November 1938]: 24.)

several variations. Thereafter, changes were made, but the essence of its dual commercial and cultural message was kept: the architectural display of Pure's blue and white colors and the image of a home in the Romantic Suburb. To wring the fullest profit from the sign, it was protected, perfected, and adapted. Eventually the sign was revered. It became a popular icon.

Pure protected an artifact at first. The English cottage was patented to prevent its unauthorized use. Petersen's department stipulated the features that had to be removed when a station was withdrawn from the Pure chain. Pure's dealers were denied improvisations in their stations. For twenty-five years, Pure adapted its building-as-sign to meet various demands: to economize, to fit different geographical regions, to reflect changes in domestic architecture, and to react to the buildings of competitors. Petersen eventually designed many different variations (see Figs. 6.10, 6.11, and 6.12).[35]

The strongest opposition came from Pure's affiliates who did not believe the Romantic Suburb was the best image to translate into a sign. A local norm prevailed in Florida. Immigrants poured into Florida in the 1920s and the state's multiplying gasoline stations competed fiercely. During the resulting building boom, the immigrants abandoned the styles they had preferred elsewhere for the local vernacular, the Spanish style. Pure's affiliate, the Seaboard Oil Company, was convinced its stations should follow the taste in popular domestic architecture and ordered Petersen to design a series of stations in the Spanish style despite his preference for the English cottage.[36]

Modernism also began to challenge the prevailing revivalism. Then it

FIGURE 6.12 This station of the late 1930s followed the trend toward abstraction found in American domestic housing of the period. The chimneys were recessed into the plane of the gable and the bay window was enlarged. (*Source: Pure Oil News* 29 [December 1946]: 8.)

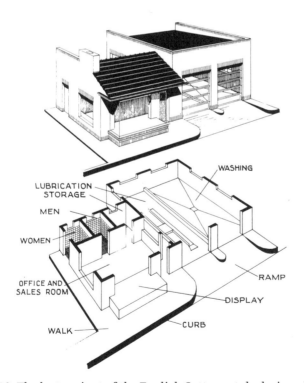

FIGURE 6.13 The last variant of the English Cottage style designed in 1946 produced a close approximation of the oblong box. The form permitted Pure Oil to build on its established image while reaching out to embrace modernism.

FIGURE 6.14 Pure Oil's modern oblong box dominated the covers of the company's road maps in the 1950s.

totally subsumed the picturesque (see Figs. 6.13 and 6.14). The reformers' attack was twofold. Their aesthetic of functionalism held that a gasoline station should look like a gasoline station instead of being disguised in residential terms. The relative simplicity of a station in the Modern mode was arguably cheaper to build than those in the Revival style, where detailing was necessary to suggest that stations were individually crafted. Walter Dorwin Teague's designs for Texaco are today perhaps the most frequently recalled expressions of modernism in 1930s and 1940s gasoline stations (see Figs. 1.3 [p. 3] and 5.20 [p. 147]. That Pure and Texaco could profit simultaneously from diametrically opposed images in station architecture confirms the great breadth of consumer taste.

Although Petersen and, accordingly, Pure while he was its chief designer never lost their emotional preference for the suburban image in gasoline stations, Petersen accepted modernism for gas stations on the grounds of economy in the 1950s. This new freedom from historical dependence did not reflect his conversion to functionalism. Rather, it echoed the continued facility of an architect trained in the various Revival styles to work in any one of them without exclusive commitment. To Petersen each style was merely applied ornament. He did not work from a central integrating theory to drive a dictated sense of beauty as did the modernists in creating quite literally a new style.[37] Petersen's brilliant decoding of suburban iconography in the 1920s left him on the verge of aesthetic cynicism by the 1950s. His intellectual path suggests a linkage to later functionalists who insisted that good design should not spring from any aesthetic preconception, but only from technical consideration.[38] Ironically, this pretended objectivity may have been the aesthetic recourse of those numbed earlier by the long battle of the styles.

Pure was determined to fix its sign firmly in the marketplace. First, Pure equated the sign with the popular image of house by pursuing a complementary maintenance program. As a result, the building-as-sign became an entire landscape unit of which the station was one part. Planting flowers, grass, and hedges was encouraged to accent the impression of the domestic refuge. Dawes himself endorsed the need for landscaping by contributing to the *Pure Oil News* photographs of an exemplary station he had seen on vacation.[39]

Clean stations were a strategy to increase business. But the degree to which Pure exhorted its dealers to keep their stations clean suggests that Pure shared the cultural conviction that cleanliness was its own reward. Cleanliness certainly meant purity at Pure. Clean toilets were the single most important tactic in the cleanliness strategy. The *Pure Oil News* admonished that "in these days of an educated public alarmed against venereal diseases, it is not going to be the brand of oil and gasoline the automobilist thinks of as he approaches a station, but, judging from the exterior of that station, what kind of toilet might be inside it."[40] Pure also demanded that everything at the stations be kept in place. Parts and tools lying around the station lot were branded as junk. Advertising signs were to be simple and few, not only to avoid confusing customers but to reinforce the message that Pure stations were neat houses.[41] Dealers who achieved Pure's standards were praised like obedient housekeepers. Housekeeping was perceived as a female chore and the house organ proudly recorded cases in which females specifically approved the company's maintenance policies.[42]

Advertising dictated that the sign be extended beyond its original application, that it refer not only to other Pure stations but to Pure itself. Thus, a one-twelfth diorama of an English cottage occupying a triangular corner lot was displayed in the reception room of the corporate headquarters (see Fig. 5.10, p. 139). Here also was an instinctive and literal reinforcement of the Anglo-American version of territoriality, the private home on the private lot separable from all others.[43]

Pure also easily integrated the sign with the image from which it had been derived. The company sold birdhouses and radios fashioned as English cottages. Petersen boasted that "these birdhouses found their way into exclusive surroundings which had not yet been invaded by competitive advertisers." The radios were intended by Petersen to get the consumer's attention at home in the evenings. Supply kept up with demand. Both items were big sellers.[44]

Pure wove its image tightly into the fabric of popular domestic thinking. Corresponding need felt for the symbolic values of the corporate image was reflected in the variety and depth of popular enthusiasm for it. In the process of applying the sign to more than Pure's gasoline stations it developed an identity independent of the original function. It began to be revered in its own right when a half-size replica of the English cottage with a child's lounge inside was placed in the Pure exhibit at the Century of Progress in 1933. Children and adults flocked to it. After the 1934 exposition closed, Gimbel Brothers' Department Store in Philadelphia borrowed the model to display in the toy section and use for an hourly

FIGURE 6.15 The Union Oil design vocabulary came to the fore when that firm absorbed Pure Oil in the 1960s.

midget show that Christmas. Crowds were so large that they disrupted sales and forced rescheduling the performances to one every two hours. This living dollhouse fired the public imagination, causing several state fairs and other public exhibitions to request its use.[45]

The English cottage became an icon. Pure attempted to encourage other automobile-related businesses, automobile dealerships and motel chains, for example, to adopt elements of the sign. A neighbor of Petersen's asked him to design a house like the English cottage, but the company never promoted its use for actual residences. Pure was satisfied when the sign fulfilled the two purposes for which it had been created, and proudly chronicled the cases in which the design was welcomed in residential neighborhoods. By 1940 the company decided that its corporate image based on the English cottage was firmly fixed in wide acceptance.[46]

The English cottage was used by Pure as long as Dawes and Petersen controlled the design process. Dawes died in 1952 and Petersen retired from Pure five years later. The new managers replaced his picturesque design when they ordered a new corporate sign by the roadside in a clearly Modern mode.[47] Of course, the Pure Oil signature disappeared totally from the roadside when the company was merged with Union Oil in the 1960s (see Fig. 6.15).

The interplay of influences determining the look of the ubiquitous gasoline station in the American landscape was quite rich. Calculations of profit from a matrix of factors determined the look of gasoline stations company to company. Carlos B. Dawes's deliberate search for an ideal building-as-sign for Pure Oil provides an example of the decisionmaking process early in the history of the gasoline station. At one level Dawes's "Standardization" idea functioned within Pure Oil to gather all the information accumulated at various places within the company relevant to station design. Low unit construction cost and efficient operation were uncontroverted tenets. Station layout, materials, equipment, and landscaping were complex considerations. But it was the overall impression of the ensemble, and especially the architecture of the station building, that drove the decisionmaking process. Carlos's advice to adapt the incumbent station architecture was rejected. Henry M. Dawes thought it unlikely to impress the consumer Pure Oil wished to target. The image of cool classicism conveyed by the incumbent architecture failed to find a sympathetic chord in Henry's personality.

Personality and social class sympathies quickly decided the issue. With the hiring of C. A. Petersen, who had already designed one gasoline station in the suburban mode, Henry M. Dawes found a kindred spirit. Petersen was given free rein to plumb the image of the Romantic Suburb. Although the English cottage was manipulated in the following thirty years, the upper-middle-class aspiration inherent in the Romantic Suburb remained Pure's essential image along the roadside so long as Dawes and Petersen were respectively the corporate patron and architect.

Recent scholarship has emphasized class underlying the popularity of the suburban image in residential architecture of the 1920s. In fact, class coincided with personality to make the English cottage the final choice for Pure. But it remains unknown whether personality influenced class or vice versa. As Elizabeth M. Douvan warns, the historian is severely hampered by the inability to establish comprehensive data on control groups to test any hypothesis about the relative weight of class and personality.[48] Yet an exhaustive search through corporate archives and interviews with participants (even though the look be retrospective) can at least outline basic issues. Various sources taken together yield insight by comparison and contrast. A synthesis is not only desirable but necessary, for corporate archives are never "complete," and complementary oral sources obtained in retrospection are always slanted by the current needs of the questioner.[49]

The same comprehensive search for sources should be undertaken to determine the respective role of consumer and entrepreneur in the development of gasoline station image. Does synchronization adequately describe the relationship of popular taste and private profit? More recent scholarship invites investigation of the assumption that roadside architecture is the product of a general popular demand undifferentiated by social class or the size of an entrepreneur's intended market. Did big entrepreneurs foist their taste on the marketplace? Furthermore, it has been recommended that future roadside scholarship distinguish between big and small entrepreneurs with the implication that small entrepreneurs may not have forced their tastes on the consumer.[50] The next chapter will deal with the small entrepreneur.

Who do entrepreneurs and corporate architects satisfy with their apparently objective studies constructing saleable images? Themselves or the consumer? In the case of Pure Oil it is clear the English cottage was

Henry M. Dawes's personal icon, albeit one that could potentially be expected to become a popular icon in the late 1920s and early 1930s. Personal fantasies have been writ large on the landscape in formulating the American roadside.

Values likely changed as time passed. Did the elitist image of the English cottage eventually appeal to a too narrow segment of the market to survive America's increasing mass automobility? Early automobile manufacturers produced the cars they wanted to drive. Was the English cottage, for example, the architectural equivalent of Duesenbergs, the Cords, or the long-vanished Lozier automobile whose price was advertised as the highest average of any car and its clientele's last consideration?[51] Were the architectural modernists eventually closer than the revivalists to a later mass instinct for utility before beauty? Was the English cottage eventually a fossil on the landscape sustained only by its elitist creators and no longer cherished as a popular icon? Did Pure's successor, Unocal, more correctly gauge the utilitarian nature of the later mass market by emphasizing truckstops and modern-style gasoline stations?

7

Gas Station Design – The Small Entrepreneur

When consumers purchased products that were hand-made by local craftsmen and/or sold in locally owned stores, consumer satisfaction tended to be higher, or so holds consumer lore as a kind of nostalgic mythology. Accordingly, it has been with the advent of mass-produced and mass-marketed products that tension has undermined the relationship between buyers and sellers. Local producers and businessmen seemed neighbors and still do. Corporations do not. Scale makes a difference to consumers and entrepreneurs alike, it is said.

The gasoline station was the essential point of contact between oil corporations and consumers. How did business size, actual or intended, influence the design of stations? Full analysis of the American gasoline station demands attention to the small as well as the large entrepreneurs. Having described the design process of a large corporation, the Pure Oil Company, we now focus on the design imperatives of two regional jobbers. Small companies also pursued place-product-packaging, out of self-defense if nothing else. That is, small entrepreneurs were also faced with creating a distinctive presence in landscape as a means of creating brand loyalty if only over limited trade areas. Especially in the depressed economy of the 1930s, when petroleum supply far outstripped demand, small entrepreneurs stressed customer satisfaction. They presented themselves as local producers and as neighbors, and marketed product and service reliability accordingly. They pretended to be everything that the large, impersonal corporations were not.

In this chapter we look at the Barkhausen Oil Company of Green Bay, Wisconsin, of the 1920s, and the Quality Oil Company of Winston-Salem, North Carolina, of the 1930s, both independent jobbers, that is, locally owned businesses that distributed petroleum products received from corporate refineries or marine terminals.[1]

Independent jobbers seem to have built their business styles more around local civic duties, thus to engender local support in the face of intensive competition from large chains. Independent jobbers were no less profit-minded than their large corporate counterparts. Their hallmarks as terse, self-made men with pride in business and commitment to civic duty only reflected more on local rather than national arenas. One jobber in St. Joseph, Michigan, could brag, "At one time [I] was a member of the St. Joseph Common Council, interested in all civic matters. Was president of several corporations and at the present time, still fighting for a living."[2] Civic pride was rarely valued sufficiently to dictate truly expensive and fully innovative gasoline station architecture. But architecture was valued as a means of making local gasoline stations distinguishable from those of the national giants.

Both Barkhausen and Quality Oil exemplify the entrepreneur's keen eye on the "bottom line." Image and its tactic—gasoline station architecture—figure into their thinking but not without supervening financial considerations. Good architecture results but not for its own sake, although both jobbers mentioned do deviate from the norm in that the architecture of their gasoline stations is, admittedly, among the most noted by historians. Both Barkhausen and Quality Oil owned gasoline stations and sold petroleum products to other similarly "branded outlets," forming local chains. How important were national trends in gasoline station design—national trends in place-product-packaging—in forming these chains? How free to develop truly local expressions were these entrepreneurs? To what extent were they merely reactive as opposed to innovative?

Barkhausen Oil and Allied Independents

Henry A. Barkhausen, more commonly known to the public as H. A. Barkhausen, was born in Westphalia, Germany, and moved to the United States in 1870. Within a decade he settled in Green Bay, Wisconsin, because of the large number of fellow countrymen in an area offering economic opportunities. Participation in community was no less important than the quest for a suitable income. Barkhausen's musical talent found him work first in a music store but his business skills led him into partnership as a grocer. It was in 1886, however, that he joined a new partner in the coal and oil business. By 1894 he was supplying gasoline from the area's first gasoline storage tank. By 1907, H. A. owned Barkhausen Brick and Tile Works, Barkhausen Coal and Wood, and the Barkhausen Oil Company. His first gasoline stations were utilitarian structures at Menominee, Michigan, site of his gasoline storage tank, and Sturgeon Bay, Wisconsin. Access to supply and position on the busiest streets were his earliest locational rationales. S. D. Hastings, senior and junior, were hired respectively as vice-president and secretary-treasurer for the new firm.[3]

Following Barkhausen's death in 1917, the Hastingses extended the

FIGURE 7.1 The Foeller, Schober, and Stephenson–designed gasoline station at the Walnut Street bridge in Green Bay, Wisconsin, circa 1922. Gasoline was sold under the local Imperial brand.

business. By 1922 Barkhausen retailed gasoline from ten garages owned by others, and from three company stations. The Hastingses calculated no advantage in aesthetics at first and their outlets were strictly utilitarian.[4] Not until 1922 did they open their first designed filling station. It was located in Green Bay on Walnut Street at the bridge (see Fig. 7.1), and the *Press-Gazette,* that city's only newspaper, noted:

> The day when a filling station was looked upon as a necessary evil, an unsightly object that detracted from any neighborhood, is past. Many persons crossing the Walnut Street bridge have paid a tribute to the new Barkhausen oil station at the west end of the bridge. The style is something unusual and altogether pleasing. It is of stucco, finished with red brick. Every detail shows the care that was put into its design and construction by the Ludolf M. Hansen Company.[5]

Personal aesthetics, evoked by calculations of market advantage, produced this landmark. Conformity with civic values thereafter resulted in a succession of stations with strong residential imagery. Green Bay's most prestigious architectural firm provided the designs. It is to the intricate interworkings of personal taste and profit calculation in the context of local civic values that Barkhausen Oil's gasoline station designs take meaning.

Boosterism was the civic value system that grew in small towns from the tension-torn 1920s. Although the 1920 census seemed to declare that the nation had become big-city urban,[6] self-styled small town and small city boosters were defensive. Against the impression of the big city as impersonal, sinful, rent by contending self-interests, and lacking a common identity, small town defenders contrasted their place as idyllic in its friendly, law-abiding, calm, and cohesive life style. Conformity was urgent and could be achieved by "hustle" and "pep," favorite booster words. Self-doubt, however, lurked not far beneath the booster's happy-go-lucky and hard-working demeanor. Countless philanthropic campaigns and ardent declarations of optimism were summarized in the counsel to boost, not knock.[7] Service clubs such as Rotary, Kiwanis, and Lions leaped in membership in the 1920s. The rollicking good fellowship of their weekly luncheons were stages to praise businessmen as social servants and launch programs for community service.[8] As boosterism revealed in Muncie, Indiana, subject of Robert and Helen Lynd's classic study of small city life in the 1920s, mass activities were emphasized as if to submerge individual doubts and differences. Unquestioning civic allegiance was promoted through participation in the Chamber of Commerce, rooting for the most prominent local sports team, and informal peer pressure against social criticism. A constant succession of official celebrations, such as "Own Your Own Home Day," indoctrinated an uncertain public. Support for local merchants versus automobiling to shop in bigger and distant markets was encouraged as a way to reinvest in the entire community. Businessmen joined not an organization but a local network.[9] Thus, boosterism was not the businessman's clever strategy to profit; rather, it was an expression of his fear that his entire way of life would end if conditions changed.

The Association of Commerce and the *Press-Gazette* were the mainspring of boosterism in Green Bay. Welcome allies were acquired in professional baseball and football teams. A three-day civic homecoming celebration in August 1921 was praised by the newspaper because it "aroused a keener affection for Green Bay and advertised it favorably," despite poor attendance. The characteristic search for a unifying purpose was made the subject of a city-wide contest for a slogan later in the year. The choice of "Gateway to the Great Waterway" reflected boosterism's strong financial overtones. Contests for a city song and logo followed quickly in early 1922. February 19 to 26 was officially designated Booster Week.[10]

Green Bay intended to become no less than northeast Wisconsin's primary trading center. Its merchants annually sponsored the Northeast Wisconsin State Fair, launched an annual industrial exposition in 1921, and regularly held special sales. In 1925, out-of-state automobile tourists, lured by northern Wisconsin's outdoor resorts, brought an estimated $110,000,000 to the region. The completed highway linking Green Bay to St. Louis in 1922 was promoted as "the longest street in the world." Green Bay boosters began to talk in 1924 of adding a winter sports season to become the "American St. Moritz." The new construction in the central business district between 1921 and 1925 was another sign of civic vitality. The YMCA, a city auditorium, a hotel, and a newspaper plant were constructed.[11]

As in other cities, suburbia offered the landscape in which Green Bay's boosters sought to resolve urban tensions. Its boosters celebrated suburban environments combining pastoral scenery with a contemporary home on the edge of a great city. They shared in the national ethic that with every family caring for its own home whole cities would be uplifted. They held congested dwellings responsible for the high crime rates of urban areas. Country living was thought conducive of "independence, competence, and release from worry." They wanted residential areas to sport shade trees and gardens in the belief that landscaping could weave the countryside into the city to outweigh its "artificial marvels." The individually owned home for the nuclear family was the healthiest setting for child rearing and guaranteed that the citizen would "feel more self-assurant, more confident, and more respectable."[12]

Zoning was the primary device Green Bay's boosters used to build their city of pastoral homes. Public discussion of zoning to separate residential and commercial areas began in 1922. Fear of commercial blight grew simultaneously. The Women's Club persuaded local merchants to remove their signs along a five-mile stretch of highway southward toward Chicago in late 1923, and joined a national campaign to regulate roadside billboards. Automobile-related businesses and grocery stores had become sources of substantial public frustration by 1925. The mayor appealed for suspension of unresolved issues in order to enact quickly a proposed ordinance against the construction of "oil stations and similar objectionable buildings in residential districts." Within ten days the city council had omitted one stage of public review to hasten enactment of the city's first zoning ordinance for which the newspaper noted public sentiment had suddenly become strong.[13]

Barkhausen Oil's father-and-son team, the Hastingses, were key boosters. Both worked on a variety of service projects, including the formation of the Green Bay Motor Club and the committee to raise an endowment for families whose income-producers were killed in World War I.[14] Residential imagery, a product of local boosterism, satisfied the need for conformity in the locally owned Barkhausen gasoline stations. The Hastingses' personal preferences as boosters for gasoline stations in the residential mode coincided with their business calculations. They adopted this image as a symbol of their company's long-standing involvement with Green Bay and shared civic faith in the present as well as (they hoped) through claims of local pride to gain a competitive edge on their major rival, Standard Oil of Indiana. Barkhausen emphasized its individuality by advertising Liberty and Imperial petroleum products and its standing as an "independent."[15] Descendant companies of the giant Standard group remained publicly suspect despite the dissolution of the trust. Standard Oil of Indiana attempted to project conformity by advertising its sense of social responsibility and bigness as a guarantee of quality.[16]

FIGURE 7.2 Gasoline station at Walnut and Oakland streets in Green Bay, Wisconsin, circa 1926.

Standard Oil's public image did not improve with time as it became the object of Wisconsin's new marketing act against rebates. The trust's pricing policies caused two sensational national attacks in 1923, including the federal investigation led by the Committee on Manufacturers whose chairman was a renowned enemy of monopoly, Wisconsin's Sen. Robert La Follette. Standard's voluntary removal of roadside signs in the West did earn congratulations from local boosters and its attempt to provide visually pleasing stations earned their tacit consent.[17]

Standard ran afoul of Green Bay boosters on the issue of civic responsiveness inside Green Bay. A minor competitor fired public resentment by locating a station dangerously close to a school in 1924. One of Standard's own stations became the only obstacle to fulfillment of the city plan for a four-block civic area in downtown Green Bay a month later. A special committee that included representatives of all the service clubs appealed unsuccessfully to Standard for the station's relocation. Barkhausen then began advertising its civic responsiveness. The two gasoline stations Barkhausen commissioned in 1924 were visual variants on that strategy. The last Green Bay station, designed on the eve of the zoning ordinance's enactment, was the most houselike (see Fig. 7.2). Within two years station design became one of Barkhausen's main advertising themes: "You Can Distinguish Barkhausen's Beautiful Service Stations. They Are Emphatically Different."[18]

Henry A. Foeller, whose architectural firm the Hastingses commis-

FIGURE 7.3 Racine, Wisconsin, site before construction of a Foeller, Schober, and Stephenson–designed gasoline station.

sioned for these stations, espoused boosterism's faith in unlimited economic expansion and the suburban aesthetic. He overcame considerable opposition as chairman of the city planning commission to insure that beauty was a leading consideration in the design of the Main Street bridge, the city's most expensive project of the early twenties. He guided the zoning ordinance through three years of discussion to enactment. His enthusiasm for flower gardens won him city-wide praise. He was also a member of the booster establishment.[19]

Clarence O. Jahn, the architect of all but the first of the Barkhausen stations, was doubtless influenced by the ardent boosterism of his boss when designing the Barkhausen stations. Jahn had been exposed to the full range of the popular picturesque style selected for the houses designed by Foeller, Schober, and Stephenson in the early 1920s.[20] He easily transferred this style to the design of the gasoline stations assigned him. Jahn further complemented the residential feeling of his designs by the regular inclusion of plantings. Jahn's work for Barkhausen Oil ended in 1924 and further commissions were precluded with the younger Hastings's death in a fire, one of Green Bay's worst, at the bulk plant in 1929. With subsequent purchase by Socony-Vacuum, that corporation introduced its own architecture in augmenting the Barkhausen chain.[21]

Jahn continued to design stations for other Wisconsin gasoline companies: Waupan Oil Company of Waupan (1924), Central Development Company of Madison (1924), Wisconsin Oil Corporation of Walworth

FIGURE 7.4 The Bratt and Lang Oil Company gasoline station constructed on the Racine, Wisconsin, site pictured above.

(1925), Pendergast Oil Company of Darien and Lake Geneva (1925), Bratt and Lang Oil Company of Racine (1926), and Hansen Oil Company of Burlington (1927). All the owners were members of a loose-knit group of independent petroleum dealers for whom the junior Hastings of Barkhausen was one of the chief coalescing forces prior to formation of the Wisconsin Independent Oil Jobbers Association in 1926. Their esteem for Hastings's business sense was probably a leading cause for their demand of Jahn's designs. Their lack of specific instructions to Jahn likely reflected a tacit acceptance of the qualities in his designs for Barkhausen. The independent jobbers' desire for individually designed stations was one way Wisconsin's independent dealers responded to the fierce competition with the larger companies which relied on uniformity in their station designs.[22]

Jahn's designs satisfied the independents' demand for unique designs while retaining variations on the theme of the picturesque house. His perfection of a questionnaire to retrieve information about prospective sites and his tendency to wrestle in the design process more with such factors as access, safety codes, and service features strongly suggest that Jahn closed the question of building styles after the design for the Green Bay location in early 1924. Jahn's later stations looked newer than the residential neighborhoods with which they were intended to harmonize (see Figs. 7.3 and 7.4). Sensitive adaptations had given way to a formula similar to the one C. A. Petersen developed for Pure. Wide public approval for Jahn's provincially conceived gas station designs

FIGURE 7.5 The introductory advertisement for Joe H. Glenn's Quality Oil Company. (*Source:* Winston-Salem *Journal and Sentinel,* June 15, 1930, p. 3A.)

also demonstrates that conformity to suburban imagery along the roadside was not restricted to those with grand entrepreneurial ambitions.[23]

Quality Oil Company

A captured market in the depressed economy of the 1930s brought forth a different response from Shell Oil's jobber in Winston-Salem, North Carolina, the Quality Oil Company. Shell Eastern Petroleum Products officially opened in Boston on April 19, 1929, and used various means to wedge into the competitive eastern seaboard market. Principally, Shell Eastern purchased the services of existing small jobbers with chains of existing stations and agreed not to open company stations where converted jobbers agreed to sell only Shell. Not only did this strategy spare capital from new construction but it benefited from cooptation of existing reputations rooted in local credibility. With the onset of the Depression in 1930, Shell additionally attempted to overcome decreased sales by increasing the number of outlets in the East and introducing products previously calculated as marginal in profit. In order, New England, New York, Baltimore, and then the Carolinas became the focus of Shell Eastern's expansive strategy.[24]

Winston-Salem had experienced the same rapid proliferation of gasoline outlets and their gradual concentration in the hands of a few big companies as had many American cities in the 1920s, when Shell undertook its strategy to enter the Winston-Salem market in 1929. Only three outlets were identifiable as filling stations in 1920 and none advertised branded products in the 1921 city directory, although numerous gasoline outlets likely existed at garages or stores whose primary business did not justify distinction as filling stations in the same directory. There were seventeen branded filling stations five years later: Gulf had four; Red Star Texaco had eight; and Standard had five. But the twenty-five unbranded stations still outnumbered the growing corporations and the largest number of unbranded stations owned by a company were the four each of the Pilot Oil Company and Railroad Jones. The most significant change by the start of 1929 was the parity Standard achieved with Railroad Jones by each owning seven filling stations.[25]

Two general trends in North Carolina coincided with Shell's expansion to influence filling station style. One was the state's especially strong backlash against the erosion of local businesses underlying the state's antichain-store legislation. In September 1929, the *Winston-Salem Journal* reported $51,695 in state revenue collected since July 1 for the $50 levied on every store in a chain after the first and that larger chains paid under protest pending a decision by the state Supreme Court.[26] A Southern organization of independent grocers was extended in October 1929 to Winston-Salem, and a prominent local businessman became its head. Its explicit purposes were to enable local grocers to compete in price and product quality against chain stores. Each of the local member organizations, such as Winston-Salem's, retained the right to dictate its own policies, just as the store members of the respective groups preserved their individuality. Common identity was to be achieved through advertising under a single name despite the retention of each member's distinctive store architecture and service to an established neighborhood market.[27] Even though the implications for expanding corporate oil companies were not expressed in the pages of Winston-Salem's press, antichain-store legislation alarmed the petroleum industry throughout the year. By early 1930, chain-store resentment had reached "astonishing proportions," reported the *National Petroleum News*.[28]

Another consideration of a North Carolina oil jobber would have likely been the movement to end commercialism's roadside blight and direct it instead toward roadside beautification. North Carolina was a special target of Elizabeth Boyd Lawton, the well-placed leader of the roadside beautification movement who directed a survey of abuses and proposed remedies. Cheap stations without discriminating taste and overlarge billboards or numerous little signs obscuring scenic views, as well as trees and other flora torn out for highway development, constituted problems in Lawton's mind. She lectured various groups throughout North Carolina and enlisted support for the survey from the state's departments for highways and conservation and development. Findings were published in 1930.[29]

Although Lawton's concern was chiefly rural, the bounds of commercialism also were being set inside Winston-Salem. An early step toward adoption in December 1930 of a comprehensive zoning map was taken in December 1929 with an ordinance prescribing the location of filling stations to prevent traffic congestion and to regulate proximity to public schools and other filling stations, driveway widths, and reconstruction of sidewalks lowered for driveways.[30] Aesthetics was not at issue but Winston-Salem's petroleum entrepreneurs were on notice that their private concerns had public limitations, nonetheless.

Thus, new filling stations for an ambitious entrepreneur had to satisfy a complex set of public and private, formal and informal requirements. Zoning dictated location. Roadside beautification loomed as a potential threat to any station designed without heed of the city's or state's landscape arbiters. At the same time, stiff competition required a bold strategy.

Shell entered the Winston-Salem market amid these crosscurrents on December 7, 1929. Fred W. Bonney and Walter H. Leonard opened their Shell-branded Quality Oil Company station on the corner of Northwest Boulevard and Reynolda Road. Based on the drawing that accompanied the introductory advertisement, the station was a common type, a flat-roofed brick office with flat-roofed canopy supported by brick pillars. The advertisement's appeal was to a "New 100% Service Station" where the motorists could have their cars refueled and greased in one place and the quality of service was implied by the "modern" look of the building, as a congratulating fellow merchant termed the architecture.[31] Shell affiliation was not a prominent part of the initial advertisement, perhaps to abate potential backlash against corporate invasion.

Competition increased within a month and it increased the emphasis of corporate identification by color. Texaco, which used its five-pointed red star logo in the name "Red Star Filling Stations," opened a seventh station on January 4, 1930. On the same day, Railroad Jones, the unbranded dealer with the city's most filling stations, announced his conversion to Pure by reference to its colors: "Now—It's The Blue and White Stations for Quality." Jones's stations were ordinary brick buildings with canopies.[32] Place-product-packaging as yet, however, lacked special architecture in Winston-Salem. While there is no evidence that Texaco built a unique style, it did in March 1930 leap ahead of all competitors by opening two additional stations prominently advertised as Red Star stations.[33]

The other big competitors utilized more balanced appeals in newspaper advertising. American Oil, Gulf, and Standard Oil of New Jersey attempted to verify their products' quality by reference to various scientific tests and endorsements. Gulf and Jersey Standard also introduced a gasoline claimed to be better and at a lower price.[34] Gulf did try to teach motorists to look for its orange disc signs and American and Jersey Standard similarly inserted pictures of logos carried on fuel pump globes.[35] These appeals, however, were frequently undermined by the other appeals in given advertisements, and were almost never the only or major appeal of a single advertisement.

The relative lack of visual cuing by corporate color and shape is consistent with national trends. A study of entrepreneurial and consumer appeal, rare for its public disclosure, was made for the S. F. Bowser and Company, renowned manufacturer of gasoline pumps, and appeared in 1928 in the *National Petroleum News*. Advertising and station appearance were the two least important appeals, according to motorists. Advertising was the least important calculation and station appearance was the third lowest calculation for companies, according to the report. Brand was the most important factor to motorists and station location was the most important to the companies.[36] But these were the relative weight of factors for established entrepreneurs and captive customers.

New owners brought new capital and new advertising to Quality Oil Company at the start of 1930. Fred Bonney and Walter Leonard had managed to stay in business with one station but lacked sufficient capital to gain a larger part of the Winston-Salem market. In March, Bonney quit Quality and Joe H. Glenn, Jr., a 29-year-old scion of a prominent local business family and heir to a substantial sum,[37] assumed Bonney's place as head of Shell's jobbership in Winston-Salem. However, Glenn, untrammeled by precedent, refused to expand using Quality's conventional building, and undertook a novel advertising approach: the seashell filling station.

The seashell was twenty feet at the widest point in its oval perimeter and sixteen feet high, forming the centerpiece of a landscape ensemble that also included service bays, driveways, gasoline pumps, and signs on standards (see Fig. 7.5). The elasticity and durability of concrete was selected from available building materials to apply on a wood-and-wire frame to render a seashell complete with ribbing similar to Royal Dutch/Shell's international logo. The three-dimensional shell was painted corporate yellow with red letters spelling out "Shell" above the building entrance. This unmistakable corporate symbol also became a local landmark.[38]

Precise responsibility for the final design is uncertain. Fred W. Bonney may well have encouraged the concept, perhaps even after his withdrawal from Quality's management. He had been with Texaco before his brief involvement with Shell and it was Texaco's advertising that was the most oriented to corporate color and symbol in Winston-Salem newspaper advertising. Then, too, Walter H. Leonard, surviving manager from the first Quality Oil Company, may have gotten the idea from a friend traveling through Winston-Salem, according to his son.[39] What is certain is that it was with Joe H. Glenn Jr.'s management of Quality that the seashell concept was made into a filling station. Charles R. Johnson, Winston-Salem high school graduate (1926) and a draftsman at the Frank L. Blum Construction Company, received the assignment to prepare plans for the unusual building. Glenn probably selected Blum Construction for the difficult assignment because it was the city's best known building contractor.[40] Although the final design has been attributed to the "naive literalism" characteristic of much roadside architecture in the 1920s and 1930s, it can also be argued by reference to the shape alone to have been consistent with the era's trend among professional designers toward streamlining.[41]

FIGURE 7.6 The last "seashell" station built in Winston-Salem. (*Source:* Photo courtesy of the Quality Oil Company.)

No conscious design tradition—neither professional nor vernacular—can be proven to have been at work in Quality's seashell design. Glenn likely conceived the concept in order to arrest consumer attention in a stiff market and Blum Construction and its draftsman overcame the challenges of an unprecedented building to execute the concept. Quality Oil Company's unique seashell filling station comes as close as roadside scholarship (an enterprise often forced to rely on oral sources and newspapers in the absence of entrepreneur archives) can come to declare an instance of pure spontaneity. Glenn, Johnson, and Blum Construction helped create a tradition to which subsequent observers have attributed vernacular genius.

With the creation of seashell architecture, Quality Oil Company quickly adopted an assortment of complementary techniques to enhance its market. On June 4, 1930, the first seashell was opened on Burke Street in Glenn's mother's neighborhood and was advertised for its commitment to the community.[42] As "The First of Its Kind in the World" it put "Winston-Salem Again on Top"; here was intended gratification of local pride (see Fig. 7.5). The local newspaper reprinted the advertisement's assertion of uniqueness in its news pages.[43] A photograph of the station was placed at the top of the advertisement to help clinch public awareness.

Competition quickened. By the end of 1930 Texaco and Railroad Jones added three new stations and the American Oil Company purchased two local companies.[44] It is reasonable to suspect that Glenn filed a patent for his seashell design on July 24, 1930, to block potential mimics of his

FIGURE 7.7 A Quality gasoline station of the mid-1930s. (*Source:* Photo courtesy of the Quality Oil Company.)

company's architectural stratagem. Bert L. Bennett, a successful jobber in the city's prominent tobacco industry, actively joined his nephew as vice-president of Quality Oil Company and three more seashell filling stations were under construction.[45]

In search of economy, Quality accepted Burton Construction Company's lower bid to build the fifth station but superior workmanship caused Quality to return to the original contractor for the subsequent buildings.[46] Thus, three seashell stations were open by the end of 1930. A fourth was blocked in December because it violated the zoning ordinance and Quality itself suspended replication of the small seashell for a large building downtown which combined a station and tire store. Instead, a three-foot Shell sign atop each pump was adopted to ensure brand identification and the press eagerly noted the sign as well as the pump as a local invention. A special system of accounting augmented Quality's drive for an expanded market. By April Quality had two more filling stations of seashell design under construction and advertised itself as Shell's jobber for thirty-three other dealers in the city and contiguous county.[47]

Success was not assured but Quality relaxed the architectural thrust of its place-product-packaging campaign. Newspaper advertisements were considerably reduced in size by the end of 1931 although they were published more frequently. The Shell logo with brief allusions to quality of service and product comprised the advertisements and references to seashell architecture were absent.[48] Only two more seashell filling stations were added, the last in 1933, for a total of eight (see Fig. 7.6).[49]

THE GAS STATION IN AMERICA

FIGURE 7.8 A "modern" Quality station in Winston-Salem adapted from the Shell Oil Company's design repertoire. (*Source:* Photo courtesy of the Quality Oil Company.)

Several conditions coincided by the mid-1930s to end further construction of the seashell design. While Quality had gained a foothold in the Winston-Salem market with the unique design, the buildings were too small to accommodate the various services necessary for successful competition beyond filling gasoline tanks, changing oil, and washing cars. Even the latter two functions had required an awning over a grease pit on either side of the exterior of the seashell. These services had to be provided inside a building, Shell advised, and Quality started construction of a series of stations that heeded Shell's advice yet were not identical (see Figs. 7.7 and 7.8). On the eve of World War II, Quality was Shell's jobber in fifteen North Carolina counties and claimed to sell more gallons of Shell than the next two brands combined in Winston-Salem. However, the seashell, instrumental in Quality's success, languished without lament. Quality later considered restoration of one of its original stations, out of respect for its corporate origins, but calculated that vandalism would make it impractical.[50]

Smaller entrepreneurs complement an understanding of place-product-packaging. Those who built their own stations either purchased petroleum from independent jobbers and marketed as independents or took on "branded" products. Results are stations that mimic patterns of the corporate giants but cannot fully replicate them, most obviously in the station buildings. Often built to individual plans by local building contractors, these one-of-a-kind stations once looked more like their neighboring residences in materials and form than the image-conscious station buildings of the big corporate competitors. The house with cano-

FIGURE 7.9 Dealers who retailed outside a corporate place-product-packaging system were disadvantaged by the lack of network link. They survived only where a small market niche remained otherwise unfilled.

py emerged as the most common form and within that the cube and canopy was an oft-seen sub-type; the height and width of the office closely approximated a cube located behind a canopied drive-through virtually echoing the dimensions of the office portion of the station. Here was a practical response to the opportunity to profit from the abundant petroleum and automobile mania of the 1920s and 1930s, folk architecture of the highway (see Fig. 7.9).[51]

Small "branded" dealers and independents alike have existed in every period but hardly flourish. Their logos are reduced to a few one-dimensional signs affixed to their sites or are not attempted at all. The other accoutrements of place-product-packaging are altogether lacking. Trade advantages are sought more in personal service to local clientele than regional or national recognition to a mass market. These smallest entrepreneurs, therefore, habituate themselves in very small towns and rural areas, a marketing niche willingly surrendered or unentered by the large corporations. Such "mom and pop" arrangements subsist but in decided disadvantage to the bigger entrepreneur.

Emphasis on evaluating design in place-product-packaging rather than attention to understanding the business of decisionmaking has truncated appreciation. As a result, explanations of place-product-packaging have been offered from either one of two vantage points. Architectural critics have upheld the beauty or decried the garishness of place-product-packaging's landscape implications. Theirs are exchanges of opinion about right and wrong aimed at a professional audience of architects and planners. Although they mobilize information of a historical nature, they attempt no broad explanation of cause. Either the public landscape is the victim of corporate greed or it is the beneficiary of vernacular genius.

Geographer Barbara Rubin, however, provides an alternative assessment of place-product-packaging's material aspects, although labeled variously as "Midway-style architecture" and "franchise architecture."[52] Accordingly, small roadside entrepreneurs develop architecture only with reference to strategy. Consequences seem inevitable because small entrepreneurs are shown considering no alternative designs and the implication is that choices are cynically made because they lack reference to anything but profit. Barkhausen Oil Company and its allies in Wisconsin in the 1920s and the Quality Oil Company in North Carolina in the 1930s, at least, elude Rubin's worthy inquiry but facile conclusion.

Barkhausen and Quality were sufficiently distant from each other, and from us, to permit valid historical test cases. Both illustrate a similar pattern in their use of place-product-packaging. Initial penetration in the market was achieved without concern for aesthetics. Expansion, however, evoked concern for aesthetics. None of this was inevitable. Nor was it cynical. Arguments of inevitability and cynicism derive from a distant vantage point heedless of the details of individual cases. Arguments of inevitability and cynicism might be as easily dismissed on the grounds of faith in humans as historical agents as they are held on faith in economic determinism. In fact, Barkhausen and its allies and Quality Oil reveal evidence that permits a middle ground on historical experience rather than faith in either man or matter.

In fact, they reveal a thoughtful process of decisionmaking in which individual entrepreneurs sense limits, pausing on the way to expanded markets. Tactics change while strategy grows. Rapidity of development should not be mistaken for ease of decisionmaking or inevitability. Limits sensed are community values shared by small entrepreneurs, be it boosterism in Green Bay or antichain-store sentiment in Winston-Salem. The Hastingses commissioned gasoline stations of the suburban motif both because it was a tactical recourse and because they shared the value system from which it sprang. Their architectural firm and its architect were part of that same value system and to test for cynicism by asking for a contrary result would be to ask for an absurdity. Nor can cynicism be proven in a search for the actors' unconscious, contrary values. The consistency of their words and deeds strongly suggests their honesty. Quality's seashell was a strategy to penetrate a market of large corporate domination but it was not a product of popular discontent with prevailing designs. If it was, why did other Shell jobbers not conceive the seashell or another unusual design? Quality's seashell represents a unique manipulation of a symbol of corporate bigness to achieve parity. Small entrepreneurs with no intention of aggrandizement might also retain eccentric architecture as Rubin would have it. The end to Barkhausen's suburban style and Quality's seashell designs came but from different circumstances in each case. No easily divined formula for gasoline station design or replacement is discernible. Different people at different times in different places acted in ways only broadly patterned.

Recent cases should also be studied. Marketing segmentation's advent as concept and the rise of advertising firms as instrument will likely disclose a more complicated interaction of entrepreneurs and consumers. Will the respective weight of the buyer and seller in the sale equation be found different than before?

As the complexities of each case of decisionmaking in place-product-packaging recede from memory, attitudes about the preservation of the results as historic have tended to become ahistoric. Rather than public-directed policy, historic preservation of the roadside has become an arena for conflict between aesthetes and democrats. Two camps have emerged. Either no examples of place-product-packaging should be saved on the grounds that they diminish appreciation of art or some should be preserved as evidence of popular culture in the twentieth century.[53] Didactic purpose informs both partisans. More fundamentally, conflicting perspectives underlie their faith in landscape as lesson. Aesthetes fear control lost to a world gone mad in private satisfaction and private profit. Democrats relish the chance to raise their generation's childhood delights to the level of historically significant architecture.[54] Indeed, some examples of place-product-packaging have been saved by the roadside and a few in museums. Generational conflict produces these limited results, and is hardly desirable as public policy capable of lasting beyond the generations in conflict.

Case studies of place-product-packaging above reveal a blend of entrepreneurial and consumer interests in shared architectural icons. Both parties are part of the cultural matrix which is neither right nor wrong. Place-product-packaging has mediated between willing consumers and eager entrepreneurs. Inchoate feelings in both parties are the raw stuff of the same society rendered as its culture in architectural symbols. Social action should evolve from those who already communicate through the culture debated and not only from those professionals who plan, design, or research with consequences for social policy. Historians would outreach not merely their resources but their role to foretell whether extensive place-product-packaging preservation will be or not be. History applied, however, permits the determination of future public policy in the light of past limitations and options. Light on the process of place-product-packaging may help show the way to preservation.

8

Gas Stations as a Feature of Urban Landscape

Having looked at the American gasoline station as a marketing device, an architectural form, and an object of entrepreneurial intent, we now turn more directly to geographical issues. How did gasoline stations of various types impact actual places? To answer this question we look at the cities of Champaign and Urbana in Illinois, a location with which the authors have had long familiarity. In addition to the logistical ease of working with landscape immediately at hand, Champaign-Urbana is well suited to analysis of automobile-related businesses. Thoroughfare or "strip" commercial development came rapidly to major streets connecting the "twin cities"' two major business districts. These were commercial centers that saw very early the impact of automobile-related sales and service, especially gasoline retailing. In recent decades, extensive suburbanization coupled with peripheral freeway construction has generated landscapes completely automobile-oriented. Champaign-Urbana may or may not be a typical American city, but the processes of landscape change operating there have typified and continue to typify American urban places generally.

In Champaign-Urbana, what were the prevailing types of gasoline stations at various points in time? How were these stations geographically distributed? How did the changing geography of gasoline retailing relate to the evolving morphology and changing social complexion of the two cities? Champaign and Urbana occupy a gently rolling plain at the uppermost headwaters of several rivers flowing variously to the Ohio and Mississippi. Topography provides little obstruction to modern travel and thus simple geometric grids of streets with little deviation dominate the locality: a kind of flat chessboard for conducting the game of life. Champaign's oldest plat of streets (on which its business district centers) is oriented to the Illinois Central Railroad, but the remaining plats in both Champaign and Urbana are oriented to the cardinal directions of the township and range survey. Although resultant streetscapes are thought by many to be monotonous, there is no denying that Champaign-Urbana is a very easy place in which to orient and to navigate, the vast majority of streets meeting at right angles. Two traditional business districts emerged: one in the 1830s around the courthouse in Urbana and the other in the 1850s some two miles westward in Champaign (originally called West Urbana) around the depot of the Illinois Central Railroad. The campus of the University of Illinois developed midway between these two centers and there the two cities eventually knit together in the 1870s. At that point a third business district emerged which remains partially pedestrian-oriented.

In 1920 the combined population of Champaign and Urbana stood at 26,000, growing to 37,000 twenty years later. In 1990 the two cities together had some 94,000 people, although Champaign County's total population stood at 168,000. Suburban growth spilled well beyond municipal boundaries and, in addition, nearby Rantoul, with its air base, became a small city in its own right. Champaign-Urbana has enjoyed slow but consistent growth across all decades, its fortunes driven by employment at the University of Illinois, at Chanute Air Force Base, and at food processing plants drawn to the area by its solid farm economy based on cash grain production. The two cities strike most visitors as very utilitarian. Save for the university, Champaign-Urbana is not noted for its architecture or landscape design. It is, in other words, a place where students of the commonplace can focus on the vernacular landscape largely undeterred by the high in style. Here is vernacular America fully elaborated.

The Automobile and Downtown Champaign

In 1916 a local newspaper noted:

One of Champaign's oldest landmarks has been torn down to make way for modern improvements. The oldest barn in Champaign has made way for a garage, and time rolls on over a page of history. The old barn had an atmosphere of romance about it that makes its destruction seem to an old citizen of Champaign as the destruction of Europe's cathedrals must feel to lovers of the ancient.[1]

How quickly the automobile made its inroads. Only ten years earlier the Champaign Gun and Cycle Shop had begun selling and repairing the curved-dashed Reo Motorcar as a sideline. Bert Blue's garage, the city's first, also had opened. Blue was a skilled mechanic, a repairer of contrivances from gas stoves to lawnmowers. His cryptic ad announcing his business read, "Formerly with the Wallace Machine Company, Automobiles Kept in Repair."[2] Neither business lasted out the year for automobiling was very much a novelty and the horse was still king. In 1906, Champaign's business district contained ten livery, feed, and sales

Table 8.1 Horse- and Automobile-related Businesses in Champaign, Illinois

Year	Carriage Shops	Livery, Feed, and Sales Barns	Blacksmiths[a]	Harness Shops	Auto Sales	Auto Repair and Supply
1906	4	10	9	4	1	2
1912	6	7	8	3	11	4
1916	4	6	6	4	13	17
1921	2	1	3	3	19	21
1926	0	0	3	3	15	25

[a] After 1916 the term *horseshoer* prevailed over the term *blacksmith* in describing the traditional blacksmithing business in the various city directories.

Source: City directory of Champaign-Urbana (Bloomington: Pantagraph Printing and Stationary Co., 1906; Quincy, Ill.: Samson Directory Co., 1912, 1916; Champaign, Ill.: Clark-Elwell Co., 1921; Champaign, Ill.: Flanigan-Pearson Co., 1926).

barns, four carriage shops, nine blacksmithing shops, and four harness shops (see Table 8.1).

By 1926, fifteen businesses were selling automobiles while twenty-five were engaged in automobile repair and supply. Only three horse-shoers and three harness shops remained. These statistics, not in themselves surprising, mask a significant relationship between the two kinds of businesses. Simply put, the early geography of automobile-related sales and services reflected the location of earlier horse-related businesses. It is to this relationship that we turn first.

Champaign's central business district comprised in 1906 a tight clustering of buildings in approximately twelve square blocks straddling the Illinois Central (see Fig. 8.1). Commercial activity was focused on the intersection of Main and Walnut streets west of the railroad depot. Within a block were located the city's banks, principal clothiers, grocers, hardware stores, and other merchants. Horse-related businesses were distributed throughout the district although seemingly gathered in four clusters. Three groupings framed the core of the district and included twenty-two of the city's twenty-eight enterprises related to the horse. The fourth was located in the very center of retailing activity. Each cluster provided a full range of services from livery, sales, and feed barns to blacksmiths and carriage and harness shops. Various businesses provided mutual reinforcement within each cluster and nowhere in the business district was a customer far removed from any one service required for horse or carriage.

Champaign's first automobile-related businesses were rooted, like Bert Blue's garage, in the mechanical backgrounds of their owners. Experience in the manufacture and repair of bicycles, guns, and farm machinery prepared entrepreneurs. But early automobile businesses were short-lived, especially sales dealerships. Only three of the eleven dealers operating in 1912 were in business two years later, and only one in 1916.

FIGURE 8.1 Horse-oriented and automobile-oriented business structures in downtown Champaign, Illinois, 1906.

Most motorcars were expensive and thus the local market was very limited. Dealers also failed when the companies they represented were bankrupted. Many dealers associated themselves with a repair garage or operated a repair facility. Several of these sold gasoline.

A spectrum of businesses added automobile supply and servicing to traditional lines. Downtown drug stores stocked automobile tires, oils, and greases. Carriage shops added auto painting and trimming. Available skills in wood and metal working hastened conversion of carriage shops into body shops and blacksmith shops into welding shops. As for livery stables, the suitability of the structures, rather than the operator's expertise with the lathe or welding torch, provided the principal impulse for change. Accordingly, conversion of livery stables usually resulted in a change of ownership and management as well as orientation.

As local motorcar ownership increased, totally new service facilities appeared, a function of both the high maintenance requirements of the still primitive automobiles and local entrepreneurial zeal. By 1916, shops specializing in tire sales and tire vulcanizing evolved in the fringe

THE GAS STATION IN AMERICA

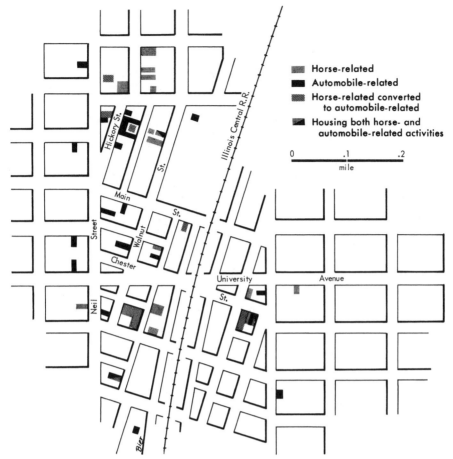

FIGURE 8.2 Horse-oriented and automobile-oriented business structures in downtown Champaign, Illinois, 1916.

of the Champaign business district (see Fig. 8.2). Gasoline, initially sold in tin containers at garages and in a variety of stores, was being pumped from curbside tanks at several garages and in front of one autoparts store. An automobile charging station serviced the Milburn Electrics then sold in town.

The middle cluster of horse-related enterprises, prosperous and self-contained in 1906 but waning in 1912, had vanished in 1916 with the exception of a single harness shop. The Miller Harness and Carriage Company, once the largest newspaper advertiser for horse-related business, had closed (see Fig. 8.3). Formerly a Studebaker Wagon distributor, Miller now operated a Studebaker Motorcar dealership in an adjacent building. Eight of Champaign's thirteen dealerships lined Hickory Street, five providing automobile repair. Here was Champaign's first "automobile row" with gasoline retailing a part of it (see Fig. 8.4)

The congregation of automobile dealers in one section of the Champaign business district had never had a counterpart among the horse-related businesses. Carriage dealers marketed the vehicles of many man-

FIGURE 8.3 Frank Miller's livery stable in downtown Champaign, circa 1906.

ufacturers, not those of only one or two companies as automobile dealers were forced to do in a more highly competitive industry. It had been possible at Miller's Carriage Shop, where fifteen different carriage brands had once been sold, to compare a variety of makes under a single roof. Consequently, the cluster of automobile dealers along "automobile row" also fostered comparative shopping of the traditional sort.

In 1921 a feed and sales barn, converted for automobile sales, storage, and repair, anchored Hickory Street on the north. Twenty-five of the city's fifty-one automobile-related enterprises were located on or within one block of Hickory Street. Champaign's first off-street gasoline station, a small station house with a canopy covering several pumps, operated at the southern periphery of the business of Neil Street. Congestion in and around "automobile row" would discourage gasoline sales and force this function to the business district's edges.

By 1926 Champaign's last two livery barns had been converted to automobile sales and storage facilities. A farm implement store, which had carried buggies and wagons, sold trucks, and a harness and saddlery shop now specialized in manufacturing automobile trunks. Only three harness and two horseshoeing shops remained of the city's once numerous horse-related enterprises. Automobile-related businesses, on the other hand, had not only increased in number to redefine the old central business district as never before, but had become the vanguard of business peripheral expansion (see Fig. 8.5). Thoroughfare "strip" development along Neil Street south from the business district's core and east

FIGURE 8.4 By 1915 a cluster of automobile supply stores had developed downtown on Champaign's Hickory Street. *Top*, A close view discloses an early curbside pump, the storage tank being buried beneath the sidewalk. *Bottom*, Horses
and wagons had not yet totally disappeared from Champaign's streets.

TABLE 8.2 The Conversion of Horse-related Businesses to Automobile-related Commerce, 1906 to 1926

Business Type	Total Number, 1906–1926	Conversion	Type of Automobile-related Activity
Horseshoers	16	4	Repair
Livery and feed barns	12	7	Sales, repair, storage
Farm machinery	8	3	Sales, repair
Bicycle shops	6	2	Sales, repair
Carriage shops	6	4	Sales, painting, manufacture of auto bodies
Harness shops	6	1	Automobile trunk manufacture
Machine shops	4	3	Sales, repair
Total	58	24	

Sources: City directories for Champaign and Urbana, Ill., 1907, 1912, 1914, 1918, 1919–20, 1922, 1923, 1924, 1925, 1926.

FIGURE 8.5 Horse-oriented and automobile-oriented business structures in downtown Champaign, Illinois, 1926.

THE GAS STATION IN AMERICA

along University Avenue followed designation of these arteries as a numbered interstate highway. Four automobile dealerships and five gasoline stations lined South Neil Street. Here was the beginning of a second-generation "automobile row," this one dominant during the 1930s and 1940s.

In summary, twenty-four of the fifty-eight horse-related facilities of the period 1906 to 1926 were converted to automobile-related enterprises (see Table 8.2). The machine tools and mechanical skills associated with farm equipment, gun, and bicycle repair inclined many businessmen to embrace some new automobile-related activity. But the physical facilities of horse-related businesses exerted the greatest influence on the emerging geography of automobile-oriented enterprise. Vacated buildings were easily converted to automobile sales and service. Built to accommodate the movement of wheeled vehicles, many of these structures, especially the livery, feed, and sales barns, required little remodeling. Where the automobile replaced the horse, gasoline retailing followed quickly.

The Growth of a Strip: University Avenue

In the 1920s new gasoline stations, repair garages, and dealer showrooms were constructed to accommodate larger and faster automobiles. Off-street driveways and parking aprons became essential and no longer were older buildings of the America's traditional business districts adequate in their conversion. New structures began to rise along the major thoroughfares leading into Champaign's downtown. University Avenue eastward from the business district became the area's principal strip connecting, as it did, with "Five Points," an intersection at the northern edge of Urbana's downtown some 1.7 miles distant (see Fig. 8.6). A new kind of commercial environment evolved on what was previously a residential street: a linear array of businesses, many related directly to the selling and repairing of motorcars. Here gasoline stations represented the single most important commercial "colonizer." Once gasoline stations intruded, other businesses followed.

The distribution of commercial land uses along University Avenue is presented for 1919 and seven subsequent dates at ten-year intervals in Figure 8.7. Selected automobile-related and automobile-convenient businesses are highlighted: gasoline stations, automobile showrooms, automobile repair and supply businesses, motels and tourist homes, and fast food restaurants. In 1919 eight businesses had already located in the three blocks adjacent to Champaign's downtown. Most of these businesses occupied small storefronts, several built in front of houses left standing. None was automobile-related or automobile-convenient since parking was restricted solely to the street. Within a decade, commerce, in particular those functions geared to the passing motorist, occupied lots

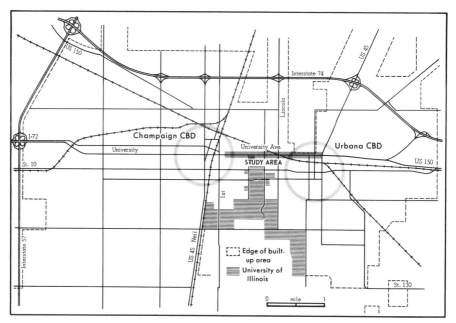

FIGURE 8.6 Champaign, Illinois, 1990. The two cities contained two traditional business districts with University Avenue offering east/west connection.

along the length of the street. On the three blocks nearest downtown Champaign a number of automobile-related businesses, including two gasoline stations, had appeared. Another gasoline station had been located at the street's midpoint at Lincoln Avenue, and two more near the Urbana business district at the eastern end of the street. Through 1929 seven residential blocks had been intruded upon by commerce. Six of these blocks had been colonized by automobile-oriented enterprises, five by gasoline stations located primarily on vacant lots. Corner lots were clearly preferred, giving, as they did, access from two streets.

Between 1929 and 1939 business expanded into six additional residential blocks, five of which were first intruded upon by gasoline stations. Gasoline stations were clustered at the street's eastern end although they were also located along the remainder of the street at rather even intervals. At Lincoln Avenue, a second gasoline station with restaurant appeared. By 1949 commercial development dominated previously vacant land near downtown Urbana. The area became more and more automobile-oriented as auto dealerships and restaurants joined existing gasoline stations and a cabin court. At the eastern end of the street near downtown Champaign, commerce not involved with the needs of the motorist began to fill the blocks. Storefronts housed several grocery stores and tailor shops, among other enterprises. Here also many small restaurants and several auto repair shops appeared.

By the late 1950s the street's character had grown increasingly automobile convenient. Parking lots, associated with new businesses such as

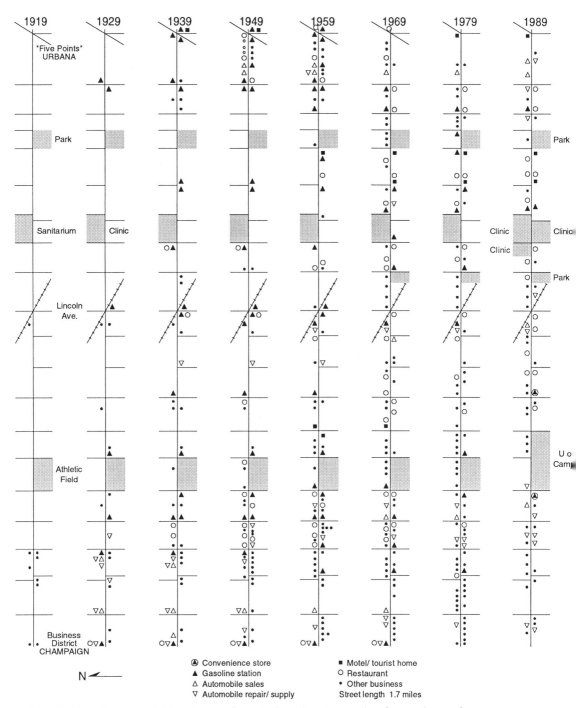

FIGURE 8.7 Commercial land uses along University Avenue in Champaign and Urbana, Illinois, 1919–1989.

TABLE 8.3 Commercial Land Use along University Avenue in Champaign and Urbana, Illinois, for Selected Years, 1919 to 1989

Year	Commercial Establishments		Gasoline Stations		Restaurants	
	Number	Size[a]	Number	Size[a]	Number	Size[a]
1919	9	1.11	0	—	0	—
1929	23	1.07	7	0.64	1	0.50
1939	50	0.69	17	0.82	6	0.66
1949	71	0.87	19	1.29	14	0.65
1959	94	0.99	23	1.17	14	1.17
1969	92	1.33	13	1.57	23	1.67
1979	96	1.76	10	2.30	12	2.25
1989	73	3.84	4	5.25	15	5.00

[a] Average size, in building lots.

TABLE 8.4 Turnover of Selected Business Types along University Avenue

Years	Mean Turnover Index[a]	
	Gasoline Stations	Restaurants
1922–1929	.835	1.100
1930–1939	.568	.768
1940–1949	.364	.431
1950–1959	.338	.376
1960–1969	.274	.150
1970–1978	.227	.220
1979–1989	.700	.466

[a] Turnover index $= \dfrac{E + D + O}{N}$ where

E = Number of new establishments which occupied a new site during a year;
D = Number of establishments which disappeared;
O = Changes in ownership (but not in business identity); and
N = Total number of respective establishments.

motels and drive-in restaurants, made their first appearance. Many older businesses also began to provide off-street parking to the rear of buildings. Commerce now dominated University Avenue, a condition that would prevail in the next two decades. By 1969 franchise restaurants with large parking lots appeared in full force. The number of gasoline stations had declined by half, although the remaining stations tended to be larger (see Fig. 8.8). The strip was clearly maturing as a commercial area with a greater variety of business types housed in larger facilities, a trend that would continue through 1989 (see Table 8.3). The number of businesses located along University Avenue stabilized through the 1950s

FIGURE 8.8 University Avenue in Urbana, Illinois, 1979.

and 1970s (94, 92, and 96 businesses, respectively); however, the size of the average business nearly doubled (.99, 1.33, and 1.76 building lots respectively). The average size of gasoline stations increased from 1.17 to 2.3 building lots between 1959 and 1979, and the average size of restaurants from 1.17 to 2.25. The average size of business establishment nearly doubled again during the 1980s.

Between 1919 and 1959 commerce tended to spread from the two ends of University Avenue toward the middle, gasoline stations serving as the prime colonizers of previously residential blocks. Perhaps of greater significance, however, a second spatial sequence developed after 1959 as a variety of businesses replaced gasoline stations and other automobile-oriented enterprises. This change also spread from each end of the street toward the middle and by the 1980s a wide range of business types, including gasoline stations, was evenly distributed along the street. In 1989, gasoline stations had clearly declined in number, reflecting the effective end of University Avenue as "gasoline alley." If anything, the avenue had become "fast food row" although the largest businesses in terms of land expropriated were motels and auto dealers.

The turnover of business functions, business establishments, and business ownerships in the early period was very high. Mean turnover rates for gasoline stations and restaurants for each decade are given in Table 8.4. The mean turnover index divides the sum of new establishments, closed establishments, and continuing establishments with new owners by the total number of establishments. The amount of instability declined steadily through time. By 1969 the strip had not only become a

TABLE 8.5 Residential Land Use along University Avenue for Selected Years, 1919 to 1989

Year	Number of Dwellings	Owner-occupied	Single-family	Multiple-family	Multiple-family/ Owner-occupied	Rented	Vacant
1919	151	76.8%	84.8%	15.2%	37.1%	37.1%	0.0%
1929	153	67.2	76.5	21.6	17.6	42.5	1.3
1939	145	68.9	72.4	24.1	17.2	44.8	2.0
1949	138	76.0	79.0	27.5	18.8	42.8	0.0
1959	112	61.6	72.3	23.2	11.6	44.6	4.4
1969	69	52.1	47.8	49.3	20.3	65.2	2.0
1979	39	25.5	10.2	74.4	15.4	59.0	17.0
1989	18	5.0	22.2	61.0	0.0	95.0	17.0

Sources: Champaign-Urbana city directories and field surveys.

TABLE 8.6 Occupations of Household Heads Resident along University Avenue for Selected Years, 1919 to 1989

Year	Total Households	Professional/ Managerial	Clerical/ Shopkeeper	Craftsman/ Operative/ Laborer	Widow/ Retired	Student
1919	150	10.0%	22.0%	40.6%	20.6%	—
1929	187	6.9	25.6	45.4	21.9	—
1949	148	10.1	21.6	47.8	17.5	3.3%
1969	140	6.4	15.0	19.2	12.8	45.7
1979	136	1.4	5.9	11.0	3.6	77.8
1989	31	0.3	0.6	—	0.6	97.6

Sources: Champaign-Urbana city directories and field surveys.

more varied commercial street, but business life-expectancy was vastly increased. Between 1969 and 1979 the overbuilding of franchise restaurants was reflected in an increased turnover rate for restaurants contrary to this general trend. However, the turnover of businesses, especially fast food restaurants, accelerated again during the 1980s. At no time since the 1920s was change in gasoline retailing so unstable as the personality of the street shifted from gasoline to food.

Commercial strip development along University Avenue can only be fully understood in terms of what the gasoline stations and other businesses displaced. In 1919 University Avenue was a residential street dominated by owner-occupied single-family housing. As indicated in Table 8.5, several slow but distinct changes occurred between 1919 and 1959. The number of housing units declined by one-quarter (or approximately 10 units each decade from a high of 151 in 1919). The proportion

THE GAS STATION IN AMERICA

of single-family houses diminished as did the proportion of owner-occupied boarding houses and apartment buildings. After 1959 these changes vastly accelerated. The number of houses declined to 25 percent of the 1919 number (at a rate nearly four times that of previous decades). Between 1959 and 1979 the proportion of single-family houses fell from 72 to 10 percent. The number of owner-occupied multiple-family dwellings increased, although they still accounted for only 15 percent of the total. Nearly 60 percent of the houses contained rental units as opposed to 45 percent in 1959, and the number of vacant houses rose substantially from 4 to 17 percent. Increasingly, the street's residential properties shifted into the hands of absentee landlords and speculators, trends all but complete by 1989.

The social character of the street changed, as summarized in Table 8.6. Although the number of structures steadily declined, the number of households remained high, fluctuating from 150 in 1919 to 187 in 1929 to 136 in 1979. There was surprising stability on the street through 1949. At least 7 percent of the heads of households held professional or managerial positions. The center of the University of Illinois campus, located six blocks south on Green Street, made University Avenue reasonably convenient for faculty families. Nonetheless, the street was traditionally dominated by household heads employed as craftsmen, operatives, or laborers (between 40 and 48 percent) and clerical workers and shopkeepers (between 22 and 26 percent). Retired couples and widows formed a third group (between 18 and 21 percent). The largest proportion of blue-collar families were renters. By 1989 university students had come to fully dominate the street. Whereas only 3 percent of the household heads had been students in 1949, 46 percent were students in 1969 and 98 percent in 1989. To the north of University Avenue lay the predominantly black "North End." But, only along the eastern section of the street adjacent to Champaign's business district did African-American families predominate among renters through the 1960s and 1970s.

Champaign-Urbana's University Avenue experienced persistent change between 1919 and 1989 although there were clear threshold points, often associated with key governmental decisions beyond which specific kinds of change accelerated. Part of the explanation for these shifts is peculiar to Champaign-Urbana, but in general the processes of commercialization on University Avenue were affected by both public and private decisionmaking based on cultural and social values universal to American cities. Gasoline stations led the way.

As individuals, property owners were interested in increasing their equity in real estate. They did not seek collectively to stabilize residential land use as a means of achieving that end. Those property owners who did not favor commercial zoning for University Avenue did not oppose it publicly. Thus commercial zoning was implemented in Champaign in 1926 and in Urbana in 1940, most property owners welcoming the decision to make University Avenue the major thoroughfare connecting the two cities' central business districts.

The first businessmen attracted to University Avenue ran automobile-oriented businesses that thrived on increased traffic flow, particularly the operators of gasoline stations. Later businesses, both those oriented and not oriented to the automobile, found the strip convenient to customers city-wide. Businesses along the strip were rarely related to one another as in the latter-day shopping center. Rather, shopping involved single-purpose trips as documented in other case studies.[3] Businessmen sought separate identities for their establishments, as clearly symbolized in elaborate signs and later with distinctive buildings and off-street parking lots. The accumulation of all of this activity greatly changed University Avenue's residential image.

Local government's concern with University Avenue was limited largely to traffic control once basic zoning decisions had been made. Increased traffic volume brought congestion. For example, by the 1960s approximately one-quarter of all accidents in Urbana occurred on University Avenue.[4] Widening of the street began in Champaign in the late 1940s and continued in Urbana through the 1950s. A four-lane pavement (with parking lanes) in Champaign and a two-lane slab (with gravel berms) in Urbana were broadened to four traffic lanes throughout with two parking lanes along most of the street. All trees adjacent to the street were stripped away and most front yards were reduced considerably in size. The placement of traffic signals started in the late 1950s and the elimination of curbside parking along portions of the street began in the late 1960s.

Nothing impacted the visual image of University Avenue more than the removal of the trees. Many houses, mostly small ones of indifferent design and poor repair, were exposed. Businesses such as gasoline stations, once partially obscured by foliage, now stood out boldly in the landscape. Not until the later 1960s did the two city governments, prodded by a private community development foundation, move to replace trees through systematic planting.[5] A new street lighting system greatly increased visibility at night, but also increased nighttime glare for residents.

Parking lots around businesses were noisy. Dirt, debris, and general commotion spilled over onto adjacent residential properties. The need for off-street parking and driveways proved a critical turning point in the shift to commercial land use. Parking lots necessitated the grouping of individual building lots for commercial purposes. As realtors acted to assemble large parcels for new businesses, existing establishments expanded onto adjacent properties. The taking of lots with houses as opposed to the taking of vacant lots sealed the street's demise as a residential place—a process that accelerated after 1959.

Changes in the social character of the street contributed to the shifts in land use. Over time, absentee landlords controlled rental housing and more buildings were owned primarily for long-term speculation. Rental housing was a transitory form of commercial enterprise that coexisted nicely with retail business. No new apartment buildings were built on University Avenue and increased rental activity was found only in converted houses. The departure of blue-collar families from the street, largely after 1949, was tied both to the changing physical character of University Avenue and to the development of newer, equivalent housing in new subdivisions. University students, transient by nature and perhaps less concerned with the street's deteriorating residential environment, proved to be a ready replacement market for landlords. The ability to rent to students contributed some stability to the area which otherwise might have been rapidly abandoned to commercial enterprise.

The evolution of a commercial strip can be understood in terms of collective and individual decisionmaking whereby private and public interests shape a linear space. Small, tentative actions accumulate to form commitments that cannot be easily reversed. Ultimately, points are reached where a majority of interested parties adjust in anticipation of a new situation, thereby bringing that situation into fruition. The idea of a commercial strip is implanted, adjustments are made by property owners, key governmental decisions are made (especially zoning changes and street improvements), and a new place is created given wholesale shifts in land use. Once gasoline stations and other businesses were established on Champaign-Urbana's University Avenue the question was not whether the street would convert to commerce, but how rapid and how orderly that conversion would be given the street's transitory social character as a residential place. Behind the commercial strips of most American cities are similar stories, the gasoline station playing the vital role as original colonizer.

Gasoline Stations in the Larger Landscape

The distribution of gasoline stations in Champaign-Urbana for 1920, 1940, 1970, and 1990 are shown in Figures 8.9, 8.10, 8.11, and 8.12. Stations are mapped by type, as identified in chapter 5, for each respective date. In 1920, the two curbside, the two house, and the four house with canopy stations were restricted to the business districts. By 1940, however, two major commercial strips had evolved. In addition to University Avenue, Green Street, upon which the university centered, had also evolved as a "gasoline alley." By coincidence, both strips contained twenty-two stations (houses, houses with canopy, houses with bays, oblong boxes, and small boxes). In addition, Neil Street ("auto dealers' row") constituted a third strip with an equally diverse array of station types reflecting several decades of changing fad and fashion in gasoline retailing. Tabulated are the various station types for the various years surveyed (see Table 8.7).

By 1970, gasoline retailing in the two traditional business districts

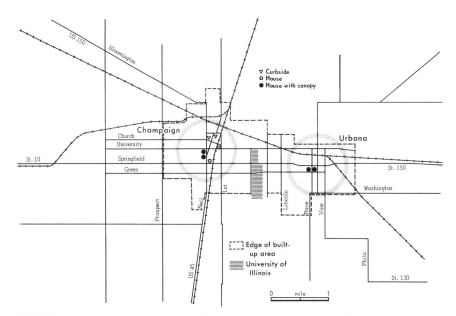

FIGURE 8.9 Gasoline retailing in Champaign and Urbana, Illinois, 1920.

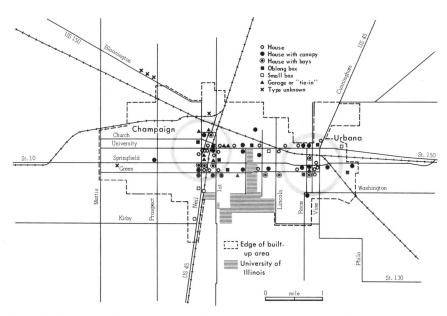

FIGURE 8.10 Gasoline retailing in Champaign and Urbana, Illinois, 1940.

was substantially eclipsed (see Fig. 8.11). But University Avenue and Neil Street were still well defined as gasoline alleys, with fifteen stations operating on the former and eight on the latter. The number of stations on Green Street had declined as other kinds of businesses, catering largely to university-oriented pedestrians, pushed expansion of "Campustown" on Green Street westward from the campus. Restaurants, bars, and other

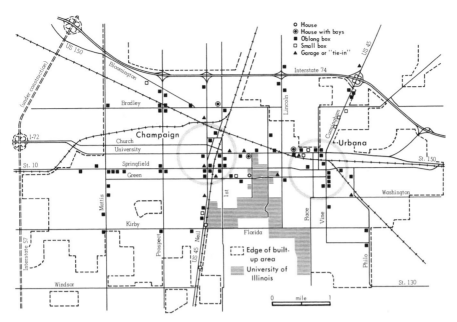

FIGURE 8.11 Gasoline retailing in Champaign and Urbana, Illinois, 1970.

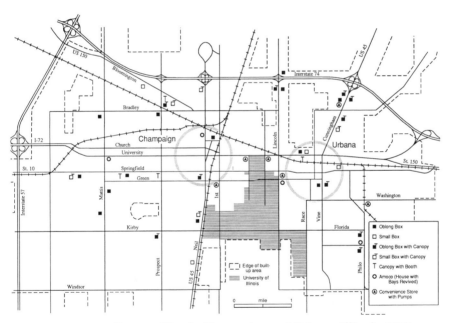

FIGURE 8.12 Gasoline retailing in Champaign and Urbana, Illinois, 1990.

places of entertainment, as well as student-oriented retail stores, drove
the growth of this, Champaign-Urbana's third "downtown," configured
substantially in the traditional manner around businesses oriented to
sidewalk traffic. Locations other than strip locations had come to characterize gasoline retailing. Neighborhood stations had evolved oriented
to post–World War II suburban subdivisions, literally all of them oblong

TABLE 8.7 Gasoline Station Types in Champaign and Urbana, 1920, 1940, 1970, and 1990

Type	1920	1940	1970	1990
Curbside	3	0	0	0
House	1	23	1	0
House with canopy	4	22	0	0
House with bays	0	7	3	0
Oblong box	0	7	68	13
Oblong box with canopy	0	0	0	10
Small box	0	5	10	4
Small box with canopy	0	0	0	5
Canopy with booth	0	0	0	4
Amoco (house with bays revived)	0	0	0	4
Garage or other "tie-in"	0	9	10	0
Convenience store with pumps	0	0	0	6

Source: Photography, insurance maps, and field survey.

boxes. Interstate highway interchanges also sported oblong boxes and, in the case of Cunningham Avenue northeast from Five Points, small boxes appeared, the latter constructed not by the major oil companies but by the independents.

The year 1990 found even more dramatic change not only in the spatial distribution of gasoline outlets, but in the addition of several new types of stations (see Fig. 8.12). Amoco (the former Standard Oil of Indiana) had sought to reinforce its presence in Champaign-Urbana by remodeling several oblong boxes into a kind of modern house with bays clad in "colonial" ornamentation (see Fig. 8.13). Several of these stations remained, but were stripped of ornamentation. But the big styling news was the arrival of the large self-standing canopies not only in association with "booths," but placed in front of and thus dominating oblong boxes and small boxes. In addition, gasoline retailing was tied to grocery sales in convenience stores with pumps (many also reinforced by canopies). These stores were operated both by oil companies (the groceries and other sundry items complementary) and by grocery retailers (the gasoline complementary). Both of these retail strategies, however, produced very similar physical facilities: large parking lots, low rectangular buildings, and adjacent pump islands.

Convenience stores in 1990 tended to reinforce the traditional strips, appearing not only on University and Cunningham avenues, but on Green Street as well. Champaign-Urbana's other stations, for the most part built over the preceding two decades, were oriented, as in 1970, to interstate highway interchanges and to peripheral neighborhood locations. The considerable decline in the overall number of stations between 1970 and 1990 was a function of the increased scale of operations at 1990 locations, the result of aggressive competition. From ninety stations the total had fallen to forty-four. Not only were the traditional business districts nearly void of gasoline retailing, but, save for Cunningham Avenue in north Urbana, the traditional strips were much reduced in importance. Gasoline stations in 1990 were rather evenly distributed geographically, a situation far removed from the tight clustering of stations in downtowns and along commercial thoroughfares during the early decades.

Throughout the twentieth century gasoline sold in the Champaign-Urbana area originated at relatively few refineries, although many of the nation's largest oil corporations and many of the Middle West's regional independents have established outlets at one time or another. Today, most of the gasoline sold originates at Amoco's refinery at Whiting, Indiana, Shell's refinery at Wood River, Illinois, and Marathon's refinery at Robinson, Illinois. It was sold under the respective national logos of the originating firms, by their "concubine" subsidiaries, and by various independents. Other national brands represented included Ashland, Phillips,

FIGURE 8.13 Two versions of the same gasoline station: (a) 1978, and (b) 1990. Amoco abandoned its architectural pretenses to "Early American" styling.

Sunoco, and Unocal, which tend to market the regional product obtained through exchange agreement. Gone were the Conoco, Exxon, Kerr-McGee, Mobil, Sinclair, and Texaco brands. Independent brands in 1990 included Super Gas (originally the local Gulf jobber), Clark, Collins (a local independent), Derby, Freedom, Site, and Wareco. Wareco marketed under both the Phillips and Coastal brands. A myriad of independent brands have come and gone over the years and are but a folk memory: Chief, Corydell, Hudson, Johnson's Brilliant Bronze, Liberty, Martin, Red Bird, Spur, Star, and Vickers, to name a very few. As in most cities, only the brand names of the majors with more than 10 percent market penetration prove durable over the long run.

It might be helpful to think in terms of evolutionary phases when considering gasoline retailing as an element of urban landscape. Initially, gasoline was made available in central business districts. For downtown Champaign four stages are apparent. Stage 1 represented the preautomobile circumstance where travel was pedestrian-, bicycle-, wagon-, carriage-, or streetcar-oriented. Stage 2 saw a host of horse-oriented, bicycle-related, or machine-oriented businesses taking on automobile sales and repair as sidelines as well as establishment of the first garages. The sorting of horse-related activities into four geographical clusters in part drove the distribution of early garages and, consequently, much gasoline retailing. Horse-oriented activities were housed in buildings that accommodated vehicles easily and thus converted readily to the needs of the automobile. Stage 3 saw the rise of a specialized automobile row where sales, service, and autoparts supply concentrated. Again, gasoline was sold in conjunction with these enterprises, but from curbside pumps rather than from tins. When sufficient market prompted construction of specialized gasoline stations with pumps in off-street driveways, a fourth stage was reached, leading ultimately to commercial strip development on the major approaches to the business district.

Strips evolved directly out of changes taking place in downtown. With increased congestion, curbside pumps became impractical. With the coming of chain stores, retail establishments grew in size and number, pushing out of central locations both residual horse-related and new automobile-related enterprises. Cheaper land at the peripheries of downtown, especially in previously residential spaces, made logical seedbeds for the new gasoline stations.

The case of Champaign-Urbana's University Avenue suggests a six-stage model of commercial strip evolution. A stable residential street comprised primarily of single-family dwellings constituted stage 1. A few neighborhood businesses were oriented to pedestrian traffic and did not detract from the quiescent quality of a predominantly residential street. In stage 2, gasoline stations formed the vanguard of an intrusive commercial development. Stations served traffic moving to and from a nearby business district. They were located primarily on previously vacant corner lots. Investments in buildings and driveways were modest and gave these businesses an impermanent, transient look.

Gasoline station development continued in stage 3, where it peaked. Indeed, descriptions such as "gasoline alley" were appropriated. However, the addition of other business types brought commercial diversity to the street. Except where business establishments located in the middle of blocks, residences and businesses still coexisted in relative stability. Although the number of dwellings declined, the number of residents remained much the same as more buildings were divided into multiple units. Fewer landlords lived in their buildings and increasingly housing became a business in its own right.

Commercial functions clearly dominated in stage 4. A significantly larger number and wider variety of businesses characterized the strip. Largely because of competition, gasoline stations declined numerically, resulting in stations being more evenly distributed in linear array. Especially evident in stage 4 was the growth of automobile-convenient establishments such as drive-in restaurants and motels with off-street parking facilities. The sizes of business parcels increased largely through the configuring of parking lots. Business buildings tended to be larger and better constructed and a sense of commercial permanence pervaded the thoroughfare. Street widening and the removal of trees substantially altered the street's personality in favor of commercialism. The number of residences declined in favor of multiple-unit rental housing owned by absentee landlords.

In stage 5, residential functions along the street all but disappeared. Only a few relic rental units survived in what was otherwise a totally commercial landscape. Matters of street beautification and traffic improvement dominated public action. Commercial properties increased in size as more businesses provided off-street parking and expanded their layouts to accommodate larger scale operation. Change introduced by gasoline stations ran its course.

The rise and fall of gasoline retailing in traditional business districts and on commercial strips form but part of the equation by which an overall historical geography of gasoline stations in Champaign-Urbana and other cities may be understood. Again, let us think in terms of evolutionary phases to sketch the overall patterns of geographical distribution across the whole of city space. Again, stage 1 was essentially a preautomobile circumstance. If stage 2 represented a concentration of early gasoline stations in and around central business districts, then stage 3 reflected fully the gasoline station as colonizer of various commercial strips. On the other hand, the decline of gasoline stations numerically on those strips marked stage 4. Interestingly, different gasoline station types seemed to have characterized the fulfillment of each stage: the second by house and canopy stations, the third by oblong boxes, and the fourth by oblong and small boxes upgraded by canopies as well as by convenience stores with pumps often under canopies as well. The changing geography of gasoline stations, therefore, is linked integrally with changing gasoline station form.

The place-product-packaging of competing gasoline interests has played out in Champaign-Urbana, driving change around the margins of the area's traditional business districts and along its emergent commercial strips. Distinctive local geographies of gasoline retailing have come and gone, gasoline stations now oriented primarily to interstate freeway interchanges and suburban locations. The trend in gasoline retailing in Champaign and Urbana has been toward larger volume outlets, some tied in with the sale of convenience items such as groceries. The newest stations tend to be of the latter type, again suggesting that the traditional gasoline station, as represented by the oblong box, for example, may be a waning feature of the American scene. Of course, during the 1980s many older stations were renewed, either restyled as Amoco simplified many of its local outlets, or reinforced by large canopies striking to the eye and thus dominating other station characteristics. Through the addition of the canopy, the traditional gasoline station in Champaign-Urbana does survive.

We should note that study of the gasoline station as a feature in the Champaign-Urbana landscape confirms earlier observations made regarding changing station form and function as revealed in the pages of the *National Petroleum News*. Trends reported in the trade literature do indeed reflect in the landscapes of actual places. The classification scheme developed from that journal does have relevancy in understanding an actual built environment.

Gasoline retailing in any city is marked by a constant ebb and flow of stations opening and closing. The urban geography of gasoline stations is one of constant flux having to do not only with changing form and function of cities generally, but with the internal makeup of the petroleum industry. The territorial competitiveness of corporate suppliers informs the viability of specific stations as much as (if not more than) location, quality of station management, and other variables decidedly local in nature. Place-product-packaging orchestrated largely at national and regional scales plays out at the scale of the city in profound landscape ephemerality. Corporate territoriality is translated into a drama of business enterprise highly mercurial. In the context of one city, Champaign-Urbana, change in the past played out in phases of clear morphological imprint: central business district reorganization, the rise and maturation of commercial strips, suburban decentralization, and freeway reinforcement.

9

Conclusion

> With all their speed forward they may be a step backward in
> civilization—that is, in spiritual civilization. It may be that they
> will not add to the beauty of the world, not to the life of men's
> souls. I am not sure. But automobiles have come, and they bring
> a greater change in our life than most of us suspect.

Thus spoke Eugene Morgan in Booth Tarkington's *The Magnificent Ambersons*. Tarkington's character might well have been right—with reference alone to symbolism's interplay with the automobile's chief servant,
the gasoline station. Too provocative to be dismissed as only locations
where gasoline-driven vehicles are serviced, gasoline stations have become, since Tarkington's prophecy, places to cue consumers' eager antic-
ipations. Gasoline stations achieved this power in a series of steps. At
first their meaning was utilitarian. They were a collection of pumps and
reservoirs to replenish needed gasoline and oil. Unadorned sheds and
machines conveyed their meaning instantly to the expectant consumer.
These settings may have implied a romance with technology and the
promise of the future to which many early automobilists were wed. But
gasoline stations soon won larger audiences with more broadly based
cultural affections. Beginning in the 1910s, gasoline stations were styled
for deeper cultural purpose. This contrivance may have profoundly affected America through a rivalry of visual image and spoken and written
word.

Critics have attacked the use of visual icons in communicating.[1] Ste-
reotypical behaviors encouraged can be disturbingly irrational. Consumers are motivated more by the little-reasoned, unquestioned values
implicit in surficial appearances than by facts deeply pondered. But symbolized representations of cherished values are among every culture's
prime motivators. In the case of the American gasoline station, visual
display, coupled with the written and spoken word in advertising, seized
on basic American impulses regarding the good and proper life. On the

FIGURE 9.1 Petroleum companies sought to communicate basic American values in engendering brand loyalty through place-product-packaging.

road map pictured, Tide Water-Associated strove to link its Tydol brand with friendliness (see Fig. 9.1). "Our Creed," reads the plaque held by the smiling attendant clothed in company colors, his hat displaying the Flying A logo, is "Friendliness, cleanliness, honest values, sustained quality and service." Above all, gasoline stations promised mobility. On the second road map pictured, Standard Oil of New Jersey featured an American family trusting their leisure travels to the Esso brand (see Fig. 9.2). "Happy motoring!" is what the company assured.

Perhaps nothing set American society apart from peoples elsewhere quite like the profound geographical mobility enjoyed. Geographical mobility, engendered by automobile use, symbolized social status among other meanings. In landscape, the triumph of the powerful over the powerless is ultimately registered. In twentieth-century America, corporate capital led the way in transforming landscapes by proposing material progress seen as culminating, at least in the 1930s, in a utopian modernity. An unintended consequence of automobility was the devalued sense of traditional place. Localities came to be valued less for their distinctive, unique traits and more for characteristics shared universally with other places in systems of modern connectedness. Localities came to be dominated by sets of standardized behavior settings, such as gasoline stations, universally adopted. Large corporations led this march toward standard universals. Prime among these corporations were the large petroleum companies whose gasolines fueled the new automobility.

Competing oil corporations staked out their markets with chains of look-alike gasoline stations. In the third road map pictured, Canada's Husky Oil Company champions its territorial inroads in the United States in the 1960s through Frontier and Beeline brands (see Fig. 9.3). Although it is true that every large enterprise has broad geographical implications, the oil companies sought to create an overt presence in the American scene. There was nothing subtle about the place-product-packaging of gasoline marketing or the corporate territoriality that it engendered. Forward integration on the part of the large crude oil pro-

Happy Motoring!

FIGURE 9.2 The gasoline station was the center fixture of each company's marketing program built around place-product-packaging as a total design concept.

ducers and refiners produced the system. None could avoid its tyranny. Small entrepreneurs were forced to join established networks or create new networks of their own. Those who resisted did not prevail. Supporters of antichain-store legislation and "divorcement" proposals numbered among the subdued if not the failed. Their sense of parochialized space went down with their ambitions for small but steady profits outside the system.

The gasoline station came to symbolize change. Not only the ephemeral, cosmetic modifications as easily forgotten as last year's advertising campaign, but the wholesale turnover of gasoline station businesses as the major oil companies overbuilt their chains in the heady enthusiasms of territorial competition. The vacant station in transition or, in more recent times, the altogether abandoned gasoline station have brought measures of dereliction into almost every American neighborhood. More important, gasoline stations were in the vanguard of commercial strip development. They were the colonizers whereby commerce invaded previously residential neighborhoods in cities. They were the pioneers whereby commerce expanded outward at the edge of cities. Gasoline stations have always stood for flux in the American scene.

Gasoline stations came to represent business opportunity. Until recently, small entrepreneurs were readily established pumping gas and repairing cars at service stations. But profit margins were always very slim and dealers and jobbers were always at the mercy of the large corporations. Profits in the industry were pyramided to the top and rapid turnover at the retail level was always problematic. Much of the change that gasoline stations represented was, indeed, that of failure—the promise of opportunity unfulfilled. The idea of the small business person operating independently was an illusion. It spoke of the American dream of independence. In reality, it was big business masquerading. The gasoline station may have provided opportunities for local business people to link with national systems of marketing, but those linkages always worked to the favor of the corporations.

A relatively few large companies came to dominate gasoline retailing.

FIGURE 9.3 Through chains of look-alike gasoline stations, the petroleum corporations, both large and small, built trade territories in intense competition.

Since 1911 the federal government has acted to keep different corporations in competition, leveling the playing field so that no single interest will dominate the petroleum industry as once did Standard Oil. But a kind of oligopoly does exist, greatly curtailing the energy options of the American motorist as consumer. Alternatives to gasoline have been slow to emerge in an energy market fully dominated by the large integrated oil companies. There is nearly a total commitment to petroleum-oriented technologies in ground (as well as air) transportation today. American degrees of freedom are restricted as regards transportation options. Yet automobility has come to symbolize quite the opposite to Americans.

The automobile's inherent flexibility presupposes a kind of freedom of action. Our national anthem celebrates "the land of the free." If we accept that conclusion, then we can find its ample satisfaction in the gasoline station's implications. Other automobile-related icons may serve more fully—for example, the automobile itself or, perhaps, the "open road"—but the gasoline station is not without important claim. As a servant of automobility, the gasoline station fosters the illusions of a carefree reality that many Americans associate with freedom. The constitutional right to freedom of action is seemingly served by the gasoline station, which makes it possible for Americans—at least those in possession of an automobile—to travel whenever and wherever they like. Automobility appears to be inherently liberating. Access to remote corners of the nation may no longer imply courage—"home of the brave" is another line from the "Star Spangled Banner." Freedom in comfort is assured everywhere across the various far-flung marketing territories of the oil giants.

The gasoline station symbolizes other things as well. The gasoline station partially counteracts the motorcar's tendency to atomize society. The automobile, as a steel, glass, and plastic container, cocoons drivers, isolating them from one another. At gasoline stations drivers can mingle with attendants and with one another. In travel the gasoline station is always a potential point of pause. It is a place of anchor where movement stops for direct, personal socialization. The maneuvers of the machine are displaced by face-to-face interactions. Every gasoline station is potentially a center of social interest that speaks of community, if only communities of commuters or recreational or business travelers. At gasoline stations individualists come together.

The gasoline station traditionally carried a masculine implication. Here was a place where males squarely confronted the automobile age. It was a place of machines. It was a place of greases and lubricants and, of course, of gasoline. Operations required not only technical intelligence, but muscular strength thought to be more common to men than to women. At gasoline stations males congregated in ways reminiscent of livery stables and blacksmith shops. The traditional gasoline station could be crude and earthy despite the latter-day gloss of glass and porcelain enamel. Gasoline stations were intimidating places for many women. The rise of the convenience store has wrought a new era. The merger of gasoline and groceries has wrought places where both men and women are comfortable. The convenience store tends to be staffed and run by women as well as men. Perhaps that fact substantially explains the popularity of this new place-type along the American roadside.

At certain times the gasoline station has been immersed in residential associations. To blend into residential landscapes, gasoline stations were made houselike. Regardless of architectural rendering, however, the gasoline station has always functioned as a "home away from home," especially for motorists in trouble. The gasoline station has been a place for problem solving, be it mechanical—the overcoming of "car trouble"— or geographical—the directing of lost travelers to places found. In everyday rounds of movement in the twentieth century, gasoline stations were probably the most frequently encountered kind of commercial place save, perhaps, for grocery stores. In highway travel, gasoline stations were a periodic necessity in the rhythm of driving. Gasoline stations punctuated variously the hustle and bustle of America's highly mobile society. Frequency of encounter makes of them a kind of "second home." It is a place of strong behavior expectation as is one's home.

None of this was new when the automobile debuted. Americans valued the mobility of horse and wagon and railroad travel. Large railroad corporations were in the ascendancy. Livery stables and railroad depots were places for social interaction. But it was the automobile let loose in vast numbers that drove mobility to extremes accelerating profound change in American society. The 1920s brought the "red scare," Sacco and Vanzetti, the Scopes "Monkey trial," the "Return to Normalcy." It was a time when Americans searched for roots, not in Southern or Eastern Europe from where the flood of new immigrants derived, but in Britain and in America's colonial past, seen as predominantly "Anglo." The automobile was a device to escape into new suburbs contrived architecturally in the image of English and colonial revivalism. Gasoline stations, similarly designed, furthered association with the emergent upper middle class.[2] The gentry were most likely to own cars, to use them in commuting or in business, or to take frequent trips. The change that automobility drove was fundamental to the whole idea of what America ought to be. The vision was not new, but it was driven with an intensity as never before.

Culture's very essence is in the communication of shared basic assumptions. Visual images convey assumptions and thereby provide social cohesion. They are part of the symbolic interaction that is society. To the degree that certain landscape elements, such as residentially styled gasoline stations, are commonly seen, they become the very essence of culture—things to which emotional and other attachments are made in association. The cultural values symbolized by building types invite scholarly explanation. Why do some forms—some images—persist? Why do others fade and get replaced? Why did historically styled gasoline stations of the 1920s give way to futuristic styles in the 1930s? Did the economic depression so rock American confidence that an accelerated and eventual total embrace of modernism seemed necessary? What really lies behind the rise of the convenience store today?

Gasoline stations of all periods share essential architectonic features that render them unmistakable as gasoline stations: buildings, pumps, signs, and driveways, most especially. Each period has seen varying emphases placed on structures of different size, shape, and spatial organization. Variation has been a function of ephemeral fad and fashion packaged as style. Style has been manipulated to reflect changing taste. Much change in gasoline station design has involved quest only for "difference in sameness" whereby slight variations are introduced on basic themes. The deliberately unique has not fared well. The tepees, windmills, and lighthouses were driven out by the modernist tendency to plane away differences and achieve uniformity. Place-product-packaging co-opted wacky individualism. Change was carefully contrived as a kind of planned obsolescence whereby change-for-change's-sake gave, sustained through advertising, a sense of improvement or progress. Out of place-product-packaging came a sense of choice, another illusion of freedom. Although the gasoline sold was very much the same from one company to another, place-product-packaging convinced customers otherwise. Americans relished the sense of choice implicit.

Designers participated as a professional class in the supply of gasoline station schemes. Entrepreneurs fostered change to keep corporate images fresh and inviting. Successful marketers were those who synchronized with changing popular moods, the timing of change being as critical as the change itself. Cosmetic alteration suggested growth, renewal, progress—all basic drives in the American experience. Generational sensibilities are rooted in such synchronized alteration. Things made obsolete stand symbolic of points in time filled with diverse associations of strong emotive power. Occluding fads and fashions speak of a generation's past. Emerging fads and fashions speak of a still expansive future. The design process, of course, is calculated to move a product—gasoline most specifically. Again, it was a calculation to the expanded fortunes of the relatively few—the corporations, their managers, and their stockholders.

Corporate territoriality through place-product-packaging also benefited consumers, for with it came cheap petroleum products readily accessible. Low prices as derived from economies of scale swept the consumer along. Americans embraced the system willingly. They were not pawns in some ineluctable Marxist pageant. They embraced the automobile fully with all of its known implications and they readily adapted to the implications unforeseen. Perhaps the gasoline tax offers proof. Have Americans ever accepted any other form of taxation so readily?[3] The American nation's founding was entwined with resistance to taxation. Nevertheless, Americans have accepted agreeably the gasoline tax as a means of building highways. In the process they have enhanced their gasoline dependency. This automobile/highway syndrome is fully accepted by the vast majority. It is questioned only by the few.

Students of gasoline retailing have tended to ignore the cultural symbolisms implicit in gasoline stations. Geographers have viewed gasoline stations more as real estate, the locating of stations in urban markets and the decisionmaking underlying same being emphasized. The gasoline station as location has received its due, but not the gasoline station as place. Location has been but one dimension of retailing success, albeit an important one. No amount of "packaging" could salvage a gasoline outlet poorly located. But reliance on systems of place-product-packaging was generally necessary to success. Historians of the petroleum industry have tended to focus on the big questions of oil exploration, the development of refinery technologies, and the financing of integrated oil companies. Perhaps it is their preference for questions of conventional power. Receiving special emphasis in recent years has been the role of "big oil" in world geopolitics.[4] The ephemeral shifts of marketing strategy as translated through changing gasoline station cosmetics may have seemed too insignificant previously for serious historical analysis. Only when extreme shifts in the market occurred were substantially new gasoline station prototypes designed. Design departments were preoccupied with incremental adaptations insufficiently dramatic, perhaps, to capture the attention of historians.[5] Thus also have historians ignored the gasoline station as a kind of place.

Silence on place-product-packaging in monographs of the petroleum industry is also attributable to the fact that scholars have shared with entrepreneurs modernist sensibilities. They have shared a faith in the quantifiable. Marketing has been calculated in terms of costs and mechanical systems. Less tangible factors, such as the cultural values implicit in design, may have seemed too elusive to analyze. Design was intuitive. Rationalizations for the relative merits of particular color schemes, forms, or decorative details generally went unrecorded. Scholars have little penetrated corporate archives in search of such comprehension. Most corporate histories serve to showcase corporate leaders, emphasizing personalities basking in degrees of business success.[6]

Silence on corporate territoriality is more difficult to assess. Although the subject represents the classic capitalist's struggle to penetrate and hold markets, the silence may be a function of a kind of myopic blindness, corporations valued only to the extent that they succeed. Market contractions or reorientations from one region to another suggest a more complicated kind of corporate history to be avoided as corporate embarrassment. Empires that do not triumph are not worth studying. Corporate moguls steer fearlessly into the waves of economic peril and tend always to emerge as captains of their destiny. Certainly this is the impression that many corporate oil histories leave. Perhaps the surging fortunes of risk capital with its frequent surprises (including losses as well as profits), and dramatized by corporate logos carried like flags into battle, are a kind of adventure the corporate historian is reluctant to treat.

The post–World War II generation, of which the authors are a part, is the first to focus systematically on the automobile's influencing of people's landscape decisions. We have gained for the study of roadside architecture a certain scholarly creditability. The study of gasoline stations, for example, has been made impelling. Stories have been told that beg elaboration. Understanding, if not approval, of roadside architecture likely will grow, although this is obviously a tentative prediction. It seems very likely that roadside landscapes will continue to expand. Too much American geography has been reoriented to the nation's roadsides for them to suddenly recede and disappear. Indeed, a major revolution in transportation would be necessary. Certainly, abandonment of the automobile would be even more momentous than the automobile's adoption. Capital formation along the roadside seems to have its own imperatives.

The twentieth century has spawned a consumerist society in the United States. Always materialistic, Americans have turned from life styles based on work (profession or occupation) to life styles based on consuming. It is more what people consume that defines their lives and gives them status today. It is less what they produce. For more affluent Americans, purchase of goods and services has become an end in itself. In the aggregate, consumption would seem to loom as a kind of national destiny. Material satisfactions from goods and services obtained is important, but so also are the psychic rewards. Important is the aggrandized consumer. Places have been packaged to be consumed. Psychic rewards accrue from buying in specific kinds of places. The rise of the American gasoline station provides clear evidence.

The gasoline station is a carefully contrived behavior setting created to induce categories of consumption tied to automobility. Its structuring as a feature of built environment reflects foremost the logistics of retailing gasoline. Its styling and its signage (indeed, architecture as signage) carries universalizing corporate messages into every locality. The gasoline station, as the other commercial form-types of the roadside, redefines localities intruded upon according to the fashionable universals of modern economy. In everyday lives Americans have come to accept such places as part of the "natural" fabric of life. Around such common places lives are configured, remembered, and anticipated.

Gasoline stations, like everything else in the American scene, invite interpretation. As part of American landscape they beg to be read for cultural and social meaning. What is it that they tell us in broadest outline? Certainly they tell us that we live in a world of increased place-product-packaging. Perhaps our environment is more thoroughly engineered for consumption than we are wont to realize? Gasoline stations tell us of a world of enhanced corporate dominance. Perhaps advantage is pyramided up the economic hierarchy more than we would like to think? Gasoline stations tell us of a world of accelerated change. Perhaps our material world is less stable than we would like to believe?

The landscape is a mirror. It reflects what we have been, what we are, and what we are becoming as a society. But it is much more than that. Creation of the built environment is integral to a society's becoming. People are socialized through institutional fabrics necessarily contained in a material world of geographical dimension. Places for their structure and their symbolism represent settings for behavior. Every society encodes in its places the expectations for ongoing, regularized behaviors that make life reasonably predictable, and thus sustainable as taken-for-granted world. Social life is both enabled and constrained by the systems of place constantly emerging and occluding in the symbolic interactions that sum to society. Power relations play out through the competitions of place, often with clear territorial dimension. Thus it has been our intention to position readers to see the American gasoline station as a distinctive place type. Thus it has been our intention to excite readers to think seriously about the American roadside, using the gasoline station as focus. The automobile, indeed, may have brought greater change to our lives than most of us suspect. Undoubtedly, the automobile will continue to influence our lives, perhaps playing an increasingly central role in who we profess ourselves to be as individuals and as community.

So where has all of this brought the two authors—the geographer and the historian in search of landscape meaning? Where has it brought them in their consideration of the American gasoline station? This book completes a cycle of initial discovery, tentative exploration, and intensive investigation. Herein we have shared our findings, focusing on place-product-packaging and corporate territoriality as concerns capable of putting gasoline stations in more meaningful perspective. We have sought to go beyond the largely descriptive efforts that tend to characterize study of the vernacular landscape and its elements. Our work has been a playing out of impulses—a taking seriously of childhood interests, a gambling on subject matter not highly valued in our professional circles, a questing for more theoretical grounds by which to appreciate. We have brought ourselves to the point of completing this book and, accordingly, would invite our readers to help carry on the search for meaning in America's most common places. It is time to look at and take seriously the American gasoline station as a part of the American experience.

Notes

Abbreviations

GBPG   *Green Bay Press Gazette*
NPN   *National Petroleum News*
PAST   *Pioneer America Society Transactions*
PON   *Pure Oil News*
WSJ   *Winston-Salem Journal*

Notes in abbreviated form at first reference appear in full in the bibliography.

Preface and Acknowledgments

1. Sharon Zukin, *Landscapes of Power: From Detroit to Disney World* (Berkeley: University of California Press, 1991), 268.
2. Robert David Sack, *Place, Modernity, and the Consumer's World: A Geographical Framework for Analysis* (Baltimore: Johns Hopkins University Press, 1993).

Chapter 1. Gas Stations in Generational Perspective

1. The geographer already owned by age 10 Stewart's *U.S. 40: Cross Section of the United States of America*. That book and Schlereth's *U.S. 40: A Roadscape of the American Experience* make excellent introductions to landscape study for the uninitiated. For excellent overviews applicable anywhere see Meinig, ed., *The Interpretation of Ordinary Landscapes*, especially Peirce S. Lewis, "Axioms for Reading the Landscape," 11–32; and Lewis, "Learning from Looking."
2. See Johnson, *Geography and Geographers*.
3. This impulse surfaced in Jakle, Brunn, and Roseman, *Human Spatial Behavior*.
4. Susan Sontag in her book, *On Photography*, said it best. "The American landscape has always seemed too varied, immense, mysterious, fugitive to lend itself to scientism" (65).
5. This line of argumentation is elaborated in Jakle, *The Visual Elements of Landscape*.
6. An example would be Semple, *American History and Its Geographical Conditions*.
7. Perhaps the most convenient synopsis of what modern historical geography is all about appears as Preston, *Historical Analysis in Geography*.
8. Turner, "The Significance of the Frontier in American History."
9. The dissertation was condensed as Jakle, "Salt on the Ohio Valley Frontier, 1770–1820."

10. The notion of the "geographic past" is elaborated in Jakle, "Time, Space and the Geographic Past."

11. For a classical statement defining "cultural landscape" see Sauer, "The Morphology of Landscape."

12. See Harris, "The Historical Mind and the Practice of Historical Geography."

13. See Prince, "Real, Imagined and Abstract Worlds of the Past."

14. Jakle, *The Tourist*.

15. This penchant for the distant past is painfully evident in a recent overview of the field of historical geography. See Earle et al., "Historical Geography."

16. See Riley, "Vernacular Landscapes."

17. A review of the literature on vernacular houses is contained in Jakle, Bastian, and Meyer, *Common Houses in America's Small Towns*.

18. Ibid.; Jakle, "Gasoline Stations in the Champaign-Urbana Landscape"; Jakle, "The American Gasoline Station, 1920 to 1970"; Jakle and Mattson, "Goodbye to the Horse"; Jakle, "Motel by the Roadside"; Jakle and Mattson, "The Evolution of a Commercial Strip"; Jakle, "Roadside Restaurants."

19. Kammen, "Introduction."

20. Sculle, "French Anticlericalism after the Separation of Church and State, 1906–1910."

21. Goubert, "Local History."

22. Von Ranke, *The Theory and Practice of History,* xix–xxx.

23. For example, see Keith A. Sculle, "A Look at the Past: Gas Stations Important Yale-to-Casey Landmarks," *Casey Daily Reporter* (Casey, Ill.), April 10, 1975, p. 4.

    Comprehensive survey findings were reported in Keith A. Sculle, "Interim Report of Historic Landmarks" for the Illinois Department of Conservation in each of the following counties: Bond, Champaign, Clark, Coles, Crawford, Cumberland, DeWitt, Douglas, Edgar, Edwards, Effingham, Fayette, Ford, Iroquois, Jasper, Kankakee, Livingston, McLean, Macon, Moultrie, Piatt, Shelby, Stark, Tazewell, Vermilion, and Woodford. Mimeographed, September 1972 through June 1975.

24. Thompson, *The Voice of the Past,* 5.

25. Administrative responsibility and intellectual curiosity are discussed in Sculle, "Keeping the National Register Honest," and Sculle, "A Case for Local Significance."

26. An existential argument for historic preservation is contained in Sculle, "A Case for Self-preservation, Bob's Place."

27. The first Wisconsin effort resulted in a sidebar for an article by Sculle and Derr, "Fill'er Up."

28. Sculle, "The Pure Sign"; Sculle, "C. A. Petersen"; Sculle, "Boosterism and Architecture"; and Sculle, "The Vernacular Gasoline Station."

29. Jakle, "The Writing of Scholarly Books in Geography."

30. Novick, *That Noble Dream,* 577–92.

31. Sculle, "Registers of Historic Places," and Sculle, "Another Roadside Attraction"; Flink, "The Automobile Revolution."

32. Neustadt and May, *Thinking in Time*.

Chapter 2. Place-Product-Packaging

1. Architects coined the term *place-product-packaging*. See Oliver and Ferguson, "The Environment Is a Diary."

2. See Giddens, *The Constitution of Society;* Cohen, "Structuration Theory and Social Praxis."

3. Mead, *Mind, Self, and Society*. See also Stone and Faberman, eds., *Social Psychology through Symbolic Interaction*.

4. Dicke, *Franchising in America,* 3.

5. See Relph, *Place and Placelessness*.

6. Much of our thinking on postmodernism stems from Kolb, *Postmodern Sophistication*. See also Harvey, *The Condition of Postmodernity*, and Soja, *Postmodern Geographies*.

7. Venturi, Brown, and Izenour, *Learning from Las Vegas*. See also Venturi and Brown, *A View from the Campidoglio*.

8. "The Great American Roadside"; and Steinbeck, *The Grapes of Wrath*.

9. Nabokov, *Lolita*; Dettelbach, *In the Driver's Seat*, 36–39; Jack Kerouac, *On the Road* (New York: Viking Press, 1959), 156.

10. Liebs, *Main Street to Miracle Mile*, 3–7.

11. For a perceptive understanding of J. B. Jackson, see D. W. Meinig, "Teachers," in Meinig, ed., *The Interpretation of Ordinary Landscapes*, 195–244. Jackson, "Other-Directed Houses."

12. Jackson, "Other-Directed Houses," 30.

13. Pellegrini, "Design for Travel"; and Snow, "The New Road in the United States."

14. Wolfe, *The Kandy-Kolored Tangerine-Flake Streamline Baby*; Hess, *Googie*, 119; Kouwenhoven, *The Beer Can by the Highway*; Susman, ed., *Culture and Commitment 1929–1945*, 45–46; and Boorstin, *The Image*, 279–80.

15. Keller, *The Highway as Habitat*. See also Plattner, *The Standard Oil (New Jersey) Photography Project*. Amateur photography is also a source of past roadside imagery. See Paster, "The Snapshot, the Automobile, and the Americans."

16. See Vale and Vale, *U.S. 40 Today*; Watson and Gillon Jr., *New York Then and Now*.

17. Hokanson, *The Lincoln Highway*. See also Scott and Kelly, *Route 66*, and Wallis, *Route 66*.

18. Scott and Kelly, *Route 66*, 179–81.

19. For an example of an effective use of oral history see Bodnar, *Worker's World*. Regarding oral history and the roadside see Sculle, "Oral History."

20. Belasco, *Americans on the Road*; Marling, *The Colossus of Roads*; Horwitz, *The Strip*.

21. For example, see Blake, *God's Own Junkyard*.

22. Venturi, Brown, and Izenour, *Learning from Las Vegas*; Hirschorn and Izenour, *White Towers*; Vieyra, *"Fill'er Up"*; Witzel, *The American Gas Station*.

23. Andrews, *The Well-built Elephant and Other Roadside Attractions*; Hess, *Googie*, 40; Langdon, *Orange Roofs, Golden Arches*; Liebs, *Main Street to Miracle Mile*, 10.

24. Jakle, *The Tourist*; Relph, *Place and Placelessness*, and Riley, *Rational Landscapes and Humanistic Geography*; Vale and Vale, *U.S. 40 Today*, and Vale and Vale, *Western Images, Western Landscapes*.

25. Rae, *The Automobile*; Rae, *The Road and the Car in American Life*; and Flink, *The Automobile Age*.

26. Jennings, ed., *Roadside America*.

27. Dicke, *Franchising in America*, 13–18; Mandell, *The Great Credit Card Industry*, 14–17; and Marburg, "The Organization of Distribution and Marketing."

28. Dicke, *Franchising in America*, 3–5.

29. "Where Oil Got Its Trademarks."

30. "Introducing the New Pure Oil Co. Seal," 5.

31. Advertisement, *NPN* 52 (October 1960): 26.

32. Advertisement, *NPN* 17 (May 20, 1925): 28.

33. "Exclusive Right to Pump Color Scheme Upheld in Court Ruling."

34. Schroeder, "Brand Identification Is Taking on a Professional Look."

35. Chatfield, "Cities Service Ads Build Goodwill among Customers and Employees."

36. Ibid.

37. "Pure Oil Advertising Reaches New High Peak."

38. Dicke, *Franchising in America*, 9.

Chapter 3. Marketing Strategies in the Petroleum Industry

1. Pierson, *The Moving American*. Sources to which we are indebted for the overview of the automobile and highway throughout chapter 3 are following: Abernathy, *The Productivity Dilemma*; Flink, *The Automobile Age*; Labatut and Lane, eds., *Highways in Our National Life*; Rae, "The Internal Combustion Engine on Wheels"; Rae, *The Road and the Car in American Life*; Rose, *Historic American Roads*; Seely, *Building the American Highway System*; and U.S. Department of Transportation, Federal Highway Administration, *America's Highways, 1776–1976*.
2. Bailey, "The Other Revolution," 52–64.
3. For the relationship of the automobile and the highway through the 1920s see Hugill, "Good Roads and the Automobile in the United States," 327–49. For the highway through the 1920s see MacDonald, "The History and Development of Road Building in the United States," 1181–1206.
4. Economic reasons giving rise to the gasoline station are best treated in Williamson et al., *The Age of Energy, 1899–1959*, 210–40. A brief overview emphasizing the experience of the Atlantic Refining Company is in McLean and Haigh, *The Growth of Integrated Oil Companies*, 267–70.
5. U.S. Department of Transportation, Federal Highway Administration, "Highway Statistics: Summary to 1985" (hereafter USDOT 1985), Table MV-201; Flink, "The Ultimate Status Symbol," 157–58; USDOT 1985, Table MF-221; Mandell, *The Great Credit Card Industry*, 16–19.
6. See Beaton, *Enterprise in Oil*, 279–81.
7. Freitag, "Wofford Oil Company of Alabama"; Stafford, "Oil Companies Pushed to Keep Abreast of Florida's Growth"; Barringer, "His Initials are RR."
8. Beaton, *Enterprise in Oil*, 420.
9. "Money to be Made," 116.
10. Guthrie, "'Super' Stations and Oil Companies Compete for Gasoline Business," 64–65.
11. "Kind of Highway Determines Type of Successful Station."
12. Halbert, "Tendency Is Toward Better Stations Rather than More of Them."
13. "Sun Introduces Public to Octane Ratings in Selling Gasoline."
14. Advertisement, *NPN* 20 (February 20, 1924): 94.
15. USDOT 1985, Tables MV-201, MF-221.
16. For interstate highway policy through the 1980s see Rose, *Interstate*.
17. Anderson, *Fundamentals of the Petroleum Industry*, 30.
18. Pew, "Against Marketing Divorcement."
19. "What the Gasoline Tax Is Doing to the Oil Industry."
20. Barringer, "Standard of Indiana Announces Extension of 'Iowa Plan.'"
21. "A Gasoline Station Is Not a Store," *NPN* 26 (April 4, 1934): 30–32.
22. Marvin Reid, "America Enters the Gasoline Era," *NPN* 76 (February 1984): 52.
23. USDOT 1985, Table MV-201; Reid, "America Enters the Gasoline Era." For the automobile industry in the quarter century after World War II, see White, *The Automobile Industry since 1945*.
24. USDOT 1985, Table MF-210.
25. O'Connor, *The Empire of Oil*, 148.
26. Reid, "America Enters the Gasoline Era," 51.
27. Reid, "How Phillips Marched into Dixie," 104–5.
28. USDOT 1985, Tables MV-201 and MF-221.
29. Anderson, *Fundamentals of the Petroleum Industry*, 280.
30. Reid, "America Enters the Gasoline Era," 53.
31. Ibid., 55.
32. "Truckstops: Multibillion-dollar Business."

33. "Motels Chancy, but . . ."

34. "How Kyso Stakes a Big, Bold Interstate Claim."

35. "Hard Lessons and Big Changes in the Market."

36. USDOT 1985, Table MV-201.

37. U.S. Department of Energy, Energy Information Administration, "U.S. Gasoline Consumption."

38. Reid, "America Enters the Gasoline Era," 58.

39. Ibid., 57.

40. Ghosh, *Competition and Diversification in the United States Petroleum Industry,* 4.

41. Flynn, "The Small Business Motor Fuel Marketer Preservation Act of 1981 . . . ," 115.

42. "Distributors Before/After Oil Shock."

43. Dicke, *Franchising in America,* 52.

44. Allvine, Houston, and Phillips, "The Case for Legislative Relief from the Impending Destruction of Small Business and Competition in the Gasoline Industry," 66.

45. For 1981 see USDOT 1985, Table MV-201. For 1990 see U.S. Department of Transportation, Federal Highway Administration, "Selected Highway Statistics and Charts 1990," tables SS90-4, SS90-17. For trends in the fuel economy of the late 1980s see U.S. Congress, Office of Technology Assessment, *Improving Automobile Fuel Economy,* 31.

46. Reid, "Oil Product Imports," 36.

47. "Percent Self-Service Motorist Gasoline Sold by Brand," 138.

48. "Car Care Center Growth Slows, But Developers See Bright Future."

49. "Why C-Stores Lead Gasoline Markets," 35.

50. Reid, "The Majors Brush Up Their Public Images."

Chapter 4. Corporate Territoriality

1. Greene, *Strategies of the Major Oil Companies,* 50.

2. Breese, "How to Stay Youthful at Fifty," 96.

3. Barringer, "S.O. Indiana Files Suit Against Use of 'Esso' in 14 States," 24.

4. "Humble Oil: 'Esso' or 'Enco'?" 68.

5. "The Day of Big Sellouts."

6. "Branded Retail Outlets," 48.

7. Dedman, *Challenge and Response,* 61.

8. "How Indiana Standard Will Go National," 81.

9. McLean and Haigh, *The Growth of Integrated Oil Companies,* 304.

10. "Richfield Out, Sinclair In," 123.

11. "Atlantic-Richfield," 46.

12. White, *Formative Years in the Far West,* 507.

13. Guthrie, "'Super' Stations and Oil Companies Compete for Gasoline Business," 64.

14. "The California-Kentucky Merger," 95.

15. "How Fledgling Chevron USA Was Hatched," 29.

16. "Fewer Outlets for Gulf Oil," 9; "Merger Frenzy," 24.

17. "BP Oil to Sohio to BP," 67.

18. "Beyond Fanfare, BP Must Face Reality and Challenge."

19. Shaner, "'New' BP Launches Image Campaign in U.S. Markets."

20. "Battle for No. 1."

21. Greene, *Strategies of the Major Oil Companies,* 129.

22. Ibid., 130, 139.

23. "Mobil's Marathon Tender," 30.

24. Reich, *The Next American Frontier,* 147.

25. "Conoco-Dupont," 44.

26. Beaton, *Enterprise in Oil*, 56.

27. Ibid., 273.

28. Ibid., 478.

29. James, *The Texaco Story*, 39.

30. Greene, *Strategies of the Major Oil Companies*, 201.

31. "Getty-Skelly Merger Close at Hand."

32. "Cities Shuffle Names in ID Change."

33. Giebelhaus, *Business and Government in the Oil Industry*, 150.

34. Ibid., 77.

35. "Sunray Aims Marketing Push," 55.

36. "1918—The Company Then and Now—1938," 55.

37. "Southwest," 25.

38. "Is Total Shooting for No. 1 Midwest Spot?" *NPN* 72 (October 1980): 41.

39. "By Being Bold, Murphy Becomes a Baby International," 71.

Chapter 5. The Gas Station as Form

Note: The content of this chapter first appeared as Jakle, "The American Gasoline Station, 1920 to 1970," and Sculle, "The Enduring Best."

1. See, e.g., Kniffen, "Louisiana House-Types," and "Folk Housing: Key to Diffusion." Recent works include Noble, *Wood, Brick, and Stone,* and Jakle, Bastian, and Meyer, *Common Houses in America's Small Towns.*

2. The literature on gasoline station location is summarized in Claus and Hardwick, *The Mobile Consumer.* See also Claus, *Spatial Dynamics of Gasoline Service Stations.* The early literature on gasoline station design appears mainly in the trade journals of the American petroleum industry. See especially the *NPN.*

3. Lohof, "The Service Station in America"; Vieyra, *"Fill'er Up!"*; Liebs, "Gasoline Stations," in *Main Street to Miracle Mile,* 95–115.

4. "Now the No-service Station."

5. "Money to be Made," 114–15.

6. "Around the Filling Stations," 8.

7. "Money to be Made," 133.

8. Ibid., 115.

9. Ibid., 116.

10. Breese, "How to Stay Youthful at Fifty," 90.

11. Truesdell, "Highest New York State Court Rules Out Curb Pumps in Buffalo."

12. Advertisement of the Arthur B. Shepard Co., *NPN* 15 (October 31, 1923): 94.

13. Stafford, "Jenney Builds Stations to Fit New England Settings"; Guthrie, "Bostonian Can Purchase His Gasoline and Not Offend Aesthetic Sense"; Halbert, "Merchandise Display Window Features Pure Oil Co.'s New Stations."

14. Williamson et al., *The Age of Energy, 1899–1959,* 219.

15. For a brief history of gasoline pump design see Meikle, "Refining the Roadside," 72–73. Collections permit inductive study and Anderson, *Check the Oil,* 39–52, is useful regarding the history of the gasoline pump as artifact.

16. The terms *overhang, covered drive,* and *driveway shed* were also used to describe canopies.

17. "Here's Standard's Model for Steel Service Stations." The most frequent advertisers of prefabricated "house and canopy" stations in the *NPN* were Blaw-Knox Company (Pittsburgh), Butler Manufacturing Company (Kansas City, Mo.), J. R. Doelker Company (Columbus, Ohio), Edwards Manufacturing Company (Cincinnati), Marion Machine Foundry and Supply Company (Marion, Ind.), Metal Shelter Company (St. Paul), J. E. Moss Iron Works (Wheeling, W.V.), W. F. Norman Sheet Metal Manu-

facturing Company (Newark, N.J.), and Ohio Body and Blower Company (Cleveland).

18. "Standard Type of Service Station"; "Station Type Adopted by N.Y. Standard."

19. "Pattern Stations on Old Missions"; "Stucco, Tile Lead to Pleasing Station Architecture."

20. "Greasing Equipment Takes to Cover in Modern Super Service Station." The Edwards Manufacturing Company of Cincinnati was the most frequent advertiser of lubritoriums in the *NPN*.

21. The term *stall* was also used to describe enclosed bays.

22. Olson, "Sign of the Star." See also "Standardized Service Stations Designed by Walter Dorwin Teague."

23. Liebs, 106.

24. "Mid-Continent Builds Ultra-Modern Station."

25. The most frequent advertisers of prefabricated "oblong box" gasoline stations were: The Austin Company (Cleveland), B. and M. Corporation (Columbus, Ohio), Butler Manufacturing Company (Kansas City, Mo.), Cincinnati Manufacturing Company, Columbian Steel Tank Company (Kansas City, Mo.), Dresser Engineering Company (Tulsa, Okla.), Erie Meter Systems, Inc. (Erie, Pa.), Functional Buildings, Inc. (Cleveland), Madison, Inc. (Conyers, Ga.), W. A. Park, Inc. (Angola, Ind.), Stefco Steel Company (Michigan City, Ind.), and Truscon Steel Company (Youngstown, Ohio).

26. Porcelain enamel was made from a soft sheet of steel, called "enameling stock," covered with a layer of "frit" (minute particles of shattered glass resulting from the contact of molten glass with cold water). The frit-covered steel was then placed in fusing ovens at high temperatures.

27. "Shell Tailors Stations to Fit"; "Plastic Provides a Built-in Spectacular"; "Not All Masonry Is Masonry."

28. Anderson, *Check the Oil*, 41–44, and Meikle, "Refining the Roadside," 89–90.

29. Barringer, "Better Materials and Fittings Make Stations More Attractive"; Thompson, "Uniformity Is Trend in Station Design"; Sturtevant, "Marketers Design Stations to Reduce Building Costs."

30. "Shell Oil's Newest 'Blend-in,'" and "How Ranch Style Is Taking Over Service Station Design."

31. "How Old Stations Get the New Look."

32. "Are These Stations What's Ahead for Texaco?"

33. "East Coast: From Box to Colonial."

34. "Bulk Stations Started in Buffalo, Thrive There Now."

35. The most frequent advertisers of the prefabricated "small box" were Avoncraft Division of Marine Ways, Inc. (New Orleans), Porcelain Buildings, Inc. (Metaire, La.), Trans-View Structures, Inc. (Lake George, N.Y.), and Valentine Manufacturing, Inc. (Wichita, Kan.).

36. Truesdell, "How Re-designing of a Filling Station Doubled Its Business."

37. "Canopies: What's Behind an Old Standby's New Appeal."

38. "Now the No-service Station."

39. "Around the Filling Stations."

40. For example, Mobil introduced "Big Bi" and "Hi Val" gasoline in selected areas.

41. The number of illustrations varied from year to year: 140 in 1920, 89 in 1930 (non-advertising materials only), 142 in 1940, 118 in 1950, 193 in 1960, and 91 in 1970, 1980, and 1990. The mix of advertising and nonadvertising illustrations depicting gasoline stations also varied: for example, 86 percent were advertisements in 1920, 47 percent in 1940, 36 percent in 1970. Throughout the *NPN*'s history, innovations in gasoline station design generally appeared first in advertisements. How-

ever, most advertising illustrations depicted the typical or commonplace as opposed to the unique. Illustrations depicting gasoline stations also appeared with articles concerned with gasoline marketing, in general, and gasoline station management, more specifically. An average of three articles each year dealt exclusively with gasoline station design.

42. For examples see "Super Service Station Designed as Mosque"; "Tourist Camp Stations Patterned after Dutch Windmills," *NPN* 22 (April 30, 1930): 105; Weller, "Indian Village to Grow around Station." For a history of the last see Sculle, "Roadside Business."

43. Advertisement in *NPN* 46 (January/March 1954): 11; "Portable Country Stations Are Replicas of Famous Lighthouse," *NPN* 22 (June 25, 1930): 68; "Sell Gasoline from Greek Temple."

44. "Stucco, Tile Lead to Pleasing Station Architecture"; "Details of Modern Station Design Given by Union Oil Co."; "Pattern Stations on Old Missions."

45. "Station Type Adopted by N.Y. Standard"; Guthrie, "Bostonian Can Purchase His Gasoline and Not Offend Aesthetic Sense."

46. Larson, Knowlton, and Popple, *New Horizons, 1927–1950,* 266. Members of the Beacon board also formed a subsidiary chain called Colonial Filling Stations. See *Moody's Analyses of Investments* (New York, 1925), 377.

47. Crandall, "Correct Lighting Is Both Convenience and Good Advertising."

48. Richard B. Fox, telephone interview with Keith A. Sculle, March 14, 1985.

49. Larson et al., *New Horizons, 1927–1950,* 266.

50. McCarthy, "Public Calls 'Em 'Colonial Stations' So Beacon Changes Name."

Chapter 6. Gas Station Design—The Large Corporation

Note: This chapter represents an updating and elaboration of "The Pure Sign," with the addition of C. B. Dawes, "Standardization of Service Stations: Report," Dawes Arboretum, Newark, Ohio, which was unavailable when the article was published.

1. Butsch, "Introduction: Leisure and Hegemony in America," 3–27; Clarke, "Pessimism versus Populism: The Problematic Politics of Popular Culture," 28–44; and Marchand, *Advertising the American Dream.*

2. Flink, *The Automobile Age,* 132–35; Lears, "From Salvation to Self-Realization."

3. Notable literature by scholars unaffiliated with petroleum companies albeit with different perspectives than the authors' includes a short analysis of one style, Wadhams Oil and Grease Company's "Japanese 'Tea Garden'": Attoe and Latus, "Buildings as Signs." Wheeler, "Frank Lloyd Wright Filling Station, 1958," was a well-documented but essentially brief reflection on its architect's diversity and is not offered as a comprehensive treatment of the station. All the styles of a corporation include Lohof, "The Service Station in America," about the Marathon Oil Company, and Wolf, "The Gasoline Station," about Sun Oil's various stations. Vieyra, *"Fill'er Up,"* explores the role of image in gasoline station architecture and largely overlooks those not designed by architects. A synthesis of primarily secondary works distinguished significantly by its lavish color illustrations which make of the gas station with its associated memorabilia an artifact of nostalgia is Witzel, *The American Gas Station.*

4. Liebs, *Main Street to Miracle Mile,* 101.

5. "Wide Expansions in Marketing."

6. Uncle Pat, "Twenty Years in Retrospect."

7. Dawes, "Standardization of Service Stations."

8. "1877—Henry May Dawes—1952," 4.

9. Dawes, "Service Station Buildings, Principles," 4–5, in "Standardization of Service Stations"; "George T. Wofford Dies"; Uncle Pat, "Twenty Years in Retrospect," 7.

10. Dawes, "Standardization of Service Stations," 2.
11. Dawes, "Proposal for a System of Landscaping Service Stations," August 3, 1925, in ibid.
12. Vieyra, *"Fill'er Up!"* 28–29.
13. C. A. Petersen, letter to Keith A. Sculle, October 16, 1978.
14. C. A. Petersen, interview with Keith A. Sculle in Eustis, Fla., February 19, 1979 (hereafter Petersen interview).
15. Petersen to Sculle, October 16, 1978, and Petersen interview.
16. C. A. Petersen, autobiography, chapter entitled "Pittsburgh," n.p., Petersen papers, Library of Congress, Washington, D.C.; Petersen to Sculle, letter, September 25, 1978.
17. Petersen insisted that it was he who chose Ludowici-Celadon (Petersen interview, February 19, 1979), and, in the sense that the final selection of roofing tile for Pure's standard station awaited Pure's adoption of Petersen's English cottage, Petersen's claim can be accepted. However, it is clear from a series of interrogatory letters to roofing tile suppliers starting May 21, 1925, that by June 9, 1925, Carlos B. Dawes had winnowed alternative suppliers and was prepared to recommend Ludowici-Celadon (Dawes, "Standardization of Service Stations," section entitled "Roofing.")
18. Halbert, "Merchandise Display Window Features Pure Oil Co.'s New Stations," 23, and C. A. Petersen, unpublished manuscript.
19. See especially Jackson, *Crabgrass Frontier,* a wide-ranging synthesis of not only the economic and social development of the suburb through the American past but its landscape elements as well. Earliest origins are emphasized in Archer, "Country and City in the American Romantic Suburb" and "Ideology and Aspiration." The idealized suburb's middle-class roots are not only confirmed but its implications are brilliantly explored in two social histories of vernacular architecture: Wright, *Building the Dream,* and Clark, *The American Family Home.* Many of these books' conclusions are echoed but also with equally new insights from the different perspective of a vernacular architectural historian with elitist preferences: Gowans, *The Comfortable House.* Stilgoe, *Borderland,* ably offers a geographer's perspective. Questions and directions for future suburban design couched in a historical discussion of the values giving rise to suburbs are well stated in Rowe, *Making a Middle Landscape.*
20. Gowans, *The Comfortable House,* 184, 213; Clark, *The American Family Home,* 83, 189; Wright, *Building the Dream,* 210; and Lynes, *The Tastemakers,* 285.
21. Clark, *The American Family Home,* 179, 192; Lane, "The Period House in the Nineteen-twenties," 172.
22. Lynes, *The Tastemakers,* 245–46; Jackson, *Crabgrass Frontier,* 78; Wright, *Building the Dream,* 212–14; Cheney, *The New World Architecture,* 232.
23. An adequate yet brief description of the Romantic Suburb is still to be found in Kidney, *The Architecture of Choice,* 43–45, although subsequent scholarship has expanded considerably on it. See especially Archer, "Country and City in the American Romantic Suburb" and "Ideology and Aspiration," and Jackson, *Crabgrass Frontier,* 73–86, for a discussion of the first few Romantic Suburbs. Tunnard, "The Romantic Suburb in America," remains a helpful, brief introduction to the first Romantic Suburb, Llewellyn Park.
24. Kidney, *The Architecture of Choice,* 44; Lynes, *The Tastemakers,* 237.
25. Halbert, "Merchandise Display Window Features Pure Oil Co.'s New Stations," 23; Petersen interview; and Kidney, *The Architecture of Choice,* 48.
26. Field observations by Keith A. Sculle, August 6, 1979. The stations were built at the corners of Morris and Harding and Tenth and Rural: Petersen, letter to Sculle, October 16, 1978.

27. Petersen, "Transforming an Eyesore to a Thing of Beauty."

28. Halbert, "Merchandise Display Window Features Pure Oil Co.'s New Stations," 23.

29. Glassie, "Artifacts," 104; Petersen, autobiography, "English Cottage," n.p.; Petersen, *The Station Ahead,* 66; and Petersen, letter to Sculle, October 16, 1978.

30. Petersen, letter to Sculle, October 16, 1978; Halbert, "Merchandise Display Window Features Pure Oil Co.'s New Stations," 22.

31. Withey and Withey, *Biographical Dictionary of American Architects (Deceased),* 402; and Evanston Preservation Commission, "Historic Resources Survey."

32. Hinman, *Population Growth and the Demands upon Land for Housing in Evanston, Illinois;* Reeling, *Evanston,* 11; and Tennerstedt, "Evanston—'The City of Homes.'"

33. "1877—Henry May Dawes—1952," 4–5; Eaton, *Two Chicago Architects and Their Clients,* 62–63, 178–81, 246–51.

34. Halbert, "Merchandise Display Window Features Pure Oil Co.'s New Stations," 22.

35. Design patent 77,857 (February 26, 1929); "Court Enjoins Dealer's Use of Patented Station Design," 16; The Pure Oil Company, 1-2-37, Engineering Dept., Chicago, Ill., an unpublished drawing; C. B. Watson to Petersen, letter, October 13, 1935, Petersen papers, Library of Congress; and "Gilding the Lily."

36. Barringer, "Most Oil Companies Rent Stations in Florida to Operators"; Edgell, *The American Architecture of To-Day,* 101; Petersen interview.

37. Petersen, *The Station Ahead,* 33, 34, 89.

38. Clark, *The American Family Home,* 201.

39. Regarding complementary plants see as an example "Your Competitor Says 'Kindly Omit Flowers.'" Dawes underscored the advice in "Cultivate More Attractive Surroundings."

40. "Clean Service Stations Mean Better Business."

41. Legend with photograph, *PON* 23 (April 1941): 32; J.T.B., "Neat Snappy Appearance"; and "Every Pure Oil Outlet Is an Advertisement."

42. For an example of Pure's praise for standards achieved see Leslie, "Model Service Station"; and, for an example of female certification of these standards, see "The Front Yard . . . and the Back."

43. Petersen, "A Model of a Model Station," and Rapoport, *House Form and Culture,* 133–34.

44. Petersen interview, February 19, 1979.

45. Legend with photograph, *PON* 16 (August 1933): 30; Bowman, "A Finer Pure Oil Exhibit at the Century of Progress"; and "Department Store Features Miniature Pure Oil Station."

46. "Ford Men Call This Ideal Super Set-Up"; D.J.T., "The 'English Village'"; and Petersen interview. Evidence of Pure's satisfaction is in the following: Bodine, "Glorifying the American Service Station," 17; Petersen, "Transforming an Eyesore to a Thing of Beauty"; H. H. S[tevenson], "Beautiful Hudson Station"; and Pettengill, "The First Fifty Years."

47. Watkins, "Third 'Big One' Opened."

48. Clark, *The American Family Home;* Gowans, *The Comfortable House;* Wright, *Building the Dream;* Eaton, *Two Chicago Architects and Their Clients,* 246.

49. For example, Walter Dorwin Teague's Texaco type is a singularly intriguing subject for research. This first application of modernism by a major corporation (Olson, "Sign of the Star," 1) achieved the status of the archetypal gasoline station in popular culture (Vieyra, *"Fill'er Up!"* 69). Its origins at Texaco cannot be fully examined, however, because only excerpts from earlier decisions and none of its

principals survive (Stafford Acher [Texaco historian], letter to Keith A. Sculle, September 24, 1985).

50. Upton, "The Power of Things," 276–77.
51. Davis, *Conspicuous Production,* 74–75, 207.

Chapter 7. Gas Station Design—The Small Entrepreneur

Note: The section on the Barkhausen Oil Company and its allies is a revision of the article "Boosterism and Architecture."

1. "Platt Defines 'Oil Jobber,'" 24.
2. " . . . Michigan Marketer Plans for Future," 26.
3. *Green Bay Press Gazette* (hereafter *GBPG*), October 10, 1954; Donn P. Quigley (chief curator, Neville Public Museum, Green Bay, Wis.) to Keith A. Sculle, letter, January 3, 1980.
4. *GBPG*, September 6, 1922, p. 3; S. D. Hastings (son of S. D. Hastings, Jr.), letter to Keith A. Sculle, May 7, 1979.
5. *GBPG*, May 27, 1922, p. 17.
6. Carter, *Another Part of the Twenties,* 1–2.
7. Leuchtenberg, *The Perils of Prosperity,* 198, 226–27.
8. Allen, *Only Yesterday,* 178.
9. Lynd and Lynd, *Middletown,* 395, 486, 487.
10. *GBPG*, August 8, 1921, p. 6.
11. Ibid., February 10, 1921, p. 1; October 6, 1922, p. 3; April 23, 1925, p. 1; November 6, 1922, p. 3; February 1, 1924, pp. 1–2; January 1, 1925, p. 1.
12. Handlin, *The American House,* 140–41; *GBPG*, April 26, 1922, p. 7; August 31, 1921, p. 1; October 28, 1921, p. 6.
13. *GBPG*, May 18, 1925, p. 6; November 7, 1925, p. 1; November 17, 1925, p. 1.
14. "Special Green Bay Edition"; *GBPG*, June 16, 1925, p. 1.
15. *GBPG*, October 27, 1923, p. 5.
16. For example, see *GBPG*, July 11, 1922, p. 4.
17. *GBPG*, July 10, 1922, p. 2; Giddens, *Standard Oil Company (Indiana),* 314–22; *GBPG*, December 4, 1924, p. 5.
18. *GBPG*, March 25, 1924, p. 15; April 16, 1924, p. 6; August 25, 1925, p. 3; and *Wright's Green Bay Directory,* 69.
19. *GBPG*, April 13, 1921, p. 1; April 24, 1925, p. 1.
20. Ross and Catlin, *Landmarks of Wayne County and Detroit,* 171, 187; Moore, *History of Michigan,* 2:1100.
21. S. D. Hastings to Keith A. Sculle, May 7, 1979; *GBPG*, August 30, 1969.
22. Joseph Hansen (owner of Hansen Oil Company), letter to Henry A. Foeller, January 6, 1924, Berners, Schober, and Kilp archives; Powell, ed., *Past Is Prologue,* 15–16; Williamson et al., *The American Petroleum Industry,* 493; "Service Station Field Is Playground for Architectural Design"; Clarence O. Jahn, interview with Keith A. Sculle, Green Bay, Wis., August 2, 1979.
23. "Service Station Field Is Playground for Architectural Design," 74; Clarence Jahn, letter to Bratt and Lang, March 23, 1926, Berners, Schober, and Kilp archives; King, "Public Comfort Stations"; Guth, "Small Buildings"; Barringer, "'If I Ever Built A Station It Will Have Clean Rest Rooms . . . ' It Has," 54.
24. Beaton, *Enterprise in Oil,* 314–20, 418.
25. *Winston-Salem, N.C., City and Suburban Directory 1921,* 679–80, 698; *Winston-Salem, N.C. City Directory 1926,* 845; *Miller's Winston-Salem, N.C. City Directory 1930,* 941–42.
26. Taylor, "Prices in Chain and Independent Grocery Stores in Durham, North Carolina," 413; *Winston-Salem Journal* (hereafter *WSJ*), September 18, 1929, p. 4.

27. *WSJ*, October 11, 1929, p. 1.

28. "Higher Gas Taxes the Cry in the States, Chain Store Bills Are New Levies"; Chatfield, "Independent Marketers Make Capital of Anti–Chain Store Feeling," 55.

29. Lawton and Lawton, *The Roadsides of North Carolina*. For a discussion of Lawton's work throughout the nation, see Bluestone, "Roadside Blight and the Reform of Commercial Architecture."

30. *WSJ*, December 7, 1929, pp. 1, 16; December 13, 1930, p. 1.

31. Ibid., December 6, 1929, pp. 21, 27.

32. Ibid., January 4, 1930, pp. 4, 11; January 8, 1930, p. 9; October 25, 1930, p. 2.

33. Ibid., March 29, 1930, p. 12.

34. *WSJ*, October 23, 1929, p. 3; February 5, 1930, p. 9.

35. For example, *WSJ*, April 2, 1930, p. 11; November 24, 1929, p. 10A; October 11, 1929, p. 19.

36. "Almost Half of Motorists Buy on Brand Marketing Survey Finds."

37. James K. Glenn, Sr., telephone interview with Keith A. Sculle, August 14, 1979 (hereafter Glenn interview).

38. *WSJ*, April 4, 1930, p. 11; April 11, 1930, p. 16.

39. Walter H. Leonard, Jr., telephone interview with Keith A. Sculle, January 8, 1983.

40. Lillian M. (Mrs. Charles R.) Johnson, telephone interview with Keith A. Sculle, June 5, 1983.

41. Vieyra, *"Fill'er Up!"* 19, claims "naive literalism" and, alternatively, Taylor, *From Frontier to Factory*, 69, claims streamlining was the seashell's origin. Bishir, *North Carolina Architecture*, 403, is content to claim the visually verifiable origin of the seashell as an "attention getting advertisement." Considerable confusion exists as to Quality's possible inspiration by Shell's exhibition architecture. Quality's seashell (1930) antedated Shell's information booth in the form of a seashell at the California Pacific International Exposition (1935) by five years. Thus, the assertion of Barbara Rubin, "Aesthetic Ideology and Urban Design," 351, that Quality was inspired by amusement-zone architecture at world fairs must be taken as symbolic association at best and not causation through literal mimicry. Vieyra (p. 18) mistakenly dates Shell's information booth at the California Pacific International Exposition to 1936. The year 1935 is given in the *Official Guide: California Pacific International Exposition*, 24. Phil Patton, *Open Road: A Celebration of the American Highway* (New York: Simon and Schuster, 1986), 192, erroneously attributes Shell's information booth to the San Diego Exposition of 1915 and consequently "Shell shell-shaped stations" to it.

42. "Building with Shell"; Glenn interview.

43. *WSJ and Sentinel* (Sunday edition), June 15, 1930, pp. 3A, 8B.

44. *WSJ*, May 3, 1930, p. 13; October 25, 1930, p. 2; December 4, 1930, p. 4.

45. Design patent 82,644 (November 25, 1930); *WSJ*, March 28, 1941, September 22, 1954; "Building with Shell."

46. James K. Glenn, Sr., to Keith A. Sculle, letter, September 26, 1979.

47. *Miller's Winston-Salem, N.C., City Directory 1931*, 925; *WSJ*, December 20, 1930, p. 14; February 1, 1931, p. 6B; and April 23, 1931, p. 13; "Perpetual Inventory for All Stocks at Each Station."

48. For example, see *WSJ*, October 18, 1931, p. 3B; November 6, 1931, p. 30.

49. Glenn interview.

50. James K. Glenn, Sr., to Keith A. Sculle, letter, July 24, 1979; "Platt Defines 'Oil Jobber,'" 25; Glenn interview.

51. Sculle, "The Vernacular Gasoline Station," 60.

52. Rubin, "Aesthetic Ideology and Urban Design."

53. Fitch, *Historic Preservation*, 3–4; and Liebs, *Main Street to Miracle Mile*, 225–27.

54. Margolies, *The End of the Road*, 11–13.

Chapter 8. Gas Stations as a Feature of Urban Landscape

Note: This chapter represents an updating and elaboration of three articles: Jakle, "Gasoline Stations in the Champaign-Urbana Landscape: 1920 to 1970"; Jakle and Mattson, "Goodbye to the Horse"; and Jakle and Mattson, "The Evolution of a Commercial Strip."

1. *Champaign Daily News,* May 17, 1916.
2. Ibid., May 21, 1906.
3. Boal and Johnson, "The Functions of Retail and Service Establishments on Commercial Ribbons."
4. Wolfe, "Effects of Ribbon Development on Traffic Flow"; *Champaign-Urbana News-Gazette,* December 28, 1961.
5. Ibid., March 17, 1967.

Chapter 9. Conclusion

1. Consider, for example, Ellul, *The Humiliation of the Word,* 208–15.
2. Rhoads, "Roadside Colonial."
3. Burnham, "The Gasoline Tax and the Automobile Revolution," 459.
4. Yergin, *The Prize.*
5. For example, see ibid.
6. Giddens, "Writing a Corporate History," 18.

Select Bibliography

Private Collections

C. A. Petersen Papers in Manuscripts Division, Library of Congress, Washington, D.C.

Unpublished Materials

Dawes, C. B. "Standardization of Service Stations: Report." Typescript in possession of Dawes Arboretum, Newark, Ohio.

Evanston Preservation Commission. "Historic Resources Survey." Evanston, Ill., n.d.

Sculle, Keith A. "French Anticlericalism after the Separation of Church and State, 1906–1910." Ph.D. diss., University of Illinois, 1972.

Wolf, Gary Herbert. "The Gasoline Station: The Evolution of a Building Type as Illustrated through a History of the Sun Oil Company Gasoline Station." M.Arch. thesis, University of Virginia, 1974.

Government Documents

U.S. Congress, Office of Technology Assessment. *Improving Automobile Fuel Economy: New Standards, New Approaches.* OTA-E-504. Washington, D.C.: U.S. Government Printing Office, October 1991.

U.S. Department of Energy, Energy Information Administration. "U.S. Gasoline Consumption." *Energy Fact Sheet* No. 29 (March 29, 1982).

U.S. Department of Transportation, Federal Highway Administration. *America's Highways, 1776–1976: A History of the Federal Aid Program.* Washington, D.C.: U.S. Government Printing Office, 1976.

——. "Highway Statistics: Summary to 1985." Washington, D.C.: U.S. Government Printing Office, n.d.

——. "Selected Highway Statistics and Charts 1990." Washington, D.C.: U.S. Government Printing Office, n.d.

Books

Abernathy, William J. *The Productivity Dilemma: Roadblock to Innovation in the Automobile Industry.* Baltimore: Johns Hopkins University Press, 1978.

Allen, Frederick L. *Only Yesterday: An Informal History of the Nineteen-twenties.* Reprint. New York: Harper and Row, 1957.

Allvine, Fred C., Jackson W. Houston, and Otis D. Phillips. "The Case for Legislative Relief from the Impending Destruction of Small Business and Competition in the

Gasoline Industry." In *Gasoline Marketing since Decontrol,* Hearings before the Subcommittee on Energy, Environment, and Safety Issues Affecting Small Business, House of Representatives, 97th Cong., 2d sess., 1982, pp. 55–123. Washington, D.C.: U.S. Government Printing Office, 1983.

Anderson, Robert O. *Fundamentals of the Petroleum Industry.* Norman: University of Oklahoma Press, 1984.

Anderson, Scott. *Check the Oil: Gas Station Collectibles with Prices: A Pictorial History of the American Filling Station.* Lombard, Ill.: Wallace-Homestead Book Co., 1986.

Andrews, J.J.C. *The Well-built Elephant and Other Roadside Attractions.* New York: Congdon and Weed, 1984.

Bailey, L. Scott, "The Other Revolution: The Birth and Development of the American Automobile." In *The American Car since 1775: The Most Complete Survey of the American Automobile Ever Published,* Automobile Quarterly Editors, 10–93. New York: L. Scott Bailey, 1971.

Beaton, Kendall. *Enterprise in Oil: A History of Shell in the United States.* New York: Appleton-Century-Crofts, 1957.

Belasco, Warren James. *Americans on the Road: From Autocamp to Motel, 1910–1945.* Cambridge: MIT Press, 1979.

Bishir, Catherine W. *North Carolina Architecture.* Chapel Hill: University of North Carolina Press, 1990.

Blake, Peter. *God's Own Junkyard: The Planned Deterioration of America's Landscape.* New York: Holt, Rinehart and Winston, 1964.

Bluestone, Daniel M. "Roadside Blight and the Reform of Commercial Architecture." In Jennings, ed., *Roadside America,* 170–84.

Boal, F. N., and D. B. Johnson. "The Functions of Retail and Service Establishments on Commercial Ribbons." In *Internal Structure of the City,* edited by Larry S. Bourne, 368–79. New York: Oxford University Press, 1971.

Bodnar, John. *Worker's World: Kinship, Community, and Protest in an Industrial Society, 1900–1940.* Baltimore: Johns Hopkins University Press, 1982.

Boorstin, Daniel J. *The Image: A Guide to Pseudo-Events in America.* New York: Atheneum, 1962.

Butsch, Richard. "Introduction: Leisure and Hegemony in America." In *For Fun and Profit: The Transformation of Leisure into Consumption,* edited by Richard Butsch, 3–27. Philadelphia: Temple University Press, 1990.

Carlyle, Thomas. *The French Revolution: A History.* London: Fraser, 1837.

Carter, Paul A. *Another Part of the Twenties.* New York: Columbia University Press, 1977.

Cheney, Sheldon. *The New World Architecture.* London: Longmans, Green and Co., 1930.

Clark, Clifford E., Jr. *The American Family Home, 1800–1960.* Chapel Hill: University of North Carolina Press, 1986.

Clarke, John. "Pessimism versus Populism: The Problematic Politics of Popular Culture." In *For Fun and Profit: The Transformation of Leisure into Consumption,* edited by Richard Butsch, 28–44. Philadelphia: Temple University Press, 1990.

Claus, R. James. *Spatial Dynamics of Gasoline Service Stations.* Vancouver: Tantalus Research Ltd., B.C. Geographical Series No. 10., 1969.

Claus, R. James, and Walter G. Hardwick. *The Mobile Consumer, Automobile-Oriented Retailing and Site Selection.* Don Mills, Ontario: Collier-MacMillan Canada, n.d.

Cohen, Ira J. "Structuration Theory and Social Praxis." In *Social Theory Today,* edited by Anthony Giddens and Jonathan Turner, 273–308. Stanford, Calif.: Stanford University Press, 1987.

Davis, Donald Finlay. *Conspicuous Production: Automobiles and Elites in Detroit, 1899–1933.* Philadelphia: Temple University Press, 1988.

Dedman, Emmett. *Challenge and Response: A Modern History of Standard Oil Company (Indiana).* Chicago: Mobium Press, 1984.

Dettelbach, Cynthia Golomb. *In the Driver's Seat: The Automobile in American Literature and Popular Culture.* Westport, Conn.: Greenwood Press, 1976.

Dicke, Thomas S. *Franchising in America: The Development of a Business Method, 1840–1980.* Chapel Hill: University of North Carolina Press, 1992.

Earle, Carville, et al. "Historical Geography." In *Geography in America,* edited by Gary L. Gaile and Cort J. Willmott, 155–91. Columbus, Ohio: Merrill, 1989.

Eaton, Leonard K. *Two Chicago Architects and Their Clients: Frank Lloyd Wright and Howard Van Doren Shaw.* Cambridge: MIT Press, 1969.

Edgell, G. H. *The American Architecture of To-Day.* New York: Scribner's, 1928.

Ellul, Jacques. *The Humiliation of the Word.* Translated by Joyce Main Hanks. Grand Rapids, Mich.: William E. Eerdmans Publishing, 1985.

Fitch, James Marston. *Historic Preservation: Curatorial Management of the Built World.* New York: McGraw-Hill, 1982.

Flink, James J. *The Automobile Age.* Cambridge: MIT Press, 1988.

——. "The Ultimate Status Symbol: The Custom Coachbuilt Car in the Interwar Period." In *The Car and the City: The Automobile, the Built Environment, and Daily Urban Life,* edited by Martin Wachs and Margaret Crawford, 154–66. Ann Arbor: University of Michigan Press, 1991.

Flynn, John J. "The Small Business Motor Fuel Marketer Preservation Act of 1981 . . . " In *Divorcement of Motor Fuel Service Stations,* Hearings before the Committee on the Judiciary, U.S. Senate, 97th Cong., 1st sess., 1981, pp. 104–20. Washington, D.C.: U.S. Government Printing Office, 1982.

Ghosh, Arabinda. *Competition and Diversification in the United States Petroleum Industry.* Westport, Conn.: Quorum Books, 1985.

Giddens, Anthony. *The Constitution of Society: Outline of the Theory of Structuration.* Berkeley: University of California Press, 1984.

Giddens, Paul H. *Standard Oil Company (Indiana): Oil Pioneer of the Middle West.* New York: Appleton-Century-Crofts, 1955.

Giebelhaus, August W. *Business and Government in the Oil Industry: A Case Study of Sun Oil, 1876-1945.* Greenwich, Conn.: JAI Press, 1980.

Glassie, Henry. "Artifacts: Folk, Popular, Imaginary and Real." In *Icons of Popular Culture,* edited by Marshall Fishwick and Ray B. Browne, 103–22. Bowling Green, Ohio: Bowling Green University Popular Press, 1970.

Gowans, Alan. *The Comfortable House: North American Suburban Architecture 1890–1930.* Cambridge: MIT Press, 1986.

Greene, William N. *Strategies of the Major Oil Companies.* Ann Arbor, Mich.: UMI Research Press, 1985.

Handlin, David P. *The American House: Architecture and Society, 1815–1915.* Boston: Little, Brown, 1979.

Harris, R. Cole. "The Historical Mind and the Practice of Historical Geography." In *Humanistic Geography: Prospects and Problems,* edited by David Ley and Marwyn Samuels, 123–37. Chicago: Maaroufa Press, 1978.

Harvey, David. *The Condition of Postmodernity.* Cambridge, Mass.: Basil Blackwell, 1989.

Hess, Alan. *Googie: Fifties Coffee Shop Architecture.* San Francisco: Chronicle Books, 1985.

Hinman, Albert G. *Population Growth and the Demands upon Land for Housing in Evanston, Illinois.* Evanston, Ill.: Evanston News-Index, 1931.

Hirschorn, Paul, and Steven Izenour. *White Towers.* Cambridge: MIT Press, 1979.

Hokanson, Drake. *The Lincoln Highway: Main Street across America.* Iowa City: University of Iowa Press, 1988.

Horwitz, Richard. *The Strip: An American Place.* Lincoln: University of Nebraska Press, 1985.

Jackson, Kenneth T. *Crabgrass Frontier: The Suburbanization of the United States.* New York: Oxford University Press, 1985.

Jakle, John A. *The American Small Town: Twentieth-century Place Images.* Hamden, Conn.: Archon Books, 1982.

——. *Images of the Ohio Valley: A Historical Geography of Travel, 1740 to 1860.* New York: Oxford University Press, 1977.

——. *The Tourist: Travel in Twentieth-century North America.* Lincoln: University of Nebraska Press, 1985.

——. *The Visual Elements of Landscape.* Amherst: University of Massachusetts Press, 1987.

——. "The Writing of Scholarly Books in Geography." In *On Becoming a Professional Geographer,* edited by Martin S. Kenzer, 124–34. Columbus, Ohio: Merrill, 1989.

Jakle, John A., Robert W. Bastian, and Douglas K. Meyer. *Common Houses in America's Small Towns: The Atlantic Seaboard to the Mississippi Valley.* Athens: University of Georgia Press, 1989.

Jakle, John A., Stanley D. Brunn, and Curtis C. Roseman. *Human Spatial Behavior: A Social Geography.* Belmont, Calif.: Wadsworth, 1976; Prospect Heights, Ill.: Waveland Press, 1985.

James, Marquis. *The Texaco Story: The First Fifty Years, 1902–1952.* New York: The Texas Co., 1953.

Jennings, Jan, ed. *Roadside America: The Automobile in Design and Culture.* Ames: Iowa State University Press, 1990.

Johnson, R. J. *Geography and Geographers: Anglo-Human Geography since 1945.* London: Edward Arnold, 1983.

Kammen, Michael. "Introduction: The Historian's Vocation and the State of the Discipline in the United States." In *The Past Before Us: Contemporary Historical Writing in the United States,* edited by Michael Kammen, 1–21. Ithaca, N.Y.: Cornell University Press, 1980.

Keller, Ulrich. *The Highway as Habitat: A Roy Stryker Documentation, 1943–1955.* Santa Barbara, Calif.: University Art Museum, 1986.

Kidney, Walter C. *The Architecture of Choice: Eclecticism in America, 1880–1930.* New York: Braziller, 1974.

Kolb, David. *Postmodern Sophistication: Philosophy, Architecture, and Tradition.* Chicago: University of Chicago Press, 1990.

Kouwenhoven, John A. *The Beer Can by the Highway: Essays on What's "American" about America.* New York: Doubleday, 1961.

Labatut, Jean, and Wheaton J. Lane, eds. *Highways in Our National Life: A Symposium.* Princeton: Princeton University Press, 1950.

Langdon, Philip. *Orange Roofs, Golden Arches: The Architecture of American Chain Restaurants.* New York: Alfred A. Knopf, 1986.

Larson, Henrietta M., Evelyn H. Knowlton, and Charles S. Popple. *New Horizons, 1927–1950: History of Standard Oil Company (New Jersey),* Vol. 3. New York: Harper and Row, 1971.

Lawton, Elizabeth, and W. L. Lawton. *The Roadsides of North Carolina.* New York: National Council for the Protection of Roadside Beauty, 1930.

Lears, T. J. Jackson. "From Salvation to Self-Realization: Advertising and the Therapeutic Roots of the Consumer Culture, 1880–1930." In *The Culture of Consumption: Critical Essays in American History, 1880–1980,* edited by Richard W. Fox and T. J. Jackson Lears, 1–38. New York: Pantheon Books, 1983.

Leuchtenberg, William E. *The Perils of Prosperity, 1914–32.* Chicago: University of Chicago Press, 1958.

Lewis, Peirce S. "Axioms for Reading the Landscape." In Meinig, ed., *The Interpretation of Ordinary Landscapes,* 11–32.

Liebs, Chester H. *Main Street to Miracle Mile: American Roadside Architecture.* Boston: Little, Brown, 1985.

Logan, John R., and Harvey L. Molotch. *Urban Fortunes: The Political Economy of Place.* Berkeley: University of California Press, 1987.

Lynd, Robert S., and Helen M. Lynd. *Middletown: A Study of American Culture.* New York: Harcourt, Brace, 1929.

Lynes, Russell. *The Tastemakers.* New York: Harper, 1949.

McLean, John G., and Robert W. Haigh. *The Growth of Integrated Oil Companies.* Boston: Harvard University, Graduate School of Business Administration, 1954.

Mandell, Lewis. *The Great Credit Card Industry: A History.* Boston: Twayne Publishers, 1990.

Marburg, Theodore F. "The Organization of Distribution and Marketing." In *Technology in Western Civilization,* Vol. 2: *Technology in the Twentieth Century,* edited by Melvin Kranzberg and Carroll W. Pursell, Jr., 77–91. New York: Oxford University Press, 1967.

Marchand, Roland. *Advertising the American Dream: Making Way for Modernity, 1920–40.* Berkeley: University of California Press, 1985.

Margolies, John. *The End of the Road: Vanishing Highway Architecture in America.* New York: Penguin Books, 1981.

Marling, Karal Ann. *The Colossus of Roads: Myth and Symbol along the American Highway.* Minneapolis: University of Minnesota Press, 1989.

Mead, George. *Mind, Self, and Society.* Chicago: University of Chicago Press, 1934.

Meinig, D. W., ed. *The Interpretation of Ordinary Landscapes: Geographical Essays.* New York: Oxford University Press, 1979.

Miller's Winston-Salem, N.C. City Directory 1930. Winston-Salem, N.C.: E. H. Miller, 1929.

Miller's Winston-Salem, N.C., City Directory 1931. Winston-Salem, N.C.: E. H. Miller, 1931.

Moore, Charles. *History of Michigan,* Vol. 2. Chicago: Lewis Publishing, 1915.

Nabokov, Vladimir. *Lolita.* New York: Olympia Press, 1955.

Neustadt, Richard E., and Ernest R. May. *Thinking in Time: The Uses of History for Decision-Makers.* New York: Free Press, 1986.

Noble, Allen G. *Wood, Brick, and Stone: The North American Settlement Landscape,* Vol. 1: *Houses.* Amherst: University of Massachusetts Press, 1984.

Novick, Peter. *That Noble Dream: The "Objectivity Question" and the American Historical Profession.* Cambridge: Cambridge University Press, 1988.

O'Connor, Harvey. *The Empire of Oil.* New York: Monthly Review Press, 1955.

Official Guide: California Pacific International Exposition. San Diego: Office of Publications, California Pacific International Exposition, 1935.

Paster, James E. "The Snapshot, the Automobile, and the Americans." In Jennings, ed., *Roadside America,* 55–61.

Petersen, C. A. *The Station Ahead: A Service Station Manual.* n.p.: n.p., 1952.

Pierson, George W. *The Moving American.* New York: Alfred A. Knopf, 1973.

Plattner, Steven W. *The Standard Oil (New Jersey) Photography Project.* Austin: University of Texas Press, 1983.

Powell, Margaret E., ed. *Past Is Prologue.* Madison: Wisconsin Petroleum Press, 1976.

Preston, William. *Historical Analysis in Geography.* London: Longman, 1984.

Prince, Hugh C. "Real, Imagined and Abstract Worlds of the Past." In *Progress in Geography, International Review of Current Research,* 3:4–86. London: Edward Arnold, 1971.

Rae, John B. *The American Automobile: A Brief History.* Chicago: University of Chicago Press, 1965.

———. "The Internal Combustion Engine on Wheels." In *Technology in Western Civilization,* Vol. 2: *Technology in the Twentieth Century,* edited by Melvin Kranzberg and Carroll W. Pursell, Jr., 119–37. New York: Oxford University Press, 1967.

———. *The Road and the Car in American Life.* Cambridge: MIT Press, 1971.

Rapoport, Amos. *House Form and Culture.* Englewood Cliffs, N.J.: Prentice-Hall, 1969.

Reeling, Viola Crouch. *Evanston: Its Land and Its People.* Hammond, Ind.: W. B. Conkey, 1928.

Reich, Robert. *The Next American Frontier.* New York: Penguin Books, 1983.

Relph, Edward. *Place and Placelessness.* London: Croom Helm, 1976.

Riley, Robert. *Rational Landscapes and Humanistic Geography.* London: Croom Helm, 1981.

———. "Vernacular Landscapes." In *Advances in Environment, Behavior, and Design,* Vol. 1, edited by Ervin H. Zube and Gary T. Moore, 129–58. New York: Plenum Press, 1987.

Rose, Albert C. *Historic American Roads: From Frontier Trails to Superhighways.* New York: Crown Publishers, 1976.

Rose, Mark H. *Interstate: Express Highway Politics, 1939–1989.* Rev. ed. Knoxville: University of Tennessee Press, 1990.

Ross, Robert B., and George B. Catlin. *Landmarks of Wayne County and Detroit.* Detroit: Evening News Association, 1898.

Rowe, Peter G. *Making a Middle Landscape.* Cambridge: MIT Press, 1991.

Sack, Robert David. *Place, Modernity, and the Consumer's World: A Geographical Framework for Analysis.* Baltimore: Johns Hopkins University Press, 1993.

Schlereth, Thomas J. *U.S. 40: A Roadscape of the American Experience.* Indianapolis: Indiana Historical Society, 1985.

Scott, Quinta, and Susan C. Kelly. *Route 66: The Highway and Its People.* Norman, Okla.: University of Oklahoma Press, 1988.

Seely, Bruce E. *Building the American Highway System: Engineers and Policy Makers.* Philadelphia: Temple University Press, 1987.

Semple, Ellen C. *American History and Its Geographical Conditions.* Boston: Houghton Mifflin, 1903.

Soja, Edward W. *Postmodern Geographies: The Reassertion of Space in Critical Social Theory.* London: Verso, 1989.

Sontag, Susan. *On Photography.* New York: Farrar, Straus, and Giroux, 1973.

Steinbeck, John. *The Grapes of Wrath.* New York: Viking, 1939.

Stewart, George R. *U.S. 40: Cross Section of the United States of America.* Boston: Houghton Mifflin, 1953.

Stilgoe, John R. *Borderland: Origins of the American Suburb, 1820–1939.* New Haven: Yale University Press, 1988.

Stone, Gregory P., and Harvey A. Faberman, eds. *Social Psychology through Symbolic Interaction.* New York: Ginn-Blaisdell, 1970.

Susman, Warren I., ed. *Culture and Commitment 1929–1945.* New York: George Braziller, 1973.

Tarkington, Booth. *The Magnificent Ambersons.* New York: Doubleday, Page, 1918.

Taylor, Gwynne Stephens. *From Frontier to Factory: An Architectural History of Forsyth County.* Winston-Salem: North Carolina Department of Cultural Resources, 1981.

Thompson, Paul. *The Voice of the Past: Oral History.* Oxford: Oxford University Press, 1978.

Vale, Thomas R., and Geraldine R. Vale. *U.S. 40 Today: Thirty Years of Landscape Change in America.* Madison: University of Wisconsin Press, 1983.

———. *Western Images, Western Landscapes.* Tucson: University of Arizona Press, 1989.

Venturi, Robert, and Denise S. Brown. *A View from the Campidoglio: Selected Essays, 1953–1984.* New York: Harper, 1984.

Venturi, Robert, Denise S. Brown, and Steven Izenour. *Learning from Las Vegas.* Cambridge: MIT Press, 1977.

Vieyra, Daniel I. *"Fill'er Up!": An Architectural History of America's Gas Stations.* New York: Collier Books, 1979.

Von Ranke, Leopold. *The Theory and Practice of History.* Edited with an introduction by Georg G. Iggers and Konrad von Moltke. Translated by Wilma A. Iggers and Konrad von Moltke. Indianapolis: Bobbs-Merrill, 1973.

Wallis, Michael. *Route 66: The Mother Road.* New York: St. Martin's Press, 1990.

Watson, Edward B., and Edmund V. Gillon, Jr. *New York Then and Now.* New York: Dover, 1976.

White, Gerald T. *Formative Years in the Far West.* New York: Century-Crofts, 1962.

White, Lawrence J. *The Automobile Industry since 1945.* Cambridge: Harvard University Press, 1971.

Williamson, Harold F., Ralph Andreano, Arnold R. Daum, and Gilbert C. Klose. *The American Petroleum Industry,* Vol. 2: *The Age of Energy, 1899–1959.* Evanston, Ill.: Northwestern University Press, 1963.

Winston-Salem, N.C., City and Suburban Directory 1921. Asheville, N.C.: Commercial Service Co., 1921.

Winston-Salem, N.C., City Directory 1926. Asheville, N.C.: Commercial Service Co., 1926.

Withey, Henry F., and Elsie Rathbun Withey. *Biographical Dictionary of American Architects (Deceased).* Los Angeles: Hennessey and Ingalls, 1970.

Witzel, Michael K. *The American Gas Station: History and Folklore of the Gas Station in American Car Culture.* Osceola, Wis.: Motorbooks International, 1992.

Wolfe, Tom. *The Kandy-Kolored Tangerine-Flake Streamlined Baby.* New York: Farrar, Straus, and Giroux, 1965.

Wright, Gwendolyn. *Building the Dream: A Social History of Housing in America.* New York: Pantheon Books, 1981.

Wright's Green Bay Directory. Milwaukee: Wright Directory, 1927.

Yergin, Daniel. *The Prize: The Epic Quest for Oil, Money, and Power.* New York: Simon and Schuster, 1991.

Periodicals

"Almost Half of Motorists Buy on Brand Marketing Survey Finds." *NPN* 20 (April 25, 1928): 27–29.

Archer, John. "Country and City in the American Romantic Suburb." *Journal of the Society of Architectural Historians* 42 (May 1983): 139–56.

——. "Ideology and Aspiration: Individualism, the Middle Class, and the Genesis of the Anglo-American Suburb." *Journal of Urban History* 14 (February 1988): 214–53.

"Are These Stations What's Ahead for Texaco?" *NPN* 58 (February 1966): 98–100.

"Around the Filling Stations." *NPN* 14 (March 1, 1922): 8.

"Atlantic-Richfield: Anatomy of a Merger." *NPN* 61 (January 1969): 46–48.

Attoe, Wayne, and Mark Latus. "Buildings as Signs: An Experiment in Milwaukee." *Journal of Popular Culture* 7 (Fall 1973): 462–65.

B., J. T. "Neat Snappy Appearance." *PON* 11 (October 1928): 17.

Barringer, E. L. "Better Materials and Fittings Make Stations More Attractive." *NPN* 24 (May 4, 1932): 47, 49–52.

——. "His Initials Are RR—So It's the Railroad Jones Oil Co." *NPN* 23 (February 4, 1931): 41–42.

——. " 'If I Ever Built a Station It Will Have Clean Rest Rooms . . . ' It Has." *NPN* 24 (June 8, 1932): 53–54.

——. "Most Oil Companies Rent Stations in Florida to Operators." *NPN* 23 (March 25, 1931): 69–70.

——. "S.O. Indiana Files Suit Against Use of 'Esso' in 14 States." *NPN* 27 (May 22, 1935): 23–24.

——. "Standard of Indiana Announces Extension of 'Iowa Plan.'" *NPN* 28 (April 22, 1936): 11–12.

"Battle for No. 1: Are BP and Shell in a Showdown for Gasoline Supremacy?" *NPN* 83 (October 1991): 30–34.

Baum, Arthur W. "The New American Roadside." *Saturday Evening Post* 233 (July 30, 1960): 32–33, 48–50.

Bodine, H. E. "Glorifying the American Service Station." *PON* 12 (January 1930): 17.

Bowman, Heath. "A Finer Pure Oil Exhibit at the Century of Progress." *PON* 17 (July 1934): 8–9.

"BP Oil to Sohio to BP." *NPN* 61 (July 1969): 65–67.

"BP Wants In, 'the American Way.'" *NPN* 61 (June 1969): 69–70.

"Branded Retail Outlets." *NPN Factbook* 83 (Mid-June 1991): 44–51.

Breese, Frank. "How to Stay Youthful at Fifty: The NPN Story." *NPN* 51 (February 1959): 90–92.

"Building with Shell." *Sign of the Shell* (September 1930): 13.

"Bulk Stations Started in Buffalo, Thrive There Now." *NPN* 19 (October 26, 1927): 125–26.

Burnham, John Chynoweth. "The Gasoline Tax and the Automobile Revolution." *Mississippi Valley Historical Review* 48 (December 1961): 435–59.

"By Being Bold, Murphy Becomes a Baby International." *NPN* 59 (January 1967): 70–73.

"California-Kentucky Merger: Here's What It Will Mean." *NPN* 53 (July 1961): 95–98, 100, 198.

"Canopies: What's Behind an Old Standby's New Appeal." *NPN* 50 (November 1958): 98–104.

"Car Care Center Growth Slows, But Developers See Bright Future." *NPN* 83 (May 1991): 32.

Chatfield, J. C. "Cities Service Ads Build Goodwill among Customers and Employees." *NPN* 19 (October 5, 1927): 46.

——. "Independent Marketers Make Capital of Anti–Chain Store Feeling." *NPN* 22 (March 19, 1930): 55–56.

"Cities Shuffle Names in ID Change." *NPN* 57 (June 1965): 98.

"Clean Service Stations Mean Better Business." *PON* 20 (May 1938): 13.

"Conoco-Dupont: Will 'Merger Fever' Spread?" *NPN* 73 (November 1981): 43–45.

"Court Enjoins Dealer's Use of Patented Station Design." *NPN* 31 (April 26, 1939): 16.

Crandall, R. J. "Correct Lighting Is Both Convenience and Good Advertising." *NPN* 17 (May 13, 1925): 133–34, 139.

"Cultivate More Attractive Surroundings." *PON* 27 (May 1945): 11.

"The Day of Big Sellouts." *NPN* 56 (January 1964): 61–66, 107.

"Department Store Features Minature Pure Oil Station." *PON* 17 (January 1935): 18.

"Details of Modern Station Design Given by Union Oil Co." *NPN* 19 (November 16, 1927): 31–32.

"Distributors Before/After Oil Shock." *NPN* 76 (February 1984): 58.

"East Coast: From Box to Colonial." *NPN* 61 (June 1969): 37–38, 42, 44–45.

"1877—Henry May Dawes—1952." *PON* 35 (November 1952): 4–5.

"Every Pure Oil Outlet Is an Advertisement." *PON* 17 (October 1934): 14.

"Exclusive Right to Pump Color Scheme Upheld in Court Ruling." *NPN* 22 (May 7, 1930): 27–28.

"Fewer Outlets for Gulf Oil." *NPN* 66 (November 1974): 9.

Flink, James J. "The Automobile Revolution." *Illinois History* 44 (April 1991): 121–26.

"Ford Men Call This Ideal Super Set-Up." *PON* 19 (September 1936): 11.

Freitag, J. V. "Wofford Oil Company of Alabama." *PON* 13 (October 1930): 4–5.

"The Front Yard . . . and the Back." *PON* 22 (April 1940): 15.

"George T. Wofford Dies." *PON* 24 (October 1941): 45.

"Getty-Skelly Merger Close at Hand." *NPN* 69 (February 1977): 29–30.

Giddens, Paul H. "Writing a Corporate History: A Personal Memoir." *Journal of the Illinois State Historical Society* 74 (1981): 17–30.

"Gilding the Lily." *PON* 18 (December 1935): 21.

Goubert, Pierre. "Local History." *Daedalus* 100 (Winter 1971): 113–27.

"Greasing Equipment Takes to Cover in Modern Super Service Station." *NPN* 22 (March 19, 1930): 103.

"The Great American Roadside." *Fortune* 10 (September 1934): 53–63, 172, 174, 177.

Guth, Alexander C. "Small Buildings: The Automobile Service Station." *Architectural Forum* 45 (1926): 33–56.

Guthrie, V. B. "Bostonian Can Purchase His Gasoline and Not Offend Aesthetic Sense." *NPN* 15 (July 25, 1923): 34–36, 38.

——. "'Super' Stations and Oil Companies Compete for Gasoline Business." *NPN* 18 (March 10, 1926): 64–66, 68.

Halbert, Ward K. "Merchandise Display Window Features Pure Oil Co.'s New Stations." *NPN* 19 (August 17, 1927): 22–23.

——. "Tendency Is Toward Better Stations Rather than More of Them." *NPN* 17 (May 13, 1925): 75–76.

Hancock, L. B. "Erection, Operation and Maintenance of Filling Stations." *NPN* 14 (March 30, 1921): 35–36.

"Hard Lessons and Big Changes in the Market." *NPN* 71 (August 1977): 50.

"Here's Standard's Model for Steel Service Stations." *NPN* 8 (June 1916): 42.

"Higher Gas Taxes the Cry in the States, Chain Store Bills Are New Levies." *NPN* 21 (March 27, 1929): 19–20.

"How Fledgling Chevron USA Was Hatched." *NPN* 68 (November 1976): 29–30.

"How Indiana Standard Will Go National." *NPN* 52 (August 1960): 81–83.

"How Kyso Stakes a Big, Bold Interstate Claim." *NPN* 60 (August 1968): 78–82.

"How Old Stations Get the New Look." *NPN* 59 (October 1967): 77–78.

"How Ranch Style Is Taking Over Service Station Design." *NPN* 58 (May 1966): 95–101.

Hugill, Peter J. "Good Roads and the Automobile in the United States 1880–1929." *Geographical Review* 72 (July 1982): 327–49.

"Humble Oil: 'Esso' or 'Enco'?" *NPN* 55 (August 1963): 67–68.

"Introducing the New Pure Oil Co. Seal." *PON* 12 (April 1930): 5–6.

Jackson, J. B. "Other-Directed Houses." *Landscape* 6, no. 2 (Winter 1956–57): 29–35.

Jakle, John A. "The American Gasoline Station, 1920 to 1970." *Journal of American Culture* 1 (1979): 521–42.

——. "Childhood on the Middle Border: Remembered Small Town America." *Journal of Geography* 85 (1986): 159–63.

——. "Gasoline Stations in the Champaign-Urbana Landscape: 1920 to 1970." *Bulletin, Illinois Geographical Society* 20 (1978): 3–15.

——. "Motel by the Roadside: America's Room for the Night." *Journal of Cultural Geography* 1 (1980): 34–49.

——. "Roadside Restaurants: The Evolution of Place-Product-Packaging." *Journal of Cultural Geography* 3 (1982): 76–93.

——. "Salt on the Ohio Valley Frontier, 1770–1820." *Annals, Association of American Geographers* 59 (1969): 687–709.

——. "Time, Space and the Geographic Past: A Prospectus for Historical Geography." *American Historical Review* 76 (1971): 1084–1103.

Jakle, John A., and Richard L. Mattson. "The Evolution of a Commercial Strip." *Journal of Cultural Geography* 1 (1982): 76–93.

——. "Goodbye to the Horse: The Transition from Horse-related to Automobile-related Businesses in an Urban Landscape." *PAST* 2 (1979): 31–51.

"Kind of Highway Determines Type of Successful Station." *NPN* 20 (June 6, 1928): 29–30.

King, Frank R. "Public Comfort Stations." *The American City* 33 (1925): 613–19.

Kniffen, Fred B. "Folk Housing: Key to Diffusion." *Annals, Association of American Geographers* 55 (1965): 549–77.

——. "Louisiana House-Types." *Annals, Association of American Geographers* 26 (1936): 179–93.

Lane, Jonathan. "The Period House in the Nineteen-twenties." *Journal of the Society of Architectural Historians* 20, no. 4 (1961): 169–78.

Leslie, W. T. "Model Service Station." *PON* 18 (September 1935): 12.

Lewis, Peirce S. "Learning from Looking: Geographic and Other Writings about the American Cultural Landscape." *American Quarterly* 35 (1983): 242–61.

Lohof, Bruce A. "The Service Station in America: The Evolution of a Vernacular Form." *Industrial Archeology* 11 (1974): 1–13.

Lovejoy, F. W. "Chain Filling Stations to be Future Development of Industry." *NPN* 18 (June 9, 1926): 21–23.

McCarthy, John J. "Public Calls 'Em 'Colonial Stations' So Beacon Changes Name." *NPN* 22 (September 10, 1930): 98.

MacDonald, Thomas H. "The History and Development of Road Building in the United States." *Transactions of the American Society of Engineers* 92 (1928): 1181–1206.

Meikle, Jeffrey. "Refining the Roadside." *Industrial Design* 31, no. 6 (November-December 1984): 70–73, 89–91.

"Merger Frenzy: Supplier Fallout Begins to Shake Industry." *NPN* 76 (April 1984): 20–25.

" . . . Michigan Marketer Plans for Future." *NPN* 33 (March 12, 1941): 25–27.

"Mid-Continent Builds Ultra-Modern Station." *NPN* 23 (August 12, 1931): 65.

"Mobil's Marathon Tender: How Many More Sitting Ducks amid Second-Tier Companies?" *NPN* 73 (December 1981): 29–30.

"Money to be Made: The Oil-Marketing Story, A Quick History of Oil Marketing." *NPN* 61 (February 1969): 111–30.

"Motels Chancy, but . . . " *NPN* 56 (March 1964): 106–14.

"1918—The Company Then and Now—1938." *PON* 21 (June 1938): 10–11.

"Not All Masonry Is Masonry." *NPN* 60 (April 1968): 124–25.

"Now the No-Service Station." *Time* 110, no. 8 (August 22, 1977): 43.

Oliver, Richard, and Nancy Ferguson. "The Environment Is a Diary." *Architectural Forum* 131 (July 1978): 115–20.

Olson, Charles D. "Sign of the Star: Walter Dorwin Teague and the Texas Company." *Society for Commercial Archeology News Journal* 11 (1990): 1, 3–6.

"Pattern Stations on Old Missions." *NPN* 7 (November 10, 1919): 50.

Pellegrini, J. V. "Design for Travel." *Landscape* 11, no. 3 (Spring 1962): 6–8.

"Percent Self-Service Motorist Gasoline Sold by Brand." *NPN Factbook* 83 (Mid-June 1991): 138.

"Perpetual Inventory for All Stocks at Each Station." *NPN* 23 (February 25, 1931): 69–70.

Petersen, C. A. "A Model of a Model Station." *PON* 12 (June 1929): 21.

——. "Transforming an Eyesore to a Thing of Beauty." *PON* 14 (April 1932): 18.

Pettengill, Samuel B. "The First Fifty Years." *PON* 46 (April 1964): 1–33.

Pew, J. Howard. "Against Marketing Divorcement." *NPN* 31 (July 12, 1939): 31–34, 36, 38.

"Plastic Provides a Built-in Spectacular." *NPN* 49 (March 1957): 101.

"Platt Defines 'Oil Jobber.'" *NPN* 33 (September 17, 1941): 24–25, 30.

"Portable Country Stations Are Replicas of Famous Lighthouse." *NPN* 20 (September 26, 1928): 68.

Price, H. Wayne, and Keith A. Sculle. "The 'Doughnut' and 'Oval' Barns of Ogle and Stephenson Counties, Illinois: An Architectural Survey." *PAST* 9 (1986): 31–38.

——. "The Failed Round Barn Experiment: Horace Duncan's Experience As Carpenter." *PAST* 6 (1983): 1–7.

——. "Observations on the Pennsylvania German Barns of Stephenson County, Illinois." *PAST* 8 (1985): 45–53.

"Pure Oil Advertising Reaches New High Peak." *PON* 22 (August 1919): 8–9.

Reid, Marvin. "America Enters the Gasoline Era." *NPN* 76 (February 1984): 44–59.

——. "How Phillips Marched into Dixie: Jobbers Led the Way." *NPN* 48 (November 1956): 104–6.

——. "The Majors Brush Up Their Public Images." *NPN* 75 (April 1983): 36–39.

——. "Oil Product Imports: The Industry's Next Big Problem." *NPN* 77 (February 1985): 36–39.

Rhoads, William. "Roadside Colonial: Early American Design for the Automobile Age, 1900–1940." *Winterthur Portfolio* 21, nos. 2–3 (1986): 133–52.

"Richfield Out, Sinclair In." *NPN* 56 (September 1964): 122–24, 126, 128.

Rubin, Barbara. "Aesthetic Ideology and Urban Design." *Annals, Association of American Geographers* 69, no. 3 (1979): 339–61.

Sauer, Carl O. "The Morphology of Landscape." *University of California Publications in Geography* 2 (1925): 19–54; reprinted in *Land and Life: A Selection from the Writings of Carl Ortwein Sauer,* edited by John Leighly, 315–49. Berkeley: University of California Press, 1963.

Schroeder, Richard C. "Brand Identification Is Taking on a Professional Look." *NPN* 48 (November 1956): 90–93.

Sculle, Keith A. "Another Roadside Attraction." *Illinois History* 41 (April 1988): 145–47.

——. "Boosterism and Architecture: The Origins of Foeller, Schober, and Stephenson's Gasoline Station Designs." *Pioneer America* 14 (1982): 1–14.

——. "C. A. Petersen: Pioneer Gas Station Architect." *Historic Illinois* 2, no. 1 (1979): 11–13.

——. "A Case for Local Significance." *Historic Illinois* 1, no. 4 (1978): 8–9.

——. "A Case for Self-Preservation, Bob's Place." *Society for Commercial Archeology News Journal* 2 (November 1985): 12–13.

——. "Diners." *Historic Illinois* 5, no. 6 (1983): 2–4.

——. "The Enduring Best: Beacon Oil Company's 'Watertown' Filling Stations." *PAST* 9 (1986): 1–8.

——. "Keeping the National Register Honest." *Historic Illinois* 1, no. 2 (1978): 6.

——. "Oral History: A Key to Writing the History of American Roadside Architecture." *Journal of American Culture* 13, no. 3 (1990): 79–88.

——. "The Pure Sign." *Journal of American Culture* 5, no. 1 (1982): 84–92.

——. "Registers of Historic Places." *Illinois History* 36 (March 1983): 126–28.

——. "Roadside Business: Frank W. McDonald and the Origins of the 'Indian Village.'" *Kansas History* 14 (Spring 1991): 15–25.

——. "The Vernacular Gasoline Station: Examples from Illinois and Wisconsin." *Journal of Cultural Geography* 1, no. 2 (1981): 56–74.

Sculle, Keith A., and Michael Derr. "Fill'er Up: Wisconsin Motorists Get Gas." *Wisconsin Trails* 21 (1980): 32–35.

"Sell Gasoline from Greek Temple." *NPN* 10 (April 17, 1918): 18–20.

"Service Station Field Is Playground for Architectural Design." *NPN* 17 (May 13, 1925): 72, 74.

Shaner, J. Richard. "'New' BP Launches Image Campaign in U.S. Markets." *NPN* 80 (March 1988): 20.

"Shell Oil's Newest 'Blend-in.'" *NPN* 52 (February 1960): 121.

"Shell Tailors Stations to Fit." *NPN* 50 (January 1958): 106–7.

Snow, J. Todd. "The New Road in the United States." *Landscape* 17, no. 1 (Autumn 1967): 13–16.

"Southwest." *NPN* 62 (January 1970): 25–26.

"Special Green Bay Edition." *The Wisconsin Magazine* 7 (May 1929): 17–56.

Stafford, Roger B. "Jenney Builds Stations to Fit New England Settings." *NPN* 19 (May 4, 1927): 27–28.

——. "Oil Companies Pushed to Keep Abreast of Florida's Growth." *NPN* 18 (January 6, 1926): 25–27.

"Standardized Service Stations Designed by Walter Dorwin Teague." *Architectural Record* 82 (September 1937): 69–72.

"Standard Type of Service Station." *NPN* 10 (November 9, 1918): 40.

"Station Type Adopted by N.Y. Standard." *NPN* 15 (July 18, 1923): 41.

S[tevenson], H. H. "Beautiful Hudson Station." *PON* 18 (December 1935): 16.

"Stucco, Tile Lend to Pleasing Station Architecture." *NPN* 9 (February 1917): 66.

Sturtevant, Frank C. "Marketers Design Stations to Reduce Building Costs." *NPN* 41 (April 13, 1949): 29–30, 32.

"Sun Introduces Public to Octane Ratings in Selling Gasoline." *NPN* 23 (July 8, 1931): 35–36.

"Sunray Aims Marketing Push." *NPN* 47 (June 1955): 54–55.

"Super Service Station Designed as Mosque." *NPN* 20 (April 18, 1928): 93–94, 97.

T., D. J. "The 'English Village.'" *PON* 20 (July 1937): 19.

Taylor, Malcolm D. "Prices in Chain and Independent Grocery Stores in Durham, North Carolina." *Harvard Business Review* 8 (July 1930): 413–24.

Tennerstedt, M. R. "Evanston—'The City of Homes.'" *PON* 19 (April 1937): 4–6.

Thompson, John W. "Uniformity Is Trend in Station Design." *NPN* 29 (April 21, 1937): 59–61, 63, 65.

Tise, Larry E. "Organizing America's History Business: A New Ethic and Plan of Action." *History News* 43, no. 2 (1988): 17–28.

"Travelodge Opens First Tri-Arc." *Tourist Court Journal* 33 (June 1970): 88–89.

"Truckstops: Multibillion-dollar Business." *NPN* 60 (October 1968): 71–76.

Truesdell, Paul. "Highest New York State Court Rules Out Curb Pumps in Buffalo." *NPN* 15 (June 20, 1923): 21–22.

——. "How Many Gasoline Pumps to the Mile? Question Facing Oil Companies." *NPN* 14 (August 2, 1922): 19–20.

——. "How Re-designing of a Filling Station Doubled Its Business." *NPN* 15 (June 27, 1923): 22–23, 25–26.

Tunnard, Christopher. "The Romantic Suburb in America." *Magazine of Art* 40 (May 1947): 184–87.

Turner, Frederick Jackson. "The Significance of the Frontier in American History." *Annual Report of the American Historical Association* (1893): 190–227.

Uncle Pat [Charles A. Ward]. "Twenty Years in Retrospect." *PON* 16 (April 1934): 4–8.

Upton, Dell. "The Power of Things: Recent Studies in American Vernacular Architecture." *American Quarterly* 35, no. 3 (1983): 262–79.

Walthius, R. D. "Third 'Big One' Opened." *PON* 45 (July 1962): 19.

Weller, Louis. "Indian Village to Grow around Station." *NPN* 22 (June 25, 1930): 89, 92, 94.

"What the Gasoline Tax Is Doing to the Oil Industry." *NPN* 16 (November 1933): 14.

Wheeler, Robert C. "Frank Lloyd Wright Filling Station, 1958." *Journal of the Society of Architectural Historians* 19, no. 4 (December 1960): 174–75.

"Where Oil Got Its Trademarks." *NPN* 51 (August 1959): 129, 131–32.

"Why C-Stores Lead Gasoline Markets." *NPN* 76 (April 1984): 34–37.

"Wide Expansions in Marketing." *PON* 11 (June 1928): 14.

Wolfe, R. I. "Effects of Ribbon Development on Traffic Flow." *Traffic Quarterly* 18 (1964): 105–17.

"Your Competitor Says 'Kindly Omit Flowers.'" *PON* 21 (May 1939): 14.

Index

Library of Congress Cataloging-in-Publication Data

Jakle, John A.
   The gas station in America / John A. Jakle and Keith A. Sculle.
     p.   cm. — (Creating the North American landscape)
   Includes bibliographical references.
   ISBN 0-8018-4723-0 (alk. paper). — ISBN 0-8018-4724-9 (pbk. : alk. paper)
   1. Service stations—United States—History. 2. Architecture, Commercial—United
States—History. I. Sculle, Keith A. II. Title. III. Series.
TL153.J27 1994
338.4'762928'60973—dc20   93-36917